# Interpersonal Emotion Dynamics in Close Relationships

Emotions play a powerful role in close relationships. Significant progress has been made in understanding the temporal features of emotions associated with the development and maintenance of close relationships across the life span. This advancement has revealed further questions: Which theories help conceptualize interpersonal emotion dynamics? What are the ways in which researchers can assess and model these dynamics? How do interpersonal emotion dynamics manifest in different close relationships? Do these emotion dynamics contribute to the maintenance or dissolution of relationships?

*Interpersonal Emotion Dynamics in Close Relationships* addresses these and other questions by bringing together state-of-the-art perspectives from scholars widely recognized for their contributions to the study of emotions in relationships. Each chapter defines interpersonal emotion dynamics, reviews methodological or empirical work, and offers important directions for future research. This volume will be a valuable resource for students, researchers, and practitioners interested in understanding the role of emotions in close relationships.

ASHLEY K. RANDALL is Associate Professor in Counseling and Counseling Psychology at Arizona State University, USA, and serves on the editorial boards for *Emotion*, the *Journal of Social and Personal Relationships*, and *The Counseling Psychologist*.

DOMINIK SCHOEBI is Professor in Psychology at the University of Fribourg, Switzerland, and serves on the editorial boards for the *Journal of Marriage and Family*, *Family Psychology*, and *Family Process*.

# STUDIES IN EMOTION AND SOCIAL INTERACTION
## Second Series

Series Editors

Brian Parkinson
*University of Oxford*

Maya Tamir
*The Hebrew University of Jerusalem*

*(Continued after Index)*

# Interpersonal Emotion Dynamics in Close Relationships

*Edited by*

Ashley K. Randall
*Arizona State University*

Dominik Schoebi
*Université de Fribourg*

# CAMBRIDGE
UNIVERSITY PRESS

University Printing House, Cambridge CB2 8BS, United Kingdom

One Liberty Plaza, 20th Floor, New York, NY 10006, USA

477 Williamstown Road, Port Melbourne, VIC 3207, Australia

314–321, 3rd Floor, Plot 3, Splendor Forum, Jasola District Centre,
New Delhi – 110025, India

79 Anson Road, #06-04/06, Singapore 079906

Cambridge University Press is part of the University of Cambridge.

It furthers the University's mission by disseminating knowledge in the pursuit of
education, learning, and research at the highest international levels of excellence.

www.cambridge.org
Information on this title: www.cambridge.org/9781107177703
DOI: 10.1017/9781316822944

First published 2018

Printed and bound in Great Britain by Clays Ltd, Elcograf S.p.A.

*A catalogue record for this publication is available from the British Library.*

*Library of Congress Cataloging-in-Publication Data*

Names: Randall, Ashley K., editor. | Schoebi, Dominik, editor.
Title: Interpersonal emotion dynamics in close relationships / edited by
    Ashley K. Randall, Dominik Schoebi.
Description: First Edition. | New York : Cambridge University Press, 2018. |

    Series: Studies in emotion and social interaction | Includes
    bibliographical references and index.
Identifiers: LCCN 2018013112 | ISBN 9781107177703 (hardback)
Subjects: LCSH: Emotions. | Interpersonal relations. | BISAC: PSYCHOLOGY /
    Social Psychology.
Classification: LCC BF511 .I58 2018 | DDC 158.2—dc23 LC record available at
https://lccn.loc.gov/2018013112

ISBN 978-1-107-17770-3 Hardback

# Contents

# Figures

# Tables

# Contributors

**Brian R. W. Baucom** Department of Psychology, University of Utah, USA

**Emily A. Butler** Family Studies and Human Development, University of Arizona, USA

**Jonathan E. Butner** Department of Psychology, University of Utah, USA

**Belinda Campos** Department of Chicano/Latino Studies, University of California, Irvine, USA

**Eva Ceulemans** Faculty of Psychology and Educational Sciences, KU Leuven, Belgium

**Charlie Champion** Department of Psychology, Arizona State University, USA

**Geoffrey W. Corner** Department of Psychology, University of Southern California, USA

**Alexander O. Crenshaw** Department of Psychology, University of Utah, USA

**Thomas Dishion**[†] Department of Psychology, Arizona State University, USA

**Thao Ha** Department of Psychology, Arizona State University, USA

**Tom Hollenstein** Department of Psychology, Queen's University, Canada

**Arpine Hovasapian** Department of Psychology and Social Behavior, University of California, Irvine, USA

**Alexis Keaveney** Department of Psychology, The Ohio State University, USA

**Mona Khaled** Department of Psychology, University of Southern California, USA

**Hannah Khoddam** Department of Psychology, University of Southern California, USA

**Peter Kuppens** Faculty of Psychology and Educational Sciences, KU Leuven, Belgium

**Jessica P. Lougheed** Department of Human Development and Family Studies, Purdue University, USA

**Galen D. McNeil** UCLA, Department of Psychology, University of California, Los Angeles, USA

**Ascher K. Munion** Department of Psychology, University of Utah, USA

**Ashley K. Randall** Counseling and Counseling Psychology, Arizona State University, USA

**Rena L. Repetti** UCLA, Department of Psychology, University of California, Los Angeles, USA

**Bernard Rimé** Psychological Sciences Research Institute, University of Louvain, Belgium

**Darby Saxbe** Department of Psychology, University of Southern California, USA

**Dominik Schoebi** Department of Psychology, University of Fribourg, Switzerland

**Sharon Shenhav** Department of Psychology and Social Behavior, University of California, Irvine, USA

**Laura Sels** Faculty of Psychology and Educational Sciences, KU Leuven, Belgium

**Sarah A. Stoycos** Department of Psychology, University of Southern California, USA

**Baldwin M. Way** Department of Psychology, The Ohio State University, USA

**Alexander Wong** Department of Psychology, University of Utah, USA

# Foreword

*Bernard Rimé*

When we consider our everyday experience, it seems obvious to us that our emotions and those of our loved ones are continually in dynamic interaction. With our children, our parents, our spouses and others to whom we are close, the emotional interaction is ongoing. These emotional exchanges in close relationships in fact constitute, moment after moment, the framework and the plot of the existence we share with others. It is therefore intellectually puzzling to observe that it took more than a century of developments for psychological science to echo this common observation.

At the dawn of the scientific study of emotion in the late 1800s, the impetus was clearly in line with intra-individualist concepts. The pioneers of the field, Darwin (1872), James (1884), and Cannon (1916), viewed emotions as automatic processes with an evolutionary history of service to the individual's adaptation. Later, many followed Watson's (1929) anti-vitalist positions and considered emotion as a disturbed condition of the organism during which it temporarily loses its potential for adaptive action (e.g., Claparède, 1928; Pribram, 1967; Young, 1943).

Constructive concepts of emotion came to the floor in the 1960s and 1970s with the advent of cognitive (Arnold, 1960; Frijda, 1986; Lazarus & Folkman, 1984; Scherer, 1984) and neo-Darwinian views (Ekman et al., 1972; Izard, 1971; Tomkins, 1962). Still, the focus of these theories remained essentially intra-individualist. Cognitive theories insisted upon cognitive appraisal, subjective experience and action tendencies. Though neo-Darwinian views stressed the importance of facial expression of emotion, it did not result from an interest in emotional social interaction. Facial expression was examined as embodying the signature of primary emotions. A social psychology perspective on emotions was still to come. In the spirit of these times, I remember our total surprise when in the 1980s in a collaborative study initiated by Klaus Scherer to investigate the components of emotional experience in ten European countries (Scherer et al., 1986), we faced clear evidence of the interpersonal nature of most emotions. Indeed, the antecedents of fear, anger, joy and sadness reported by our numerous respondents resided in interpersonal relationships in more than three-quarters of cases. We had not anticipated this.

In the meantime, studies of child development opened up major breaches in individualistic views of emotions. With the theory of attachment, Bowlby (1969) demonstrated that the children's emotional regulation was inseparable from an interpersonal dynamic with their caregivers. Meltzoff and Moore (1977) provoked a shock by evidencing infants' precocious capacities for imitation, and thus demonstrating infants' in-born disposition to social interaction. Many other developmental researchers (e.g., Bruner, 1977; Campos & Stenberg, 1981; Tronick et al., 1977) further documented the interactive nature of children-caregivers relationships and the essential role played by emotional exchanges in these relationships.

In the 1990s, adult research in turn began to focus on the place of social interaction in emotional life. For example, it was found that the emotional episodes were systematically shared with the entourage (Rimé et al., 1991). Social functions of emotion were highlighted (Keltner & Haidt, 1999). An examination of the cultural variations of emotions was undertaken (Mesquita & Frijda, 1992). In this context, calls for the study of the social aspects of emotions have multiplied (e.g., Fischer & Manstead, 2008, Parkinson, 1996, Van Kleef, 2009). The interest in this field then quickly spread to the point of opening even to the study of collective emotions (for review, von Scheve & Salmela, 2014) – a question that had been totally forgotten in the twentieth century.

The book that follows will reveal to its readers a well-circumscribed field of research that arose in the context of this evolution. This current volume examines precisely this fact that we all experience in everyday life but that emotion research has so far ignored: that our emotions are shaped by our close personal relationships, and reciprocally, that we constantly affect the emotions of our close ones. This book demonstrates that the investigation of interpersonal emotion dynamics in personal relationships has evolved with great steps toward its maturity. The contributions, gathered by Ashley Randall and Dominik Schoebi, allow us to discover the work of the major actors of this current. They provide extensive documentation on the rapid progress of this new field. The high level of scientific demands is their common feature. Readers will find an overview of the conceptual frameworks useful in this area of investigation. They will discover findings from studies examining bodily components of the interactive emotional dynamic, both at the biochemical and at the physiological level. They will also find abundant scientific observations on the staging of this dynamic in family relations, in interpersonal relationships, and in intimate relationships.

In the background, readers will guess the importance of the information provided by this research for a scientific lighting of clinical interventions. Obviously, problematic interpersonal relationships are at the core of many demands of the public for psychotherapeutic support. In reading this book, it becomes clear that research on the dynamics of emotional interactions can provide keys to these problematic relationships in many, if not all, cases.

Let me add that this book also gives a testimony of the scientific maturity reached today by the research on human emotion. Over the last fifty years, this research has undergone tremendous conceptual and methodological enrichments. It can now address issues that we did not dare – or that we did not imagine – addressing until recently. This evolution contradicts the many who doubted that human emotion could lend itself to scientific investigation.

## References

Arnold, M. B. (1960). Emotion and Personality. New York: Columbia University Press.

Bowlby, J. (1969). Attachment and Loss (Vol. 1): Attachment. London: Hogarth.

Bruner, J. S. (1977). Early social interaction and language acquisition. In H. Schaffer (Ed.), Studies in Mother–Infant Interaction (pp. 271–89). New York: Academic Press.

Campos, J., & Stenberg, C. (1981). Perception, appraisal and emotion: The onset of social referencing. In M. E. Lamb & L. R. Sherrod (Eds.), Infant Social Cognition (pp. 273–314). Hillsdale, NJ: Erlbaum.

Cannon, W. B. (1916). Bodily Changes in Pain, Hunger, Fear, and Rage: An Account of Recent Researches into the Function of Emotional Excitement. New York and London: D. Appleton.

Claparède, E. (1928). Feelings and emotions. In C. Murchison & M. L. Reymert (Eds.), Feelings and Emotions: The Wittenberg Symposium (pp. 124–39). Worcester, MA: Clark University Press.

Darwin, C. (1965; originally published in 1872). The Expression of the Emotions in Man and Animals. Chicago: Chicago University Press.

Ekman, P., Friesen, W. V., & Ellsworth, P. (1972). Emotion in the Human Face: Guidelines for Research and An Integration of Findings. New York: Pergamon Press.

Fischer, A. H., & Manstead, A. S. R. (2008). Social functions of emotion. In M. Lewis, J. M. Haviland-Jones, & L. F. Barrett (Eds.), Handbook of Emotions, 3rd edition (pp. 456–68). New York and London: Guilford Press.

Frijda, N. H. (1986). *The emotions*. Cambridge: Cambridge University Press.

Izard, C. E. (1971). The Face of Emotion. New York: Appleton-Century-Crofts.

James, W. (1884). What is an emotion? Mind, 9, 188–205.

Keltner, D., & Haidt, J. (1999). Social functions of emotions at four levels of analysis. Cognition & Emotion, 13(5), 505–21.

Lazarus, R. S., & Folkman, S. (1984). Stress, Appraisal and Coping. New York: Springer.

Meltzoff, A. N., & Moore, M. K. (1977). Imitation of facial and manual gestures by human neonates. Science, 198(4312), 75–8.

Mesquita, B., & Frijda, N. H. (1992). Cultural variations in emotions: A review. Psychological Bulletin, 112, 179–204.

Parkinson, B. (1996). Emotions are social. British Journal of Psychology, 87(4), 663–83.

Pribram, K. H. (1967). Emotion: Steps toward a neuropsychological theory. In D. Glass (Ed.), Neurophysiology and Emotion (pp. 2–40). New York: Rockefeller University Press and Russell Sage Foundation.

Rimé, B., Mesquita, B., Philippot, P., & Boca, S. (1991). Beyond the emotional event: Six studies on the social sharing of emotion. Cognition and Emotion, 5, 435–65.

Scherer, K. R. (1984). Emotion as a multicomponent process: A model and some cross-cultural data. In P. Shaver (Ed.), Review of Personality and Social Psychology (Vol. 5, pp. 37–63). Beverly Hills, CA: Sage.

Scherer, K. R., Wallbott, H. G., & Summerfield, A. B. (Eds.) (1986). Experiencing Emotion: A Cross-Cultural Study. Cambridge: Cambridge University Press.

Tomkins, S. S. (1962). Affect, Imagery, and Consciousness. New York: Springer-Verlag.

Tronick, E. D., Als, H., & Brazelton, T. B. (1977). Mutuality in mother–infant interaction. Journal of Communication, 27(2), 74–9.

Van Kleef, G. A. (2009). How emotions regulate social life: The emotions as social information (EASI) model. Current Directions in Psychological Science, 18(3), 184–8.

von Scheve, C., & Salmela, M. (Eds.). (2014). Collective Emotions: Perspectives from Psychology, Philosophy, and Sociology. Oxford, UK: Oxford University Press.

Young, P. T. (1943). Emotion in Man and Animal. New York: John Wiley and Sons.

Watson, J. B. (1929). Psychology from the Standpoint of a Behaviorist. Philadelphia and London: J. B. Lippincott Company.

# Introduction

*Ashley K. Randall and Dominik Schoebi*

When we ask people to describe their close personal relationships, they often tell us how their relationship affects them emotionally. They tell us how returning home to their parents makes them feel safe and loved, what a great time they had with their friends, or how their partner makes them feel happy and good about themselves. Sometimes they tell us how vacationing with their parents and siblings gets on their nerves, how spending time with friends makes them feel inferior, or how their partner makes them anxious because they do not communicate with them throughout the day.

Searching the internet for combinations between personal relationships terms (e.g., mother, father, friend, partner, spouse) and emotion words (e.g., happy, angry, sad), further emphasizes the connection between these two concepts (google.com, August 2017). For example, searching for combinations between the terms "partner," "husband," or "wife" and "happy" yields between 192 and 206 million hits. The terms "mother" or "father" yield 65 million hits when combined with "angry," and 215 (mother) and 172 million (father) hits when combined with "happy." Furthermore, "best friend" yields 73 million hits when combined with "happy," and between 22 and 25 million when combined with negative emotion words. Theory and research on emotion (Oatley & Jenkins, 1996), and the clinical field on emotional dysfunction (Mennin et al., 2007), acknowledge the key role of close relationships both in scientific work and clinical applications.

## The emerging study of interpersonal emotion dynamics

The role of emotions for relationship development and functioning has long been recognized and fueled important advances in relationship research (Bradbury et al., 2000). Furthermore, social factors have been a major focus in affective sciences (see Chapter 1). Emotional interdependence is arguably one of the most defining features of close relationships (e.g. Sels et al., 2016), and considered a key criterion for individuals to evaluate the bonds with another person as close or

1

intimate. Irrespective, comparably little attention has been devoted to the connection among two or more individuals' emotional experiences as they fluctuate across time.

Over the past three decades, however, a small but growing body of literature focusing on aspects of interdependent emotional change between two or more individuals – interpersonal emotion dynamics (IED) – has accumulated. This work has grown mainly in the slipstream of more firmly established lines of research, and is scattered across several scientific literatures and disciplines, such as social psychology, health psychology, clinical psychology and development psychology, social neuroscience and health sciences. An important driving factor in this work has been the development of sophisticated methods that produced the type of data necessary to investigate interdependent emotional change across time, that is, intensive longitudinal measures of emotions from more than one relationship member, collected either in daily life or in the laboratory (e.g., Bolger & Laurenceau, 2013; Mehl & Conner, 2011). Examples include studies on stress spillover (Bolger et al., 1989; Repetti, 1989) and emotional transmission (e.g., Larson & Almeida, 1999). Another factor that has advanced the field has been methodological refinements and the growing accessibility of analytic methods offering opportunities to utilize intensive longitudinal measures (e.g., multilevel modeling, and models for dyads and families; Kenny et al., 2006). This has produced empirical studies on IED and some of the few conceptual contributions (see Butler, 2011). Based on the chapters of this book, we believe the field is now at a point where integration of theory and methodological approaches, along with an expanded analytic toolbox for advancing our understanding of IEDs in close relationships and associated outcomes, offer evidence that an increasingly more coherent literature is developing.

## Promises and challenges of studying interpersonal emotion dynamics

If emotions evolved to facilitate adaptive responses to need-relevant situations, then they must be dynamic: they need to change across situations as function of the presence and nature of situational demands and opportunities (e.g., Niedenthal & Brauer, 2012). The study of emotional dynamics thus becomes an important window into individuals' adjustment processes when navigating their daily life, or during specific situations that pose adaptive tasks. Studying emotional change thus offers insight into a person's adaptation *processes*, rather than their momentary *state of adjustment* in given circumstances at a particular point in time.

A person's experienced adaptive challenges and their outcomes, including threats and opportunities, often originate in the relationship, or are likely relevant to the person's close relationship partner (e.g., parent, peer, or romantic partner) when originating outside the relationship. Therefore, the study of IEDs can be highly informative about the role and provisions of relationship processes for individual adjustment of its members (Schoebi & Randall, 2015). Moreover, by distilling information about the individual's adaptive processes independently of the type of situation, challenge or context in which they emerge, emotional information can serve as a "lingua franca" or "global currency," which benefits research based on heterogeneous samples of adaptation relevant episodes (e.g., daily life data or interaction tasks in laboratory settings). Yet the study of IEDs is also highly challenging, as it is a multilayered and multidimensional study object. Emotions involve different tones and intensities of subjective experience, and different channels at variable levels of consciousness (Scherer, 2005). Emotional change inherently involves a temporal dimension, with different emotional tones and different emotion channels varying in their characteristic rate of change. In addition, these dimensions and layers occur in two or more individuals living in unique relationships, and are connected in many different ways, producing a range of complex patterns of IED (Butler, 2011). The demands posed by the study of IEDs for research methods and analytic tools, and for theory for theory, are thus particularly high. The chapters of this book give evidence of this complexity, and, although non-exhaustive, cover a broad range of dimensions of interpersonal emotional experience in close relationships.

## Plan of the book

The goal of this book was to bring together knowledge on the study of IEDs in close relationships across the life-span. In developing this volume, we thought to include scholars who would bring together recent advances in the conceptual, methodological, statistical, and empirical underpinnings to understanding IEDs within personal relationships, as well as offer important directions for future research. As various conceptualizations of IEDs exist (see Butler & Randall, 2013), each contributor provides their conceptualization of IED, as informed by their review of the literature and conceptual perspective.

In Chapter 1, we provide an overview of major theories and models that lend themselves to studying IEDs. We also present the *Situation-Context-Person Framework of Interpersonal Emotion Dynamics (SCOPE)* to help contextualize IEDs based on situational, contextual, and personal factors. Central to all relationships across the lifespan, Chapter 2 provides a general framework for capturing IEDs, and their associations with relational and emotional adjustment. Sels, Ceulemans, and Kuppens illustrate four key characteristics of IEDs, specifically *emotional covariation, emotional influencing, emotional variability* and *emotional inertia,* and discuss underlying processes associated with well-being. Chapter 3 serves as a resource for simplifying the complexity of IEDs using regression graphics. Using dyadic data, Butner and colleagues exemplify various tools to graphically display IEDs and facilitate their interpretation, and they offer additional material for the reader's own applications in an appendix. Chapter 4 presents specific designs that elicit IEDs, such as dyadic interaction tasks and experimental designs. Lougheed and Hollenstein also review the various approaches to capture these dynamics, with specific attention to physiological arousal, emotional experience, and behavioral expression (e.g., State Space Grids; Hollenstein, 2013).

Chapters 5 and 6, respectively, focus on the biological and physiological correlates associated with IEDs. Chapter 5 begins with a review on the associations between serotonin and susceptibility to partner's emotions. Way and Keaveney also review the biochemical associations of empathy and discuss inflammation as a potential moderator of IEDs, highlighting the associations between chemical and behavioral outcomes. Moving from biology to physiology, Chapter 6 focuses on how the interactions with our relational partners "get under our skin." In doing so, Saxbe and co-authors review the various physiological systems linked to IED, specifically the Hypothalamic-Pituitary-Adrenal (HPA) Axis, the Autonomic Nervous System (ANS), Oxytocin, a neuropeptide associated with bonding, trust, and positive communication, and Testosterone.

The subsequent three chapters are dedicated to reviewing literature on IEDs within family (Chapter 7), young adult and peer (Chapter 8), and intimate relationships (Chapter 9). In Chapter 7, Repetti and McNeil focus on patterns of family interaction that give rise to both negative (demand-withdrawal), and positive (capitalization) IEDs. Furthermore, Chapter 7 reviews specific contexts, such as the within-family spillover and impact of daily stress on family emotion dynamics. In Chapter 8, Champion, Ha, and Dishion present a conceptual overview of coercion as a dynamic system that gives rise to IEDs, specifically within adolescence. Additionally, Chapter 8 presents recent data on the link between adolescent deviancy training and long-term effects on displays of coercion in romantic relationships ten years later. In Chapter 9, Shenhav, Hovasapian, and Campos provide an overview of emotion dynamics that are characteristic of intimate relationships. Special attention is given to emotion dynamics that contribute to the formation, maintenance, and dissolution of such relationships.

Last, Chapter 10 provides an overview of promising areas for future direction, including the need to revise within-person processes, including biological processes, and reciprocal connections with relationship quality. Butler also points to the importance of the need for greater methodological tools and mathematical sophistication to examine IEDs in a variety of contexts.

Written by scholars in the field of emotion, close relationships, and related disciplines, this book synthesizes conceptual and empirical knowledge on IED within personal relationships. The chapters can serve as a valuable resource and guide for graduate students, researchers, and clinicians alike to understand: (1) theoretical and methodological considerations to studying interpersonal emotions, (2) empirical research on IED across various personal relationships, and (3) important areas for future research in these areas.

## References

Bradbury, T. N., Fincham, F. D., & Beach, S. R. (2000). Research on the nature and determinants of marital satisfaction: a decade in review. *Journal of Marriage and the Family*, 62(4), 964–80.

Bolger, N., DeLongis, A., Kessler, R. C., & Wethington, E. (1989). The contagion of stress across multiple roles. *Journal of Marriage and the Family*, 51, 175–83.

Bolger, N., & Laurenceau, J. P. (2013). *Intensive Longitudinal Methods*. New York, NY: Guilford.

Butler, E. A. (2011). Temporal interpersonal emotion systems: the "TIES" that form relationships. *Personality and Social Psychology Review*, 15, 367–93.

Butler, E. A., & Randall, A. K. (2013). Emotional coregulation in close relationships. *Emotion Review*, 5(2), 202–10

Hollenstein, T. (2013). *State Space Grids: Depicting Dynamics across Development*. New York, NY: Springer.

Kenny, D. A., Kashy, D. A., & Cook, W. L. (2006). *Dyadic Data Analysis*. New York, NY: The Guilford Press.

Larson, R. W., & Almeida, D. M. (1999). Emotional transmission in the daily lives of families: a new paradigm for studying family process. *Journal of Marriage and the Family*, 61, 5–20.

Mehl, M. R., & Conner, T. A. (Eds.), (2011). *Handbook of Research Methods for Studying Daily Life*. New York, NY: Guilford Press.

Mennin, D. S., Holaway, R., Fresco, D. M., et al. (2007). Delineating components of emotion and its dysregulation in anxiety and mood psychopathology. *Behavior Therapy*, 38, 284–302.

Niedenthal, P. M., & Brauer, M. (2012). Social functionality of human emotion. *Annual Review of Psychology*, 63, 259–85.

Oatley, K., & Jenkins, J. M. (1996). *Understanding Emotions*. Cambridge, MA: Blackwell publishing.

Repetti, R. L. (1989). Effects of daily workload on subsequent behavior during marital interaction: the roles of social withdrawal and spouse support. *Journal of Personality and Social Psychology*, 57(4), 651.

Scherer, K. R. (2005). What are emotions? And how can they be measured? *Social Science Information*, 44(4), 695–729.

Schoebi, D., & Randall, A. K. (2015). Emotional dynamics in intimate relationships. *Emotion Review*, 7, 342–8.

Sels, L., Ceulemans, E., Bulteel, K., & Kuppens, P. (2016). Emotional interdependence and well-being in close relationships. *Frontiers in Psychology*, 7. doi: 10.3389/fpsyg.2016.00283.

# CHAPTER 1

# Conceptual approaches to studying interpersonal emotion dynamics

*Ashley K. Randall and Dominik Schoebi*

The study of how and why we experience emotion has been a focus in psychological science for quite some time, spanning well over a century, to Darwin (1872). Many theories and empirical studies have focused on the individual or intrapersonal experience, specifically as it relates to how the perception of an event elicits and shapes an emotional reaction (*appraisal theory of emotions*; e.g., Arnold, 1960; Lazarus, 1991). However, in the last two decades increased attention has been paid to conceptualizing emotion as an interpersonal experience; one that is associated with individuals' interactions and subsequent behaviors (e.g., Keltner & Haidt, 2001; Rimé et al., 1991; Schoebi & Randall, 2015), specifically in the context of close personal relationships (Clark et al., 2001; Ekman & Davidson, 1994).

Within the social sciences, interpersonal emotion dynamics have been examined in a number of ways (Butler, 2011). Here we conceptualize interpersonal emotion dynamics as two or more individuals' interdependent emotional changes across time. Exemplified by the contributions in this book, scholars are studying how an individual's emotional experiences – the biological, physiological, and experiential – are shaped by his or her close personal relationships across the life-span, such as those with parents, siblings, peers, and his or her intimate partners. Despite early work on understanding the social dimensions of emotion (Campos et al., 1989; Frijda & Mesquita, 1994), to date, no one framework, model, or theory conceptualizes the *why* and *how* of interpersonal emotion dynamics in close relationships; however, a number of theoretical frameworks offer various perspectives. As such, this chapter will first provide an overview of major theories and models that lend themselves to studying the social aspects of emotions, and then outline the *Situation-Context-Person Framework of Interpersonal Emotion Dynamics* (SCOPE) framework to conceptualize interpersonal emotion dynamics within close relationships.

## Theoretical perspectives on understanding the social side of emotions

Traditional emotion theories focus on the individual experience of emotion (e.g., physiological reactivity (James, 1894)); however, borrowing from emotion and social psychological literature, researchers can begin to draw a more nuanced picture of the social side of emotions. The *appraisal theories of emotions* (see Scherer et al., 2001) are particularly valuable in this regard, as they offer a way to conceptualize how emotions may function in social situations. According to such theories, emotions are thought to distill meaning from important transactions with the environment, to guide adaptive action. Appraisal theories can help one understand how social interactions can shape emotional dynamics, and also how emotions can influence and shape social interactions. Theoretical perspectives on the social functions of emotions are influenced by core elements of appraisal theories, as are emerging approaches to understanding the social effects of emotions, such as the *Emotions as Social Information* (EASI) model (Van Kleef, 2009, 2016). The EASI model adopts the perspective that an individual's emotion process affects their interpersonal processes, while other work, particularly theories considering the social regulation of emotions (e.g., Social Baseline Theory; Coan & Sbarra, 2015) highlights the social factors and conditions that can shape and change emotion processes. We briefly review a selection of these perspectives below.

### Appraisal theories of emotion

Appraisals are central to understanding emotions within a social context (e.g., Parkinson & Manstead, 2015). Appraisal theories suggest that emotions are responses to the assessment of an event or situations (Lazarus, 1991; Moors et al., 2013; Roseman & Smith, 2001). As such, these theories offer a way to relate the subjective meaning of a situation to a particular (adaptive) emotional response, including expressions of emotion and action tendencies. Take for example two people meeting for the first time, whether in a friendly or romantic context. If one hopes to continue their dialogue with the hopes of deepening a relationship with the other, and the other is appraised as acting in positive way, then one may feel excitement or joy and wish to continue seeing that person. If the other is perceived as acting negatively, however, then the person may feel disappointed or embarrassed, which would cause them to question the future of the relationship. Importantly, multiple appraisals can exist in a given situation, which can yield an indefinite number of emotional experiences. As such, one's emotional experiences, as a function of their appraisals, can be thought to be emotion processes that change over time.

Aspects of appraisal theories can also be applied to interpersonal situations, such as in the case of an interaction between two people (e.g., parent and child, peers, and romantic partners). Proposing particular appraisals (positive or negative) as key differentiating components of emotional experiences may offer some guidance for understanding how particular interpersonal situations may shape a specific emotional response. Specifically, the appraisals of a person's agency and motives within the interaction are important dimensions of the appraisal process (e.g., Ellsworth & Scherer, 2003). For example, in the context of a conflict interaction, if one's appraises a partner to be acting selfishly, this may be alarming and cause a specific emotional response. Along with other important appraisal dimensions, such as one's own controllability or power, we can outline interpersonal situations that are likely to shape certain emotional experiences. Expanding the earlier example with the two interaction partners, if one appraises the conflictual situation as they have the ability to influence the outcome of the situation, they may be less likely to feel anxious or fearful about the other's selfish intentions than if they perceive little control.

Furthermore, taking into consideration the notion that an interaction partners' emotional expressions may facilitate the appraisals of one's own emotions, appraisal theories may scaffold our understanding of interpersonal emotion dynamics. For example, in the conflictual situation mentioned above, the expressions of anger from the interaction partner may be appraised as signaling selfish motives, likely not conducive to the achievement of one's own goals, and may therefore have a negative valence. The appraisal one then makes of their controllability and power in the situation may contribute to whether they feel anger, anxiety, or sadness in response. The partner, in turn, will appraise this response based on verbal and nonverbal cues, which will change his or her emotion process, and so forth (e.g., feedback loops). Thus, the conceptualization of the emotion process as a transaction between a person and his or her environment is applicable to a relational context, which results in an interdependent, dynamic interpersonal process. The idea that emotions reflect meaning derived from interactions, and that emotional expressions convey meaning to an interaction partner, is an important mechanism underlying the social functions of emotion.

## Theoretical perspectives on the social functions of emotions

Emotions serve important social functions (Keltner & Haidt, 1999; Parkinson, 1996), such as helping people become aware of each other's beliefs, intentions, and emotions, evoking complimentary and reciprocal emotions, and increasing (or decreasing) subsequent behaviors

(Klinnert et al., 1983, as cited in Keltner & Haidt, 1999). Indeed, Rimé's (2007) work on the social sharing of emotion has found that people have various motives for sharing emotions, which include but are not limited to: venting ("blowing off steam"), receiving support, obtaining advice or solutions, gaining attention, or as a means of social bonding. As people tend to share more frequently with those whom they are closest to, the intensity and frequency of emotion expressed can be thought to be related to the nature and the functions we attribute to the relationship (e.g., support provider) (Clark et al., 2001; Parkinson, 1996).

The *social-functional approach to emotions* (e.g., Keltner & Haidt, 1999) conceptualizes emotions based on four basic premises. First, humans are social beings who may face threat in the context of social interaction (Baumeister & Leary, 1995). Second, emotions are related to the development and maintenance of close relationships (Schoebi & Randall, 2015). Third, emotions are dynamic processes that coordinate social interaction across a variety of lengths of time, from seconds to days or even longer periods (see Butler, 2011, for a review; see also Chapters 2 and 9). Last, the expression and experience of emotion yields social consequences for individuals and their relationships (Gable & Reis, 2001; see also Chapter 5). Utilizing the social-functional approach to emotions allows researchers to understand the functionality of emotion at different levels of analysis, including the individual (*intra*personal) and dyadic (*inter*personal) levels.

The individual unit of analysis focuses on the *intra*personal experience of emotions in a given social interaction. Oatley and Jenkins (1992) theorized that an individual's emotional response can serve two social functions. Emotions first *inform the individual* about the social interaction, and then *prepare the individual* to respond. For example, feeling anxious in an interpersonal context may convey a sense of vulnerability or weakness and prepare one for defensive actions or withdrawal. Thus, one's emotional experience provides information about the situation and conditions (e.g., whether a threat is present), or the person's relative position related to others in the setting (e.g., dominance or inferiority, opposition or alliance), which is expanded upon in the EASI model (Van Kleef, 2009) described below.

Taking into consideration two or more members of the system allows one to focus on the *inter*personal experience of emotion, specifically as it refers to understanding how "emotions organize the interactions of individuals in meaningful relationships" (Keltner & Haidt, 1999, p. 510). From a dyadic perspective, emotions help individuals discern each other's beliefs and intentions, evoke complimentary emotions in others, and serve as incentives (or deterrents) for other social behavior. Therefore, the expression of certain emotions may generate or change appraisals and action tendencies in the interaction partner, and thereby shape or stimulate the subsequent interactions.

With an interaction, emotions can serve either an *affiliative* or *distancing* function (Fischer & Manstead, 2016). The *affiliative* function of emotion refers to how emotions help us to maintain and establish bonds with others (Van Kleef et al., 2010). For example, sharing positive events with a close friend (Rimé, 2007) or romantic partner (e.g., Gable et al., 2004), or soliciting (and receiving) emotional support during times of distress, can help with relational well-being (Merz et al., 2014). The *distancing* function of emotions refers to how emotions may create distance between individuals, either physical or psychological. For example, anger and disgust can both serve to signal psychological distance (e.g., with respect to the social hierarchy) and motivate physical distance (even if anger may initially be expressed through approach behavior; Van Kleef, 2016). In certain relational contexts, however, anger and disgust may also assume affiliative functions in that they can allow for people to express their feelings and offer a space to talk things out (e.g., Fehr et al., 1999). Specifically, it is possible that emotions that assume distancing functions, creating distance between close partners and signaling relationship threat, and can serve to motivate affiliative emotions and behaviors in the partner, particularly if occurring alongside affiliative functions. For example, expressing anger and disappointment toward a parent, friend, or a romantic partner after they forgot an important event may serve to strengthen the bond and reduce relational insecurities over time. This example also points to the importance of considering that in daily life, emotional states may not always occur as single, discrete states, but often as "blends" of emotions with similar general valence (e.g., Vansteelandt et al., 2005; Wilhelm et al., 2004), and consequently, it is plausible that multiple social functions of emotions may be sought in a single affect-laden situation.

## Social functions of emotions and emotional interdependence

Understanding the interaction between emotion and social interaction is not a new phenomenon (see Campos et al., 1989; Clark, 1990; Clark et al., 2001; Frijda & Mesquita, 1994). For quite some time, relational scholars have proposed that understanding emotion dynamics in the context of close personal relationships can be thought of as a function of the degree of interconnectedness, or interdependence, between individuals (Berscheid & Amazzalorso, 2001). The term interdependence reflects the condition that a change of state of any partner in a relationship changes the state of the other partner (Levin, 1948, as cited in Van Lange & Balliet, 2014). A high degree of interdependence is generally seen as a characteristic that differentiates close relationships from other relationships (Kelley et al., 1983). The influence that constitutes interdependence between those in a close relationship is mutual and frequent, which can also mean that a change in one person's state thwarts or constrains possible changes in the other. Situations in which emotional change occurs are likely appraised as of personal significance (Lazarus, 1991), and in interdependent relationships, where an individual's everyday behaviors and goals are highly coordinated (e.g., Knobloch & Metts, 2013), it is likely the norm rather than the exception that a substantial emotional change affects the partner's emotions.

Connection between two peoples' behaviors, cognitions, and affect at experiential or physiological levels are at the core of what defines a close relationship. Furthermore, emotional change is an important element of many interpersonal situations in which interdependence manifests itself. For example, a situation where a mother and daughter capitalize on the daughter's personal success, situations in which a close friend provides emotional support to another, or situations of tensions or conflict between romantic partners about decisions that concern the relationship, are difficult to imagine without emotional change in both partners (see Chapters 6, 7, and 8). In nondistressed close relationships in particular, emotional change that assumes affiliative functions appears to stimulate emotional change with similar functions in partners (e.g., Randall & Schoebi, 2015). Such findings highlight the potential of close relationships to play a major role in emotion regulation.

### Social regulation of emotion

Social contexts – the imagined or real presence of others – and social interactions play a vital role in individuals' need fulfillment. As such, these can be an important means by which emotions are regulated or help to scaffold the regulation of emotions. Emotion regulation has been conceptualized as an interpersonal or social process (e.g., Coan & Sbarra, 2015; Zaki & Williams, 2013) or as a property emerging from interdependent relationships (e.g., coregulation; Butler & Randall, 2013; Sbarra & Hazan, 2008).

### Relationships as emotion regulation contexts

Humans have evolved to form social ties to better satisfy and manage their needs; relationships are regulators to human experiences (Field, 2012; Hofer, 1984). The closer and more interdependent a relationship becomes, the more the boundaries between the individual self and others become blurred (e.g., Aron et al., 2013). This interdependence may not only contribute to a coordination of emotions through exposure to shared environments, the sharing of goals and concerns, or vicarious appraisals, but also through the expansion of resources an individual has at her or his disposal (i.e., by pooling them with their partner's). From such a perspective, close relationships are primary sources of need fulfillment (Baumeister & Leary, 1995).

*Social Baseline Theory* proposes that proximity to others plays a vital role in the generation and regulation of emotions (Coan & Sbarra, 2015). Accordingly, the closer the proximity of others in the context of a potential or impending threat, the stronger the negative emotions are buffered. Evidence supports such effects for mothers (e.g., Seltzer et al., 2010) and romantic partners (Coan et al., 2006). One basic factor thought to be at play is a broader *risk distribution*, with individual risk being lower when encountering threat in a social context. A second factor is *load sharing*, following the logic that a threat or challenge to a shared goal is more successfully managed with shared resources (Beckes & Coan, 2011). Thus, if two relational partners share their resources to work toward a shared goal, they should be more efficient at attaining the goal than if one partner worked alone.

As a basic mechanism underlying the social regulation of emotion, the load sharing effects seem more relevant to interpersonal emotion dynamics than the effects of risk distribution. Because load sharing requires a degree of agreement or shared goals and concerns, and the willingness and capacity to cooperate and pool resources to work toward a specific goal, the motivations and state of a partner should play an important role. This possibility is supported by evidence suggesting that the buffering effects from the presence of another are enhanced if the relationship is of high quality (e.g., Coan et al., 2006). A relational partner's emotions are important signals of such motivations and individual conditions; emotions signaling affiliation might enhance social regulation capacity of the relationship, whereas emotions signaling distance or opposition may undermine it. Thus, in a situation of tension or high conflict, or with a distressed or vulnerable partner, one may be likely to make a less optimistic appraisal of the resources available to meet a challenge.

The notion that close personal relationships have evolved to enhance need fulfillment and to fulfill important emotion regulatory functions is congruent with the views of attachment theory (e.g., Mikulincer & Shaver, 2005). More recent theoretical contributions built on attachment theory propose that the close bonds we develop with our attachment figures may assume mutually stabilizing functions and lead to the coregulation of emotions (e.g., Sbarra & Hazan, 2008). Partners' emotions thus become linked at both physiological and psychological levels, and work to keep each other in homeostasis, as a means of coregulation. In their conceptual review of the literature, Butler and Randall (2013) define coregulation as a bidirectional linkage of oscillating emotional channels between partners, which contributes to emotional stability for both partners. To this end, their definition lends itself to understanding how this specific interpersonal pattern of emotion dynamics characterizes a self-regulating system (Butler, 2015). An important aspect of this definition of coregulation is that it reflects a relatively constant dynamic pattern, rather than a relational dynamic that is activated when acute emotions arise; therefore, it is less likely to emerge from situational appraisals. Importantly, coregulation reflects a form of interpersonal dependency that should buffer specific emotional episodes and contribute to the dampening and stabilization of emotion fluctuations after such episodes occur.

### Types of interpersonal regulation

Zaki and Williams (2013) differentiate between *response-dependent* and *response-independent* forms of interpersonal emotion regulation.

*Response-dependent* forms of interpersonal regulation require a particular response from an interaction partner to achieve a desired change of emotional state (e.g., a bid for support). If interpersonal emotion regulation of this kind occurs in the context of an interdependent relationship, it is likely that intended or unintended emotional change gets coordinated between the two individuals. For example, a person's display and deliberate expression of sadness to establish affiliation and solicit a friend's or partner's attention and support can lead to an empathic response in the other – one that is both characterized by concern and sympathy, and benevolence or love. This response may then soothe the person's sadness and foster similar positive emotions (and in turn, the perception of these changes may dampen the friend's or partner's concern and anxiety). Alternatively, the person's expression of sadness may annoy the interaction partner, and his or her angry response may further deepen the person's sadness, while adding anger and disappointment as a function of the rejection, possibly leading to an escalation of negative emotions (Downey & Feldman, 1996). Such misdirected (automatic) attempts of interpersonal emotion regulation, leading to negative interpersonal emotion dynamics, may play a major role in clinical patterns of emotional dysregulation, such as depression (e.g., Coyne, 1976; Joiner & Metalsky, 2001), whereas successful regulation may play an important role in establishing the beneficial effects of social support (e.g., Lakey & Orehek, 2011; Marroquín, 2011).

In contrast, *response-independent* forms of interpersonal regulation do not necessarily require a particular complementary response from the partner in order to establish the required emotional change (e.g., venting; Rimé, 2007). Similar to response-dependent emotion regulation, response-independent forms are prone to feed into interpersonal emotion dynamics if they involve the expression of emotions that are directed at an interaction partner (e.g., during conflict; Bloch et al., 2014), or at someone or something outside the particular relationship, in a relational context (e.g., coming home upset; Schulz et al., 2004). It seems that in many cases, the social contribution to response-independent forms of emotion regulation is the provision of an opportunity to express and deal with the emotion within the context of a social relationship, which highlights the important role of social relationships as emotion regulation contexts.

Taken together, theoretical perspectives on the social regulation of emotions emphasize that emotion buffering and stabilization (i.e., return to homeostasis) are important property of close and trusting relationships. Furthermore, close personal relationships offer many opportunities to regulate emotions in interactions with close others, which may entail intended and unintended effects on either partner's emotions. Therefore, close personal relationships are an important resource for the regulation of emotions, and more generally, an important source of emotional change, given the shared interdependence between the two interaction partners. Indeed, modeling partners' emotional change is a growing interest in many disciplines (see Kuppens, 2015). To date, researchers have focused on capturing the interaction between intrapersonal and interpersonal emotion processes and their associations with both individual and relational outcomes.

## Temporal interpersonal emotion dynamics

Butler's (2011) conceptualization of relationships as *Temporal Interpersonal Emotion Systems* (TIES) is of particular importance for making sense of interpersonal emotion dynamics. This model differentiates between specific patterns of interdependent emotional change that can be understood as relational processes across varying time lengths (i.e., partners' emotional interdependence across time). For example, interpersonal emotions can be examined second-by-second, as with physiological responses (Helm et al., 2012; Reed et al., 2015; see also Chapters 4 and 9), minute-by-minute, as with hormonal change (e.g., Saxbe & Repetti, 2010; see also Chapter 4), hour-to-hour, as with subjective emotional experience (e.g., Schoebi & Randall, 2015; see also Chapters 5, 6, and 8), or day-to-day, across days, or across weeks (Gonzaga et al., 2007; see also Chapter 7). Chapters 5, 6, 7, and 8 of this volume provide illustrative examples of how such processes may develop and function in varying personal relationships.

Adopting a dynamic systems perspective (see Chapter 9), the TIES model (Butler, 2011) assumes a degree of continuity in the system with prior states of the system predicting subsequent states, and change in a system occurring as a function of the interaction between the system's components (i.e., the two partners in a dyad). In addition, the mutual adjustment of the system's components during interaction provides the system with a self-organizing and self-regulating capacity, which involves both positive and negative feedback loops. These feedback loops can balance or reinforce processes that give rise to specific patterns of (coordinated) changes, contributing either to the reestablishment of homeostasis or to more enduring change.

To this point, we have highlighted literature that suggests emotions carry important social functions that help to shape and regulate one's emotions and interactions. Although several lines of theorizing and research contribute to the understanding causes, mechanisms and patterns of interpersonal emotion dynamics, the *why* and *how* of interpersonal emotion dynamics, have yet to be addressed by a single framework that conceptualizes individuals' emotional interdependence across time.

## Situation-context-person framework of interpersonal emotion dynamics (SCOPE)

Emotions are related to both the development and maintenance of close relationships (Schoebi & Randall, 2015), carry social information (Van Kleef, 2016), and are dynamic processes between individuals that coordinate social interaction across time points (Butler, 2015). While all three of these properties of interpersonal emotions have been explored independently, no one framework exists that offers relationship and emotion scholars a foundation for understanding the underpinnings of interpersonal emotion dynamics in close personal relationships. Below we offer an initial attempt to provide such a framework that distinguishes between situational, contextual, and personal factors that shape interpersonal emotion dynamics.

### *Situational factors and processes*

Emotional change occurs when a person's appraisals indicate that personal needs, goals, or concerns are at stake (see Chapter 5). Therefore, in the context of a close relationship between Persons A and B, Person A's emotional change becomes linked with Person B's emotional change if Person A's emotion expression (or, possibly, its effects) are appraised as significant by Person B, or if Person B alerted by a primary appraisal of significance attends to Person A to gauge availability of relational resources (e.g., Person A's support). During interactions, patterns of interdependent emotional change can emerge because the emotions displaced can fulfill social functions that structure the interaction sequences in which they are embedded (e.g., Fischer & Manstead, 2016). For example, mutual reinforcement of disclosures through expressions of positive emotions, or negative emotions expressed reciprocally during an escalating conflict interaction, may induce interdependent, alternating patterns of emotion display. Partners' emotional changes can also become linked if common or overlapping goals (e.g., Randall et al., 2013), concerns, or needs of two partners are at stake, and thus a particular situation elicits appraisals in both partners. As such, patterns of emotional independence do not necessarily emerge from actual interaction sequences.

## Contextual factors

One of the key premises of the SCOPE framework is that understanding interpersonal emotion dynamics can be conceptualized as a function of relational partners' interdependence (Berscheid & Amazzalorso, 2001), the felt responsibility for one another's needs (Clark et al., 2001), and the physical proximity between partners (e.g., Coan & Sbarra, 2015). Importantly, partners' interpersonal emotion dynamics are not stagnant (Butler, 2011); individuals learn over the course of the interaction and their relationship how to respond to their parent, peer, or partner to reach their desired outcome (either positive or negative) (Fischer & Manstead, 2016; Schoebi & Randall, 2015), which form the basis for the emerging interpersonal dynamics.

Factors at different levels of stability can operate as moderators to these interpersonal emotion processes. For example, a mother's momentary fatigue may moderate emotional dynamics during a dinnertime conversation, or partners' high levels of relationship satisfaction or commitment may dampen the negative transmission of emotions that might result from a stressful day at work. On the one hand, contextual factors shape individuals' appraisal processes, and thereby the intensity and quality of emotional reactions during specific situations, which may include the reactions to the partner's emotions, therefore reflecting partners' interdependence. On the other hand, these factors can be context specific and moderate or constrain emotion processes and interdependence in some contexts, and not in others. Such factors thus induce emotional interdependence on a macro level, resulting in longer-term interpersonal emotion dynamics.

## Personal factors

Importantly, we must acknowledge that not all individuals will react similarly or respond to situations in a similar manner (Smith & Lazarus, 1990), due to a number of relatively stable individual characteristics such as genes, personality, attachment style, and culture (Mesquita et al., 2017). For example, one's personality may predispose an individual to experience positive and negative affect to varying degrees (e.g., Komulainen et al., 2014). Additionally, one's attachment style, or the degree of security one feels to their primary caregiver (Bowlby, 1988; Shaver & Mikulincer, 2007), has been found to differentially predict emotional responses to the same situation. Specifically, individuals high in attachment insecurity, as defined by either high in attachment anxiety or avoidance, will respond to the threat with heightened negative affect and demonstrate hypervigilance toward or disengagement from the threat (see Simpson & Rholes, 2017 for a review).

**Interaction of situational, contextual, and personal factors.** Using an ecological systems approach (Bronfenbrenner, 1979), we propose that situational, contextual, and personal factors shape individuals' emotion dynamics and patterns of emotional experience in important ways (see Chapter 5), while also contributing to their emotional experiences over time. Therefore, in a given interaction, partners' interpersonal emotion experience can be considered a function of the situational and contextual factors common for the dyad (e.g., degree of closeness, relationship length, current relationship satisfaction, etc.), or unique to one of the interacting individuals (e.g., momentary stress level, a person's insecurities), in addition to each individual's personal factors.

Together, these factors initiate, shape and modulate emotion processes within and between partners during the interaction. Figure 1.1 displays such processes of two interaction partners, and their possible contribution to interpersonal connection. Both partners have their individual needs, goals, and concerns (N) that may be similar or dissimilar,

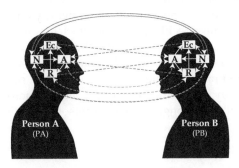

Figure 1.1. Components of emotion processes during dyadic interaction
Note: Ec = emotional change, N = needs, goals, and concerns, A = cognitive appraisals, R = regulation attempts.

and that may influence each other. Within a specific situation, the personal relevance of the situation or context is appraised (A), which may lead to or shape emotional change (Ec), upon which a person may mobilize emotion regulation efforts (R). In turn, a person's efforts to regulate emotions, both personal and interpersonal, may alter emotional change, and appraisals. Regulation efforts can be similar (or also dissimilar) between interacting partners. Regulation efforts and emotional change can be subject to appraisals by the interaction partner, whether conscious or not, and thereby shape or alter the partner's emotional change and subsequent interactions.

Recognizing the importance of situational, contextual, and personal factors in interdependent emotional change, and the multiple ways in which these factors may interact both within and between partners (contributing to interdependence), also implies that the relational significance of interpersonal emotion dynamics can barely be understood in an absolute sense. For example, patterns of mutual surges of anger in between partners can point to (and contribute to) relational dysfunction if one partner's anger, possibly accompanied with hostility or contempt, is related to an escalating interpersonal conflict. Alternatively, it can point to two partners working out a disagreement, maybe accompanied with concern and some anxiety or sadness about the future of their relationship. Or partners' surges of anger may be directed to a something or someone outside the relationship whose behavior toward one or both partners is deemed inappropriate by both partners, and the perception of a similar response by the partner may signal loyalty and support, and further strengthen the interpersonal bond. Therefore, when naturally occurring emotion fluctuations are sampled across a multitude of daily life situations (e.g., experience sampling) it should be quite difficult to identify clear links between the strength of interpersonal emotion dynamics and measures of individual or interpersonal adjustment. Experimental or quasi-experimental paradigms in the laboratory or in normative real-life situations are encouraged to be developed to identify such links (see Chapters 2 and 10). Nevertheless, a certain degree of interdependence, emerging from changes toward a more positive and less negative emotional valence, could be assumed as normative for well-functioning relationships across a wide range of emotion-relevant situations.

**Illustrative application of SCOPE**

Examining stress in the context of close personal relationships offers a unique perspective to applying concepts associated with interpersonal emotion dynamics. Applying the SCOPE framework, we present an illustrative example that is based on the systemic transactional model

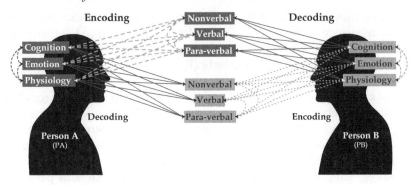

Figure 1.2. Partners' intrapersonal emotional experience (i.e., cognition, emotion, and physiology), and its communication

of a couple's interaction under stress (Bodenmann, 2005). Take a person who has experienced a stressful day. Upon coming home to share their stressful day with their parent or romantic partner they begin to communicate their stress. This stress can be communicated in a number of ways: nonverbally, such as through facial expressions (Ekman, 1993; Guerrero & Floyd, 2006), verbally (Slatcher & Trentacosta, 2011), and para-verbally, such as through the pitch and tone of voice (Baucom et al., 2012). See the dashed (Person A) and dotted (Person B) arrows in Figure 1.2 for a representation of the expression of the intrapersonal emotion experience.

Once the stress has been communicated, the interaction partner then decodes the message, which shapes his or her response. This interpersonal emotional exchange is represented by the solid gray arrows in Figure 1.2. Therefore, within a given interaction, partners' intrapersonal emotional experiences (cognition, emotion, physiology) are connected via the encoding and decoding of the messages (verbal, nonverbal, para-verbal) expressed between partners, which can occur multiple times during a given interaction, as represented by "Tx" in Figure 1.3.

Applying the SCOPE framework, Figure 1.3 depicts partners' interpersonal emotion dynamics in a given situation (e.g., during a stress conversation). During an interaction, each person brings their own personal factors to the situation, which details the what, why, and how of the information that is communicated, while each partner may have their own emotional reaction (see Figures 1.2 and 1.3; dashed and dotted arrows, respectively) which is coordinated with their partner's (represented by the solid gray arrows in Figure 1.2) through multiple interactions across time (see Figure 1.3). Therefore, in referencing both Figures 1.2 and 1.3 researchers can understand the temporal nature of different emotion

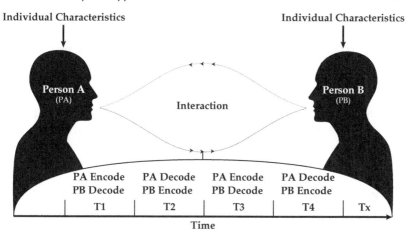

Figure 1.3. Partners' interpersonal emotion dynamics during a dyadic interaction process

channels (e.g., synchrony of physiology (see Chapter 4), transmission of experienced negative affect (see Chapters 5, 6, 7, and 8), or the oscillation of such emotional signals over time (e.g., Helm et al., 2012; Reed et al., 2015), and resulting implications for modeling emotional coregulation (or dysregulation) in the context of partners' interaction.

Future work focused on interpersonal emotion dynamics within close personal relationships is encouraged to use new technologies to examine partners' intra- and interpersonal mechanisms during interactions, in order to better predict both individual (e.g., symptoms of psychological distress) and relational (e.g., relationship length) outcomes, while taking into consideration specific situational, contextual, and personal factors that may moderate these associations. Chapter 10 provides an in-depth discussion of important areas for future research.

## Conclusion

Many of the existing theories for understanding emotional experiences lend themselves to conceptualizing interpersonal emotion dynamics. From the appraisal theories of emotion (e.g., Lazarus, 1991; Roseman & Smith, 2001), scholars can understand how emotions may be directly associated to the appraisal of situation. Furthermore, emotions serve important social functions (Fischer & Manstead, 2016; Parkinson, 1996), which can be exemplified in the social sharing of emotion (Rimé, 2007) or the regulation of such emotional experiences (e.g., Butler & Randall,

2013; Coan & Sbarra, 2015). Interestingly, until now, many of the fields interested that examine and emotion-related dynamics in the contexts of close relationships have developed independently of one another, focusing on either the intrapersonal or interpersonal emotional experience. Recent efforts, such as the EASI (Van Kleef, 2009) and the TIES (Butler, 2011) models, suggest that there is a greater need to understand the interpersonal emotion experience as it relates to both intra and interpersonal well-being, broadly defined. The SCOPE framework provides an initial attempt at conceptualizing the *why* and *how* of interpersonal emotion dynamics within close personal relationships. Our hope is that this framework, and much of the context of this book, will inspire the next generation of emotion and relational scholars to further the study of interpersonal emotion dynamics.

## References

Arnold, M. B. (1960). *Emotion and Personality.* New York, NY: Columbia University Press.

Aron, A., Lewandowski, G. W., Jr, Mashek, D., & Aron, E. N. (2013). The self-expansion model of motivation and cognition in close relationships. In J. A. Simpson & L. Campbell (Eds.), *The Oxford Handbook of Close Relationships* (pp. 90–115). Oxford: Oxford University Press.

Baucom, B., Weusthoff, S., Atkins, D., & Hahlweg, K. (2012). Greater emotional arousal predicts poorer long-term memory of communication skills in couples. *Behavior Research and Therapy,* 50, 442–7.

Baumeister, R. F., & Leary, M. R. (1995). The need to belong: desire for interpersonal attachments as a fundamental human motivation. *Psychological Bulletin,* 117(3), 497–529.

Beckes, L., & Coan, J. A. (2011). Our social baseline: the role of social proximity in economy of action. *Social and Personality Psychology Compass,* 12, 976–88.

Berscheid, E., & Ammazzalorso, H. (2001). Emotional experience in close relationships. In G. J. O. Fletcher & M. S. Clark (Eds.), *Blackwell Handbook of Social Psychology: Interpersonal Processes* (pp. 308–30). Oxford: Blackwell Publishing.

Bloch, L., Haase, C. M., & Levenson, R. W. (2014). Emotion regulation predicts marital satisfaction: more than a wives' tale. *Emotion,* 14(1), 130–44.

Bodenmann, G. (2005). Dyadic coping and its significance for marital functioning. In T. A. Revenson, K. Kayser, & G. Bodenmann, *Couples Coping with Stress: Emerging Perspectives on Dyadic Coping.* Washington, DC: American Psychological Association.

Bowlby, J. (1988). Attachment, communication, and the therapeutic process. In J. Bowlby (Ed.), *Asecure Base: Parent-Child Attachment and Healthy Human Development* (pp. 137–57). New York, NY: Basic Books.

Bronfenbrenner, U. (1979). *The Ecology of Human Development: Experiments by Design and Nature.* Cambridge, MA: Harvard University Press.

Butler, E. A. (2011). Temporal interpersonal emotion systems: the "TIES" that form relationships. *Personality and Social Psychology Review*, 15, 367–93.

(2015). Interpersonal affect dynamics: it takes two (and time) to tango. *Emotion Review*, 7, 336–41.

Butler, E. A., & Randall, A. K. (2013). Emotional coregulation in close relationships. *Emotion Review*, 5, 202–10.

Campos, J. J., Campos, R. G., & Barrett, K. C. (1989). Emergent themes in the study of emotional development and emotion regulation. *Developmental Psychology*, 25, 394–402.

Clark, C. (1990). Emotions and the micropolitics in everyday life: some patters and paradoxes of "Place". In T. D. Kemper (Ed.), *Research Agendas in the Sociology of Emotions* (pp. 305–34). Albany, NY: State University of New York.

Clark, M. S., Fitness, J., & Brissette, I. (2001). Understanding people's relationships is crucial to understanding their emotional lives. In G. J. Fletcher & M. S. Clark (Eds.), *Blackwell Handbook of Social Psychology: Interpersonal Processes* (pp. 253–78). London: Blackwell.

Coan, J. A., & Sbarra, D. A. (2015). Social baseline theory: the social regulation of risk and effort. *Current Opinion in Psychology*, 1, 87–91.

Coan, J. A., Schaefer, H. S., & Davidson, R. J. (2006). Lending a hand of the neural response to threat. *Psychological Science*, 17(12), 1032–9.

Coyne, J. C. (1976). Toward an interactional description of depression. *Psychiatry*, 39(1), 28–40.

Darwin C. (1872). *The Descent of Man and Selection in Relation to Sex*. London: Murray.

Downey, G., & Feldman, S. I. (1996). Implications of rejection sensitivity for intimate relationships. *Journal of Personality and Social Psychology*, 70, 1327–43.

Ekman, P. (1993). Facial Expression and Emotion. *American Psychologist*, 48(4), 384–92.

Ekman P., & Davidson R. J. (1994). *The Nature of Emotion: Fundamental Questions*. New York, NY: Oxford University Press.

Ellsworth, P. C., & Scherer, K. R. (2003). Appraisal processes in emotion. In R. J. Davidson, K. R. Scherer, & H. H. Goldsmith (Eds.), *Handbook of Affective Sciences* (pp. 572–95). New York, NY: Oxford University Press.

Fehr, B., Baldwin, M., Collins, L., Patterson, S., & Benditt, R. (1999). Anger in close relationships: an interpersonal script analysis. *Personality and Social Psychology Bulletin*, 25, 299–312.

Field, T. (2012). Relationships as regulators. *Psychology*, 3, 467–479.

Fischer, A. H., & Manstead, A. S. R. (2016). Social functions of emotion and emotion regulation. In L. F. Barrett, M. Lewis, & J. M. Haviland-Jones (Eds.), *Handbook of Emotions* (4th edn., pp. 424–39). New York, NY: Guilford Press.

Frijda, N. H., & Mesquita, B. (1994). The social roles and functions of emotions. In S. Kitayama & H. R. Markus (Eds.), *Emotion and Culture: Empirical Studies of Mutual Influence* (pp. 51–87). Washington, DC: American Psychological Association.

Gable, S. L., & Reis, H. T. (2001). Appetitive and aversive social interaction. In J. Harvey & A. Wenzel (Eds.), *Close Romantic Relationships: Maintenance and Enhancement* (pp. 169–94). Mahwah, NJ: Erlbaum.

Gable, S. L., Reis, H. T., Impett, E. A., & Asher, E. R. (2004). What do you do when things go right? The intrapersonal and interpersonal benefits of sharing positive events. *Journal of Personality and Social Psychology*, 87, 228–45.

Gonzaga, G. C., Campos, B., & Bradbury, T. (2007). Similarity, convergence, and relationship satisfaction in dating and married couples. *Journal of Personality and Social Psychology*, 93(1), 34–48.

Guerrero, L. K., & Floyd, K. (2006). *Nonverbal Communication in Close Relationships*. Mahwah, NJ: Lawrence Erlbaum.

Helm, J. L., Sbarra, D. A., & Ferrer, E. (2012). Assessing cross-partner associations in physiological responses via coupled oscillator models. *Emotion*, 12, 748–62.

Hofer, M. A. (1984). Relationships as regulators: a psychobiologic perspective on bereavement. *Psychosomatic Medicine*, 46, 183–97.

James, W. (1894). The physical basis of emotion. *Psychological Review*, 101, 205–10.

Joiner, T. E., Jr, & Metalsky, G. I. (2001). Excessive reassurance seeking: delineating a risk factor involved in the development of depressive symptoms. *Psychological Science*, 12(5), 371–8.

Kelley, H. H., Berscheid, E., Christensen, A., et al. (1983). Analyzing close relationships. In H. H. Kelley, E. Berscheid, A. Christensen, et al. (Eds.), *Close Relationships* (pp. 20–67). New York, NY: Freeman.

Keltner, D., & Haidt, J. (1999). Social functions of emotions at four levels of analysis. *Cognition & Emotion*, 13, 505–22.

(2001). Social functions of emotions. In T. Mayne & G. A. Bonanno (Eds.), *Emotions: Current Issues and Future Directions* (pp. 192–213). New York, NY: Guilfords.

Knobloch, L. K., & Metts, S. (2013). Emotion in relationships. In J. Simpson and L. Campbell (Eds.), *Oxford Handbook of Close Relationships* (pp. 514–34). Oxford: Oxford University Press.

Komulainen, E., Meskanen, K., Lipsanen, J., et al. (2014). The effect of personality on daily life emotional processes. *PLoS One*, 9(10), e110907.

Kuppens, P. (2015). It's about time: a special section on affect dynamics. *Emotion Review*, 7, 297–300.

Lakey, B., & Orehek, E. (2011). Relational regulation theory: a new approach to explain the link between perceived social support and mental health. *Psychological Review*, 118, 482–95.

Lazarus, R. S. (1991). *Emotion and Adaptation*. Oxford: Oxford University Press.

Marroquín, B. (2011). Interpersonal emotion regulation as a mechanism of social support in depression. *Clinical Psychology Review*, 31(8), 1276–90.

Merz, C. A., Meuwly, N., Randall, A. K., & Bodenmann, G. (2014). Engaging in dyadic coping: buffering the impact of everyday stress on prospective relationship satisfaction. *Family Science*, 5, 30–7.

Mesquita, B., Boiger, M., & De Leersnyder, J. (2017). Doing emotions: the role of culture in everyday emotions. *European Review of Social Psychology*, 1, 95–133.

Mikulincer, M., & Shaver, P. R. (2005). Attachment theory and emotions in close relationships: exploring the attachment-related dynamics of emotional reactions to relational events. *Personal Relationships*, 12(2), 149–68.

Moors, A., Ellsworth, P. C., Scherer, K. R., & Frijda, N. H. (2013). Appraisal theories of emotion: state of the art and future development. *Emotion Review*, 5, 119–24.

Oatley, K., & Jenkins, J. M. (1992). Human emotions: function and dysfunction. *Annual Review of Psychology*, 43, 55–85.

Parkinson, B. (1996). Emotions are social. *British Journal of Psychology*, 87, 663–83.

Parkinson, B., & Manstead, S. R. (2015). Current emotion research in social psychology: thinking about emotions and other people. *Emotion Review*, 7, 371–80.

Randall, A. K., Post, J. H., Reed, R. G., & Butler, E. A. (2013). Cooperating with your romantic partner: associations with interpersonal emotional coordination. *Journal of Social and Personal Relationships*, 30, 1072–95.

Randall, A. K., & Schoebi, D. (2015). Lean on me: susceptibility to partner's affect attenuates psychological distress over a 12-month period. *Emotion*, 15, 201–10.

Reed, R. G., Barnard, K., & Butler, E. A. (2015). Distinguishing emotional co-regulation from co-dysregulation: an investigation of emotional dynamics and body-weight in romantic couples. *Emotion*, 15(1), 45–60.

Rimé, B. (2007). Interpersonal emotion regulation. In J. J. Gross (Ed.), *Handbook of Emotion Regulation* (pp. 466–85). New York, NY: Guilford Press.

  (2009). Emotion elicits the social sharing of emotion: theory and empirical review. *Emotion Review*, 1, 60–85.

Rimé, B., Mesquita, B., Philippot, P., & Boca, S. (1991). Beyond the emotional event: six studies on the social sharing of emotion. *Cognition & Emotion*, 5, 435–65.

Roseman, I., & Smith, C. (2001). Appraisal theory: overview, assumptions, varieties, controversies. In Scherer, K. R., Schorr, A., & Johnstone, T. (Eds.), *Appraisal Processes in Emotion: Theory, Methods, Research* (pp. 3–19). New York, NY and Oxford: Oxford University Press.

Saxbe, D., & Repetti, R. L. (2010). For better or worse? Coregulation of couples' cortisol levels and mood states. *Journal of Personality and Social Psychology*, 98(1), 92–103.

Sbarra, D. A., & Hazan, C. (2008). Coregulation, dysregulation, self-regulation: an integrative analysis and empirical agenda for understanding adult attachment, separation, loss, and recovery. *Personality and Social Psychology Review*, 12(2), 141–67.

Scherer, K. R., Schorr, A., & Johnstone, T. (Eds.). (2001). *Appraisal Processes in Emotion: Theory, Methods, and Research*. New York, NY: Oxford University Press.

Schoebi, D., & Randall, A. K. (2015). Emotional dynamics in intimate relationships. *Emotion Review*, 7, 342–48.

Schulz, M. S., Cowan, P. A., Pape Cowan, C., & Brennan, R. T. (2004). Coming home upset: gender, marital satisfaction, and the daily spillover of workday experience into couple interactions. *Journal of Family Psychology*, 18(1), 250–63.

Seltzer, L. J., Ziegler, T. E., & Pollak, S. D. (2010). Social vocalizations can release oxytocin in humans. *Proceedings of the Royal Society of London B: Biological Sciences,* 277(1694), 2661–6.

Shaver, P. R., & Mikulincer, M. (2007). Adult attachment strategies and the regulation of emotion. In J. J. Gross (Ed.), *Handbook of Emotion Regulation* (pp. 446–65). New York, NY: Guilford Press.

Simpson, J. A., & Rholes, W. S. (2017). Adult attachment, stress, and romantic relationships. *Current Opinion in Psychology,* 13, 19–24.

Slatcher, R. B., & Trentacosta, C. J. (2011). A naturalistic observation study of the links between parental depressive symptoms and preschoolers' behaviors in everyday life. *Journal of Family Psychology,* 25(3), 444.

Smith, C. A., & Lazarus, R. S. (1990). Emotion and adaptation. In L. A. Pervin (Ed.), *Handbook of Personality: Theory and Research,* pp. 609–37. New York, NY: Guilford press.

Van Lange, P. A. M., & Balliet, D. (2014). Interdependence theory. In J. A. Simpson, & J. F. Dovidio (Eds.), *APA Handbook of Personality and Social Psychology: Interpersonal Processes and Intergroup Relations* (Volume 2). New York, NY: APA Books.

Van Kleef, G. A. (2009). How emotions regulate social life: the emotions as social information (EASI) model. *Current Directions in Psychological Science,* 18(3), 184–8.

  (2016). *The Interpersonal Dynamics of Emotion: Towards an Integrative Theory of Emotions as Social Information.* Cambridge: Cambridge University Press.

Van Kleef, G. A., De Dreu, C. K. W., & Manstead, A. S. R. (2010). An interpersonal approach to emotion in social decision making: the emotions as social information model. *Advances in Experimental Social Psychology,* 42, 45–96.

Vansteelandt, K., Van Mechelen, I., & Nezlek, J. B. (2005). The co-occurrence of emotions in daily life: a multilevel approach. *Journal of Research in Personality,* 39(3), 325–35.

Wilhelm, P., Schoebi, D., & Perrez, M. (2004). Frequency estimates of emotions in everyday life from a diary method's perspective: a comment on Scherer et al.'s survey-study "Emotions in everyday life". *Social Science Information,* 43(4), 647–65.

Zaki, J., & Williams, W. C. (2013). Interpersonal emotion regulation. *Emotion,* 13, 803–10.

CHAPTER 2

# A general framework for capturing interpersonal emotion dynamics

*Associations with psychological and relational adjustment*

Laura Sels, Eva Ceulemans, and Peter Kuppens

Emotions are fundamentally dynamic in nature as they alert us to important changes in the environment, and motivate us to cope with them (Kuppens, 2015; Scherer, 2009). The characteristics of these emotional changes over time provide crucial information about people's mental well-being and adjustment and even about the risk for the occurrence and progress of psychopathology (Houben et al., 2015; Wichers et al., 2015). For instance, the persistence of people's emotional experience over time prospectively predicts the onset of depressive disorder in adolescence (Kuppens et al., 2012).

In addition, emotions mainly occur and change in the context of social interactions and relationships (Schoebi & Randall, 2015; Tiedens & Leach, 2004). They regulate social interaction, and social processes in turn regulate the emerging emotions (Frijda & Mesquita, 1994). Over recent years, there have been calls for including social relations in the study of emotional processes (Fischer & Van Kleef, 2010; Parkinson & Manstead, 2015), resulting in a significant increase of research explicitly focusing on interpersonal emotion dynamics – the ways in which emotions emerge and change in interactions between people and can become interwoven over time (Butler, 2015; Lichtwarck-Aschoff et al., 2009; see also Chapter 1 for a conceptual review). This increase was further spurred by the growing availability of technologies and statistical techniques that allow for dyadic, multilevel, and overtime data collection and analysis (see Chapter 4). Yet, the precise nature and correlates of interpersonal emotion dynamics remain poorly understood (see also Butler, 2015; Schoebi & Randall, 2015 and Chapter 10). How can we make sense of complex interpersonal emotion patterns, and how are they related to psychological and relational adjustment?

The aim of the current chapter is help fill this gap, by providing an overview of research on interpersonal emotion dynamics, the processes that underlie these dynamics, and how these dynamics can contribute to (mal)adjustment. We propose a taxonomy that acts as a structuring framework, identifying four key characteristics of interpersonal emotion dynamics: emotional covariation, emotional influencing, emotional variability, and emotional inertia. We synthesize research findings relating these characteristics to psychological and relational adjustment; and in so doing, identify gaps in our existing knowledge of interpersonal emotion dynamics. In line with current research practices, we focus on how emotions interact between individuals in a close relationship (e.g., couples, adult-caregivers, close friends), as such relationships are principal contexts for emotion experience, expression, and regulation, and are central for people's adjustment (Berscheid & Ammazzalorso, 2001; Reis et al., 2000; see Chapter 7 for an explicit focus on families, Chapter 8 for young adult romantic and peer relationships, and Chapter 9 for intimate relationships). However, we think that the proposed concepts have applicability beyond the dyad to social relationships involving more people.

## Taxonomy of four fundamental interpersonal emotion dynamic characteristics

We introduce a novel taxonomy[1] to capture some important characteristics of interpersonal emotional dynamics. Although these dynamics can be investigated in multiple ways, the taxonomy focuses on four elementary aspects, which stem from two distinctions.

As a first organizing principle, we distinguish on studying the specific dynamics that occur between individuals, and the dynamics that characterize an interpersonal system as a whole. When individuals interact, the nature of their interaction is determined by each person's individual qualities and by the unique interplay between these qualities (Reis et al., 2000). This interplay can be studied in isolation, focusing on

---

[1] Note that the taxonomy suggested here partly mirrors a framework that Kuppens & Verduyn (2015) have proposed to grasp intrapersonal emotion dynamics. In this taxonomy, two distinctions are made that in combination result in four elementary characteristics of intra-individual emotion trajectories. A first distinction is drawn between a focus on single versus multiple emotions and a second distinction is made between two facets of emotional change, the degree of variability and time-dependency. These two distinctions result in four intrapersonal dynamic features: emotional covariation, emotional cross-lags, emotional variability, and emotional inertia. Like we propose here for the interpersonal case, these characteristics have been shown to be essential for individual well-being (e.g., Houben et al., 2015; Pe et al., 2015).

the interpersonal connections only. For instance, one can examine how the angry expressions of one partner elicit responses in the other partner during a fight. However, the whole picture can be looked at as well, taking both the individual qualities and the interpersonal connections into account. For our example above, this would mean that partners' intra-individual changes in anger (due to for instance intrapersonal regulation processes) are also considered, as well as how they combine with the interpersonal connections into an emotional state of the couple. Thus, one then focuses on how the global level of negativity that is present in the couple changes across the interaction, which results from interactions between both partners' intra-individual changes in anger and the interpersonal reciprocity in anger taking place. In this case, a systems perspective approach[2] is adopted, in which the dyadic partners are conceived as one single interpersonal system which is irreducible to the constituent partners and has properties of its own such as the state of the system being dependent on its past state, states to which the system often recurs, etc. (e.g., Lewis, 2000; Steenbeek & van Geert, 2005; see also Chapter 3 for a dynamic system approach to interpersonal emotion processes).

As a second organizing principle, we distinguish between time-dependency and time-independency of emotional change. A time-dependent perspective investigates how strongly an emotional state carries over from one moment to the subsequent moment and thus considers sequential relations, whereas time-independency does not take the temporal order of emotional states into account. For our angry fight example, a time-dependent perspective means that one investigates how anger between the partners/within the couple carries over from one moment to the next. For dynamics that occur between individuals, this means focusing on how much one person's change in anger predicts the partner's subsequent change in anger. For dynamics that characterize the interpersonal system as a whole, this means capturing the change in the couple's anger, or how long the couple maintains an angry state, resulting from each partner sustaining their own and their partner's anger during the fight.

[2] System theories (e.g., general system theory; Von Bertalanffy, 1968) focus on the study of complex systems and their characteristics, emphasizing the interactions between constituting elements which all together form one system with its own patterns of self-stabilization and organization. For instance, clinical family system theories (e.g., Minuchin, 1974) have promoted such a system view of the family, and developmental and relational researchers commonly approach human development and relationships from such a system perspective (e.g., Gottman et al., 2002; Hollenstein, 2015; Lewis et al., 1999; Reis et al., 2000).

From a time-independent stance, one focuses on how the anger of
the partners relate to each other over time or on the dispersion of anger
for the whole interpersonal system. Here, the temporal order of experienced anger in each party does not matter. For instance, whether both
partners are experiencing a constant, moderate level of angriness during
the first half of the fight and then a more extreme, elevated level at the
end of the fight, or whether they constantly switch between these moderate and extreme levels, can lead to the same results. Here, dynamics
that occur between individuals capture how much partners' changes in
anger during the fight fluctuate together. If one shows an increase in their
anger, is the other one's anger increasing as well? Dynamics that characterize the interpersonal system as a whole capture the extremity of the
anger experienced by the couple during the fight. How much does each
partner's own anger change over the course of the fight, and how much
does this change go together with a change in the partner's anger?

Together, these distinctions result in four key characteristics of
interpersonal emotion dynamics, graphically illustrated in Figure 2.1:
(1) emotional covariation, or how emotions of different individuals
covary across time, (2) emotional influencing, or how individuals' emotions at one moment predict other people's emotions at the next moment,
(3) emotional variability, indicating how much the emotional state of the
interpersonal system fluctuates across time, and (4) emotional inertia,
representing the carryover of the emotional state of the interpersonal
system from one moment to the next. In the following sections, we discuss each of the four characteristics separately, focusing on definitions,
potential underlying processes and relations with well-being, and relevant existing research.

## Emotional covariation

Interpersonal emotional covariation reflects the strength with which different individuals' emotions covary across time (Butler, 2011). It is sometimes referred to as synchrony or emotional similarity (e.g., Anderson
et al., 2003; Papp et al., 2013) and can be operationalized as the concurrent
covariation of people's emotions over time. For instance, in one study,
spouses' moods and cortisol levels were assessed four times a day for
three consecutive days, and covariation was assessed by slopes in a multilevel model predicting participants' own cortisol level and mood by
their partner's concurrent cortisol level and mood. The spouses showed
positive covariation of both cortisol and negative mood during daily
live, but not of positive mood, meaning that partners' negative emotions
concurrently increased and decreased throughout the days. In principle

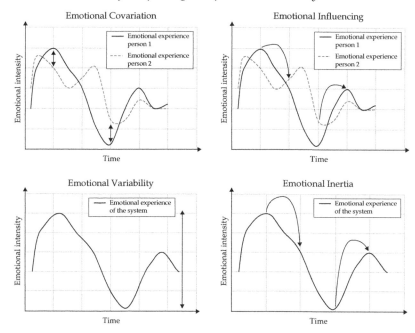

Figure 2.1. Graphical representation of the four key characteristics of interpersonal emotion dynamics

Note: The horizontal line shows the distinction between time-dependent and time-independent characteristics, the vertical line shows the distinction between dynamic characteristics that occur between individuals and characteristics of the interpersonal system. Note that the *y*-axis represents the emotional intensity of the experience and the *x*-axis represents time.

it is also possible that people show negative covariation, with increases in one person's emotion coinciding with decreases in another person's emotion. Up to now such inverse linkages have been mainly reported in studies investigating physiological linkages in close relationships (for an overview, see Timmons et al., 2015).

Concurrent covariation can arise due to two processes. First, in case of measurements across longer timescales (e.g., experience sampling), covariation may be the result of individuals influencing each other on shorter timescales and thus may reflect time-dependency rather than time-independency. Emotional influencing will be discussed in the corresponding section below. Second, emotional covariation can be explained in terms of emotional similarity, with people having shared environments or experiences that they interpret in similar fashion, or corresponding diurnal affective rhythms (Anderson et al., 2003; Gonzaga et al., 2007). Emotional similarity is especially expected to occur in close relationships with high physical proximity (e.g., families living together), mutual care and interdependence of activities, cognitions, goals, and behaviors (Fitzsimons et al., 2015; Wegner et al., 1985). Indeed, people in close relationships become increasingly emotionally similar over time, termed emotional convergence, and this convergence positively predicts relationship quality and longevity (Anderson et al., 2003).

The emotional convergence hypothesis explicitly states that it is adaptive for people in a close relationship to evidence emotional similarity, because of three primary reasons (Anderson et al., 2004). First, emotional similarity helps people to coordinate their behaviors and thoughts, and thus to respond together to environmental demands. Second, it enables people to better understand each other and therefore facilitates their interactions. Finally, it increases their closeness as they feel validated in their emotional experiences. This line of research suggests that positive emotional covariation goes together with smoother interactions between close relationship partners, and thus positively relates to relational adjustment. It has indeed been shown that people prefer to interact with persons that are experiencing similar emotions (Gibbons, 1986), that they feel more satisfied when they do (Locke & Horowitz, 1990) and that their negative emotions in stressful situations decline, compared to when they interact with persons that are experiencing dissimilar emotions (Townsend et al., 2014). Additionally, emotional similarity has been related to more relationship satisfaction, closeness, and stability (Townsend et al., 2014). Nevertheless, in daily life, emotional covariation in romantic partners is sometimes negatively related to adjustment indicators (e.g., relationship satisfaction; Saxbe & Repetti, 2010 and attachment; Butner et al., 2007). Here, emotional covariation probably does not only reflect emotional similarity processes, but also emotional influencing.

### Emotional influencing

Interpersonal emotional influencing refers to one individual's emotions predicting another individual's emotions over time, and is also known as *emotion transmission* (Larson & Almeida, 1999), *susceptibility* (Randall & Schoebi, 2015), *cross-lagged covariation* (Butler, 2011), *crossover* (Westman, 2001), or emotion transfer (Parkinson, 2011). It is usually operationalized as the extent to which the (change in the) emotional experience of one person predicts the (change in the) emotional experience of another person at a subsequent time point, for instance by cross-correlations (e.g., Feldman, 2003) or prospective change models, and thus explicitly incorporates the process of one person's emotions feeding into another person's emotions across time (Larson & Almeida, 1999).[3] For instance, people tend to bring home workplace-related stress, which impacts their partners' mood negatively (Westman, 2001; see also Chapter 7 for a review). Interpersonal influencing can result in augmentation, with emotions reinforcing each other across time or showing positive feedback loops (a change in one predicts a similar change in the other), or in blunting, with emotions counteracting each other across time or showing negative feedback loops (Pe & Kuppens, 2012; Reed, Barnard, & Butler, 2015).

Regarding the processes underlying emotional influencing, people can catch others' emotions through mirroring or mimicry processes (Hatfield et al., 1994), or the emotion of others can be evaluated and change one's own emotion through social appraisal (Parkinson & Simons, 2009). Also, people often share their emotions with others, which elicits similar emotions in the listener (Rimé, 2009). Another possibility is coordination processes. For instance, during parent–child interactions, parents are sensitive to micro-shifts in their child's affective state and behavior and match their own (Feldman, 2007), which benefits the child's emotional development and regulatory capacities (Tronick, 1989). Coordination is not only considered fundamental for child development, but also for regulating and facilitating communication and relationships in adults (Feldman, 2007; Vallacher et al., 2005). For instance, when people are motivated to have a smooth and pleasant interaction with someone else, they adjust their own emotional state to the apparent state of this person (Erber et al., 1996; Huntsinger et al., 2009). Finally, emotional influencing can result from conscious or unconscious regulation processes (Zaki & Williams, 2013). For instance, people can explicitly try to reduce the stress their partner experiences in a certain situation by distracting him or her, or they can do it unconsciously.

Because emotional influencing can be indicative of different processes, it is difficult to make overall predictions about its associations with individual and relational adjustment. It is often seen, however, as a defining characteristic of intimate relationships (Butler, 2011; Schoebi & Randall, 2015). Emotional influencing indeed suggests closeness or interdependence between persons, with individuals being able to impact each other (Kelley et al., 1983). Whether it goes together with more or less well-being might therefore be a function of which emotions or outcomes

---

[3] However, correlational findings cannot speak directly to the underlying mechanisms. As a consequence, it is also possible that a change in a receiver's emotions following the sender's emotions has nothing to do with this sender's prior emotion. For instance, in certain cases cross-lagged associations can also result from a person responding to a shared stimulus with different response times.

people end up experiencing due to this interdependence (Fitzsimons et al., 2015; Kelley, 1979). When influencing helps people to regulate their emotions better than they would do on their own, a positive association between emotional influencing and adjustment is expected, with the opposite being true for poorer emotion regulation. Imagine a patient who experiences a lot of anxiety when sitting in the waiting room before a painful treatment. If this patient's partner is present, the couple can start showing negative feedback loops between their emotions, resulting in the patient's negative emotions being reduced. However, the couple can also show positive feedback loops, reinforcing each other's anxiety, with the patient ending up with even stronger negative emotions than when waiting alone. These feedback loops pertain to the concepts of co-regulation and co-dysregulation (Butler & Randall, 2013; Reed et al., 2015; see also Chapter 3). Co-regulation refers to an oscillating, bidirectionally linked and mutually dampening emotional influencing pattern, governed by negative feedback loops, that contributes to each person's emotional stability (Butler & Randall, 2013; Field, 1985; Sbarra & Hazan, 2008). Co-dysregulation, on the other hand, refers to a positive feedback process in which partners' emotions are mutually amplifying, away from emotional stability (Reed et al., 2015). Thus, people can facilitate each other in regulating their emotions efficiently or, on the contrary, hamper each other's emotion regulation. Thus, augmentation between negative emotions might be associated with maladjustment, whereas blunting of opposite-valence emotions could play a buffering role. Additionally, for psychological adjustment, it could matter if emotional influence is reciprocal (as in co-regulation) or if one person is more dependent and consistently accommodates the other's emotions, receiving worse outcomes as a result.

Research on emotional influencing and adjustment indeed reveals mixed findings. In daily life, mainly negative emotions seem to cross-over, and the cross-over increases when the family is under chronic stress (Larson & Almeida, 1999). Relatedly, susceptibility of children to others' distress and parents' negative emotions has been related to poorer affect regulation abilities and social development (Eisenberg & Fabes, 1995; Kim et al., 2001). Also, negative affect reciprocity (negative emotions augmenting negative emotions) during conflict discussions mainly characterizes distressed romantic relationships (Gottman, 1998; Levenson & Gottman, 1983). However, focusing on overall affect, being influenced more by a romantic partner's emotions goes together with more cooperation (Randall et al., 2013) and perspective-taking (Schoebi, 2008). In parent–child dyads, affective coordination is crucial for child development as it positively predicts for instance the child's use of symbolic play and self-control later on (Feldman & Greenbaum, 1997; Feldman et al., 1999). To our knowledge, only a few studies investigated cross-lags between opposite-valence emotions (Randall & Schoebi, 2015; Sels et al., 2016), showing that individuals whose negative emotions were predicted more by their romantic partner's previous positive emotions showed less distress over a year (Randall & Schoebi, 2015), and that overall emotional influence in couples (including both cross-lags between similar and opposite-valence emotions) was positively related to higher individual adjustment in terms of life satisfaction but not depression (Sels et al., 2016). However, this association with life satisfaction was mainly driven by the extent to which people influenced their romantic partner's positive emotions, indicating that the valence of the emotions and being able to change or drive a partner's emotions versus being susceptible to a partner's emotions matters for associations with well-being.

**Emotional variability**

With interpersonal emotional variability, we move our focus to the interpersonal system level, which incorporates both individual and interpersonal emotional dynamics as well as their interactions. As in daily life, all these dynamics are likely to simultaneously exert their influence, studying the interpersonal system as a whole aligns more with reality, and is an important avenue for future research. Interpersonal emotional variability specifically is defined as the range and extremity of the interpersonal system's emotional states.[4] To our knowledge, interpersonal variability as defined here has not been investigated before, but could be construed in different ways.

First, interpersonal emotional variability can be construed unidimensionally by computing the variance of the portion of emotional experience that is shared among different individuals. To this end one factor or principal component is extracted per dyad, which captures the shared emotional state of the interpersonal system (just as extracting one factor from different items that represent a scale reflects the shared variance of

---

[4] It does not include temporal dependency and moment-to-moment changes are thus not accounted for (e.g., Ebner-Priemer & Trull, 2009). Therefore, emotional variability differs from other constructs that were previously referred to as such, but that actually also include moment-to-moment fluctuations and thus more closely represent emotional instability or inertia (Ferrer et al., 2012; Hollenstein, 2015; Van der Giessen et al., 2013; Van der Giessen et al., 2014).

the scale items). To also take possible time dependencies into account, dynamic factor analysis (e.g., Ferrer & Nesselroade, 2003) or a time series version of the common fate model (Ledermann & Kenny, 2012; Ledermann & Macho, 2014) can be applied, after which the variance or standard deviation of the scores across time on the extracted latent variable can be calculated. Given its factor-analytic basis, a necessary condition for this unidimensional approach to work adequately is that the emotions of the partners involved covary to some extent.

Second, multidimensional measures can be used, based on research on socio-emotional development, where the set of emotional states an interpersonal system such as a parent–child dyad can be in is called the emotional *state space* of the system (Granic & Lamey, 2002; Lewis et al., 1999). Concretely, for dyads, a two-dimensional state space grid is composed of two categorical variables that represent the different possible emotional states for each individual. Given this state space, the variability of the system is quantified by looking at the number of different states the system is in across time. Adopting this approach, it is not necessary that the emotions of the partners involved covary, but the amount of covariation does impact the variability score obtained. In case the emotional variables are continuous rather than categorical, we suggest using other variability indicators, such as the generalized variance of the two individuals' experienced emotional experiences, which is a multivariate measure of variability (Wilks, 1932). Using this generalized variance, interpersonal emotional variability is explicitly defined as a combination of both partners' individual variability, taking out the amount of overlap they show in emotional states (emotional covariation). Here, emotional variability becomes smaller when there is more concurrent covariation in partners' emotions. One other possible measure to assess interpersonal variability is *spin*, which is a measure originally developed to quantify how much fluctuation people show in the interpersonal circumplex (Moskowitz & Zuroff, 2004).

In both the unidimensional and multidimensional approach, interpersonal variability will be related to individual variability as well as interpersonal covariation. Specifically, in both cases the individual variabilities are positively related to interpersonal variability. However, conditional to these individual variabilities, the size of the interpersonal variability will decrease with lower interpersonal covariation in the unidimensional approach, whereas the multidimensional measures will increase.

Interpersonal emotional variability can be interpreted as a measure of the sensitivity of the system toward contextual changes. Low variability may reflect unresponsiveness toward environmental demands, as the system remains in one or a few specific emotional states[5] across time (Hollenstein, 2013). Therefore, we hypothesize that low variability relates negatively to well-being. On the other hand, high variability may reflect hypersensitivity to the context and failure to keep one's own and the other's emotions in check, indicating impaired (interpersonal) emotion regulation, which might also be considered maladaptive.

To our knowledge, interpersonal emotional variability and its association with well-being has not been studied yet, which reveals an important potential direction for future research. In research on dyadic flexibility (referring to transitions in and out of emotional states over time) in parent–child interactions and its associations with socio-emotional development, a composite flexibility measure is mostly calculated (e.g., Hollenstein, 2015). These measures encompass variability and time-dependency of the system's states, and thus capture both emotional variability and inertia. As flexibility is defined as the opposite of dyadic rigidity, the findings of this line of research will be discussed in the next section.

**Emotional inertia**

Emotional inertia refers to emotional experiences carrying over from one moment to the next, indicating an interpersonal system's self-predictivity and resistance to change. Again, interpersonal emotional inertia can be investigated in a uni- or multidimensional way, and consists of both intrapersonal and interpersonal dynamical aspects.

The unidimensional approach operationalizes interpersonal emotional inertia as the autocorrelation of the interpersonal system's scores on the extracted shared emotions factor. This measure is affected by how much the individuals' emotions persist over time, and their covariance. The autocorrelation captures the degree to which the current level of shared emotions can be predicted by its level at the previous time point, with a higher autocorrelation reflecting a more self-predictive emotional system. As was the case for emotional variability, this unidimensional approach is only meaningful if individuals' emotions covary at least to some extent.

A multidimensional version of emotional inertia involves the tendency to linger in a specific emotional state. In case of continuous data,

---

[5] Under the prerequisite that people experience a similar amount of emotional stimulation (e.g., in experiments). Without keeping the external environment constant, low variability could also reflect that individuals do not encounter many emotion eliciting events.

interpersonal inertia could be captured by a measure that combines the individuals' autocorrelations and how much their emotions are predicted by the other people's previous emotions (cross-correlations). Interpersonal emotional inertia will thus be highest for interpersonal systems whose members show high individual inertia and high emotional influencing. For categorical data, state space grid measures can be used, such as the duration that a dyad remains in a certain emotional state or cell, or the distance between consecutive emotional states (Hollenstein, 2013).

Theoretically, we expect emotional inertia to reflect a reduced ability to regulate both one's own and each other's emotions back to baseline levels, and decreased emotional recovery. The system gets "stuck" in a certain state, becomes more self-predictive, and therefore less responsive to external and internal demands and regulation efforts. Consequently, it indicates rigidity instead of resilience, which is often viewed as a hallmark of dysfunctional systems. For instance, in family system theories, a functional family system is conceived as a system that is able to appropriately adapt to both external and internal demands. Closed, rigid systems (as seen in dysfunctional families) have impermeable boundaries, and thus fail to interact with the outside environment, becoming resistant to change (e.g., Goldenberg & Goldenberg, 2012; Minuchin, 1974, 1985). Therefore, we hypothesize high interpersonal emotional inertia to relate to maladjustment.

As mentioned above, interpersonal flexibility is considered to be the opposite of interpersonal rigidity, and has been extensively studied (for an overview, see Hollenstein, 2015). More concretely, flexibility in dyads is defined as a combination of the amount of states a dyad switches between and the ability to move quickly between different emotional states (e.g., Hollenstein & Lewis, 2006). Recently, it has been advocated that dyadic emotional flexibility and individual emotional inertia are reciprocally related to each other: a change in an individual's emotional flexibility generates a change in the dyad's flexibility and vice versa (Mancini & Luebbe, 2016). More emotional flexibility in parent-child dyads has been found to go together with, and to predict more adaptive functioning in, children and adolescents, as is evident by less externalizing and internalizing of problems (Hollenstein et al., 2004; Van der Giessen et al., 2014). Because interpersonal inertia is partly determined by each person's individual inertia, the findings on interpersonal flexibility support our hypothesis on the maladaptivity of interpersonal inertia.

Additionally, Gottman et al. have shown by the use of advanced mathematical methods that intrapersonal emotional inertia in combination with certain patterns of emotional influencing seem characteristic for distressed marriages (Gottman et al., 1999). They invited married couples in their lab to discuss a problem that was a source of continued disagreement, coded the emotions that these couples expressed during the conversations, and did a follow-up on the couples' marital status. It turned out that couples that were high in individual inertia, and that showed mismatches in the emotional influence patterns they exhibited on each other, were particularly prone to divorce.

### Discussion and future directions

The purpose of this chapter was to propose a systematic taxonomy that captures key characteristics of interpersonal emotional dynamics, each providing unique information about the dynamical unfolding of emotions between different people across time. These characteristics reflect ways in which people experience, influence, and regulate their own and others' emotions, which may shed light on psychological and relational functioning.

Separately discussing each dynamic characteristic and associations found with (mal)adjustment revealed important gaps in existing research. First, much remains unknown about the precise contexts that result in positive versus negative associations between interpersonal interwovenness and adjustment. For instance, interpersonal emotional covariation and influencing may only indicate coordination or coregulation if people's emotions are also oscillating in a coordinated stable pattern (Butler & Randall, 2013; Vallacher et al., 2005). Also, it is important to know if the direction of interpersonal covariation is positive or negative, if emotional influencing is unidirectional or bidirectional, if there is high interpersonal emotional variability because of low emotional covariation or not, etc. In addition, while emotional variability and emotional inertia have been studied extensively in the context of intrapersonal emotion dynamics, they remain to be explored as dynamic characteristics of interpersonal systems. We hope that we have given some starting points for how these dynamical characteristics can be understood and investigated. More generally, there is a need for integration between intrapersonal and interpersonal emotion dynamic disciplines, because these dynamics do not operate fully independently from each other; which also became evident in the multidimensional operationalization of emotional variability and inertia (see also Chapter 10).

Finally, it needs to be underscored that the timescale on which emotions are assessed plays a critical role in interpersonal emotion dynamics, and how data can be interpreted (see also Hollenstein et al., 2013). First, it is well known that emotion dynamic characteristics observed on short time scales such as second by second (e.g., unfolding of initial response) can be driven by sometimes similar, but often also very different processes than characteristics observed on longer time scales (e.g., moods; Koval et al., 2013). Second, the timescale on which emotions are observed may sometimes obscure the processes really taking place. As mentioned above, people's emotions can seem to covary on time scales such as daily or hourly assessments, due to people's emotions influencing each other on shorter timescales. Caution is therefore needed in interpreting such results.

Interpersonal emotion dynamics are inherently complex, and we zoomed in on four basic dynamic characteristics, in order to be able to define logical relations and hypotheses in a manageable way without requiring very advanced mathematical skills. Still, one of the key characteristics of dynamic systems is nonlinearity (Lewis, 2000), and for future research it is important to incorporate nonlinear extensions and patterns to provide a complete and nuanced picture of interpersonal emotion dynamics. For instance, one could focus on interpersonal linkages in cyclical changes unfolding across a longer time span (Butner et al., 2007). To investigate such cyclical patterns, we refer the interested reader to coupled oscillator models, as described in Chapter 3 (Butner et al., 2005) and coupled nonlinear difference equations (Cook et al., 1995; Gottman et al., 2002). Other possibilities to investigate more complex nonlinear processes are the use of exploratory techniques (Ferrer, 2016), threshold autoregressive (TAR) models (Hamaker et al., 2009), or models that allow for time-varying changes in interpersonal associations (Chow et al., 2010).

In conclusion, the characteristics of interpersonal emotion dynamics are important indicators of psychological and relational functioning. However, future research is needed to test more nuanced hypotheses about which combinations of dynamical characteristics precisely reflect adaptive or maladaptive functioning. It has recently been advocated that interpersonal emotion dynamics not only flag important relationship processes (Schoebi & Randall, 2015), but also contribute to partners' health and adjustment (Butler & Randall, 2013), providing important insights into couple functioning. This will bring us closer to a true understanding of the far-reaching social dimension of emotions, and to developing successful clinical interventions for improving human relationships.

### Acknowledgments

This research was supported by the Research Fund of the University of Leuven (Grants GOA/15/003; OT/11/031), by the Interuniversity Attraction Poles programme financed by the Belgian government

(IAP/P7/06), and by a research grant from the Fund for Scientific Research-Flanders (FWO, Project No. G.0582.14 awarded to Eva Ceulemans, Peter Kuppens and Francis Tuerlinckx).

## References

Anderson, C., Keltner, D., & John, O. P. (2003). Emotional convergence between people over time. *Journal of Personality and Social Psychology*, 84(5), 1054–68.

Anderson, C., Keltner, D., Tiedens, L. Z., & Leach, C. W. (2004). The emotional convergence hypothesis. In L. Z. Tiedens & C. W. Leach (Eds.), *The Social Life of Emotions* (pp. 144–63). New York: Cambridge University Press.

Berscheid, E., & Ammazzalorso, H. (2001). Emotional experience in close relationships. In G. J. Fletcher & M. S. Clark (Eds.), *Blackwell Handbook of Social Psychology: Interpersonal Processes* (pp. 308–30). Oxford, England: Blackwell Publishers Ltd.

Butler, E. A. (2011). Temporal interpersonal emotion systems: the "TIES" that form relationships. *Personality and Social Psychology Review*, 15(4), 367–93.

  (2015). Interpersonal affect dynamics: it takes two (and time) to tango. *Emotion Review*, 7(4), 336–41.

Butler, E. A., & Randall, A. K. (2013). Emotional coregulation in close relationships. *Emotion Review*, 5(2), 202–10.

Butner, J., Amazeen, P. G., & Mulvey, G. M. (2005). Multilevel modeling of two cyclical processes: extending differential structural equation modeling to nonlinear coupled systems. *Psychological Methods*, 10(2), 159–77.

Butner, J., Diamond, L. M., & Hicks, A. M. (2007). Attachment style and two forms of affect coregulation between romantic partners. *Personal Relationships*, 14(3), 431–55.

Chow, S.-M., Haltigan, J. D., & Messinger, D. S. (2010). Dynamic infant-parent affect coupling during the face-to-face/still-face. *Emotion*, 10(1), 101–14.

Cook, J., Tyson, R., White, J., Rushe, R., Gottman, J., & Murray, J. (1995). Mathematics of marital conflict: qualitative dynamic mathematical modeling of marital interaction. *Journal of Family Psychology*, 9(2), 110–30.

Eisenberg, N., & Fabes, R. A. (1995). The relation of young children's vicarious emotional responding to social competence, regulation, and emotionality. *Cognition & Emotion*, 9(2–3), 203–28.

Ebner-Priemer, U. W., & Trull, T. J. (2009). Ecological momentary assessment of mood disorders and mood dysregulation. *Psychological Assessment*, 21(4), 463–75.

Erber, R., Wegner, D. M., & Therriault, N. (1996). On being cool and collected: mood regulation in anticipation of social interaction. *Journal of Personality and Social Psychology*, 70(4), 757–66.

Feldman, R. (2003). *Development across the Life Span*. Upper Saddle River, NJ: Prentice Hall.

  (2007). Parent-infant synchrony and the construction of shared timing; physiological precursors, developmental outcomes, and risk conditions. *The Journal of Child Psychology and Psychiatry*, 48(3–4), 329–54.

Feldman, R., & Greenbaum, C. W. (1997). Affect regulation and synchrony in mother-infant play as precursors to the development of symbolic competence. *Infant Mental Health Journal*, 18(1), 4–23.

Feldman, R., Greenbaum, C. W., & Yirmiya, N. (1999). Mother-infant affect synchrony as an antecedent of the emergence of self-control. *Developmental Psychology*, 35(5), 223–31.

Ferrer, E. (2016). Exploratory approaches for studying social interactions, dynamics, and multivariate processes in psychological science. *Multivariate Behavioral Research*, 51(2–3), 240–56.

Ferrer, E., & Nesselroade, J. R. (2003). Modeling affective processes in dyadic relations via dynamic factor analysis. *Emotion*, 3(4), 344–60.

Field, T. (1985). Attachment as psychobiological attunement: being on the same wavelength. In M. Reite & T. Field (Eds.), *The psychobiology of attachment and separation* (pp. 415–54). Orlando, FL: Academic Press.

Fischer, A. H., & Van Kleef, G. A. (2010). Where have all the people gone? A plea for including social interaction in emotion research. *Emotion Review*, 2(3), 208–11.

Fitzsimons, G. M., Finkel, E. J., & Vandellen, M. R. (2015). Transactive goal dynamics. *Psychological Review*, 122(4), 648–73.

Frijda, N. H., & Mesquita, B. (1994). The social roles and functions of emotions. In S. Kitayama & H. R. Markus (Eds.), *Emotion and Culture: Empirical Studies of Mutual Influence* (pp. 51–87). Washington, DC: Americal Psychological Association.

Gibbons, F. X. (1986). Social comparison and depression: company's effect on misery. *Journal of Personality and Social Psychology*, 51(1), 140–8.

Goldenberg, H., & Goldenberg, I. (2012). *Family Therapy: An Overview*. Canada: Cengage Learning.

Gonzaga, G. C., Campos, B., & Bradbury, T. (2007). Similarity, convergence, and relationship satisfaction in dating and married couples. *Journal of Personality and Social Psychology*, 93(1), 34–48.

Gottman, J. M. (1998). Psychology and the study of marital processes. *Annual Review of Psychology*, 49(1), 169–97.

Gottman, J., Swanson, C., & Murray, J. (1999). The mathematics of marital conflict: dynamic mathematical nonlinear modeling of newlywed marital interaction. *Journal of Family Psychology*, 13(1), 3–19.

Gottman, J., Swanson, C., & Swanson, K. (2002). A general systems theory of marriage: nonlinear difference equation modeling of marital interaction. *Personality and Social Psychology Review*, 6(4), 326–40.

Granic, I., & Lamey, A. V. (2002). Combining dynamic systems and multivariate analyses to compare the mother-child interactions of externalizing subtypes. *Journal of Abnormal Psychology*, 30(3), 265–83.

Hamaker, E. L., Zhang, Z., & Van der Maas, H. L. (2009). Using threshold autoregressive models to study dyadic interactions. *Psychometrika*, 74(4), 727–45.

Hatfield, E., Cacioppo, J. T., & Rapson, R. L. (1994). *Emotional Contagion*. Cambridge, England: Cambridge University Press.

Hollenstein, T. (2013). *State Space Grids* (pp. 11–33). New York, NY: Springer.

(2015). This time, it's real: affective flexibility, time scales, feedback loops, and the regulation of emotion. *Emotion Review*, 7(4), 308–15.

Hollenstein, T., Granic, I., Stoolmiller, M., & Snyder, J. (2004). Rigidity in parent-child interactions and the development of externalizing and internalizing behavior in early childhood. *Journal of Abnormal Child Psychology*, 32(6), 595–607.

Hollenstein, T., & Lewis, M. D. (2006). A state space analysis of emotion and flexibility in parent-child interactions. *Emotion*, 6(4), 656–62.

Hollenstein, T., Lichtwarck-Aschoff, A., & Potworowski, G. (2013). A model of socioemotional flexibility at three time scales. *Emotion Review*, 5(4), 397–405.

Houben, M., Van Den Noortgate, W., & Kuppens, P. (2015). The relation between short-term emotion dynamics and psychological well-being: a meta-analysis. *Psychological Bulletin*, 141(4), 901–30.

Huntsinger, J. R., Lun, J., Sinclair, S., & Clore, G. L. (2009). Contagion without contact: anticipatory mood matching in response to affiliative motivation. *Personality and Social Psychology Bulletin*, 35(7), 909–22.

Kelley, H. H. (1979). *Personal Relationships: Their Structures and Processes*. Hillsdale, NJ: Lawrence Erlbaum Associates.

Kelley, H., Berscheid, E., Christensen, A., et al. (1983). *Close Relationships*. New York, NY: Freeman.

Kim, K. J., Conger, R. D., Lorenz, F. O., & Elder Jr., H. G. (2001). Parent-adolescent reciprocity in negative affect and its relation to early adult social development. *Developmental Psychology*, 37(6), 775–90.

Koval, P., Pe, M. L., Meers, K., & Kuppens, P. (2013). Affective dynamics in relation to depressive symptoms: variable, unstable, or inert? *Emotion*, 13(6), 1132–41.

Kuppens, P. (2015). It's about time: a special section on affect dynamics. *Emotion Review*, 7(4), 297–300.

Kuppens, P., Sheeber, L. B., Yap, M. B., et al. (2012). Emotional inertia prospectively predicts the onset of depressive disorder in adolescence. *Emotion*, 12(2), 283–9.

Kuppens, P., & Verduyn, P. (2015). Looking at emotion regulation through the window of emotion dynamics. *Psychological Inquiry*, 26, 72–9.

Larson, R. W., & Almeida, D. M. (1999). Emotional transmission in the daily lives of families: a new paradigm for studying family process. *Journal of Marriage and the Family*, 61(1), 5–20.

Ledermann, T., & Kenny, D. A. (2012). The common fate model for dyadic data: variations of a theoretically important but underutilized model. *Journal of Family Psychology*, 26(1), 140–8.

Ledermann, T., & Macho, S. (2014). Analyzing change at the dyadic level: the common fate growth model. *Journal of Family Psychology*, 28(2), 204–13.

Levenson, W. R., & Gottman, J. M. (1983). Marital interaction: physiological linkage and affective exchange. *Journal of Personality and Social Psychology*, 45(3), 587–97.

Lewis, M. (2000). The promise of dynamic systems approach for an integrated account of human development. *Child Development*, 71(1), 36–43.

Lewis, M. L., Lamey, A. V., & Douglas, L. (1999). A new dynamic systems method for the analysis of early socioemotional development. *Developmental Science*, 2(4), 457–75.

Lichtwarck-Aschoff, A., Kunnen, S. E., & van Geert, P. L. (2009). Here we go again: a dynamic systems perspective on emotional rigidity across parent-adolescent conflicts. *Developmental Psychology*, 45(5), 1364–75.

Locke, K. D., & Horowitz, L. M. (1990). Satisfaction in interpersonal interactions as a function of similarity in level of dysphoria. *Journal of Personality and Social Psychology*, 58(5), 823–31.

Mancini, K. J., & Luebbe, A. M. (2016). Dyadic affective flexibility and emotional inertia in relation to youth psychopathology: an integrated model at two timescales. *Clinical child and family psychology Review*, 19(2)117–33.

Minuchin, S. (1974). *Families and Family Therapy*. Cambridge, MA: Harvard University Press.

Minuchin, P. (1985). Families and individual development: provocations from the field of family therapy. *Child Development*, 56(2), 289–302.

Moskowitz, D. S., & Zuroff, D. C. (2004). Flux, pulse, and spin: dynamic additions to the personality lexicon. *Journal of Personality and Social Psychology*, 86(6), 880–93.

Papp, L. M., Pendry, P., Simon, C. D., & Adam, E. K. (2013). Spouses' cortisol associations and moderators: testing physiological synchrony and connectedness in everyday life. *Family Process*, 52(2), 284–98.

Parkinson, B. (2011), Interpersonal emotion transfer: contagion and social appraisal. *Social and Personality Psychology Compass*, 5, 428–39. doi:10.1111/j.1751-9004.2011.00365.x.

Parkinson, B., & Manstead, A. S. (2015). Current emotion research in social psychology: thinking about emotions and other people. *Emotion Review*, 7(4), 371–80.

Parkinson, B., & Simons, G. (2009). Affecting others: social appraisal and emotion contagion in everyday decision making. *Personality and Social Psychology Bulletin*, 35(8), 1071–84.

Pe, M. L., Kircanski, K., Thompson, R. J., Bringmann, L. F., Tuerlinckx, F., Mestdagh, M., … Kuppens, P., (2015). Emotion-network density in major depressive disorder. *Clinical Psychological Science*, 3(2), 292–300.

Pe, M. L., & Kuppens, P. (2012). The dynamic interplay between emotions in daily life: augmentation, blunting, and the role of appraisal overlap. *Emotion*, 12(6), 1320–328.

Randall, A. K., Post, J. H., Reed, R. G., & Butler, E. A. (2013). Cooperating with your romantic partner: associations with interpersonal emotion coordination. *Journal of Social and Personal Relationships*, 30(8), 1072–95.

Randall, A. K., & Schoebi, D. (2015). Lean on me: susceptibility to partner affect attenuates psychological distress over a 12-month period. *Emotion*, 15(2), 201–10.

Reed, R. G., Barnard, K., & Butler, E. A. (2015). Distinguishing emotional coregulation from codysregulation: an investigation of emotional dynamics and body weight in romantic couples. *Emotion*, 15(1), 45–60.

Reis, H. T., Collins, W. A., & Berscheid, E. (2000). The relationship context of human behavior and development. *Psychological Bulletin*, 126(6), 844–72.

Rimé, B. (2009). Emotion elicits the social sharing of emotion: theory and empirical review. *Emotion Review*, 1(1), 60–85.

Saxbe, D., & Repetti, R. L. (2010). For better or worse? Coregulation of couples' cortisol levels and mood states. *Journal of Personality and Social Psychology*, 98(1), 92–103.

Sbarra, D. A., & Hazan, C. (2008). Coregulation, dysregulation, self-regulation: an integrative analysis and empirical agenda for understanding adult attachment, separation, loss, and recovery. *Personality and Social Psychology Review*, 12(141), 141–67.

Scherer, K. R. (2009). The dynamic architecture of emotion: evidence for the component process model. *Cognition and Emotion*, 23(7), 1307–51.

Schoebi, D. (2008). The coregulation of daily affect in marital relationships. *Journal of Family Psychology*, 22(3), 595–604.

Schoebi, D., & Randall, A. K. (2015). Emotional dynamics in intimate relationships. *Emotion Review*, 7(4), 342–48.

Sels, L., Ceulemans, E., Bulteel, K., & Kuppens, P. (2016). Emotional interdependence and well-being in close relationships. *Frontiers in Psychology*, 7(283).

Steenbeek, H., & van Geert, P. (2005). A dynamic systems model of dyadic interaction during play of two children. *European Journal of Developmental Psychology*, 2(2), 105–45.

Tiedens, L., & Leach, C. (2004). *The Social Life of Emotions* (Volume 2). New York: Cambridge University Press.

Timmons, A. C., Margolin, G., & Saxbe, D. E. (2015). Physiological linkage in couples and its implications for individual and interpersonal functioning: a literature review. *Journal of Family Psychology*. doi:10.1037/fam0000115

Townsend, S. S., Kim, H. S., & Mesquita, B. (2014). Are you feeling what I'm feeling? Emotional similarity buffers stress. *Social Psychological and Personality Science*, 5(5), 526–33.

Tronick, E. Z. (1989). Emotions and emotional communication in infants. *American Psychologist*, 44(2), 112–19. doi:10.1037/0003-066X.44.2.112.

Vallacher, R. R., Nowak, A., & Zochowski, M. (2005). Dynamics of social coordination: the synchronization of internal states in close relationships. *Interaction Studies*, 6(1), 35–52.

Van der Giessen, D., Branje, S. J., Frijns, T., & Meeus, W. H. (2013). Dyadic variability in mother-adolescent interactions: developmental trajectories and associations with psychosocial functioning. *Journal of Youth and Adolescence*, 42(1), 96–108.

Van der Giessen, D., Hollenstein, T., Hale III, W. W., et al. (2014). Emotional variability in mother-adolescent conflict interactions and internalizing problems of mothers and adolescents: dyadic and individual processes. *Journal of Abnormal Child Psychology*, 43(2), 339–53.

Von Bertalanffy, L. (1968). *General System Theory*. New York: Braziller.

Wegner, D. M., Giuliano, T., & Hertel, P. T. (1985). Cognitive interdependence in close relationships. In W. J. Ickes (Ed.), *Compatible and Incompatible Relationships* (pp. 253–76). New York: Springer-Verlag.

Westman, M. (2001). Stress and strain crossover. *Human Relations*, 54(6), 717–51.

Wichers, M., Wigman, J. T., & Myin-Germeys, I. (2015). Micro-level affect dynamics in psychopathology viewed from complex dynamical system theory. *Emotion Review*, 7(4), 362–7.

Wilks, S. S. (1932). Certain generalizations in the analysis of variance. *Biometrika*, 24(3/4), 471–94.

Zaki, J., & Williams, W. C. (2013). Interpersonal emotion regulation. *Emotion*, 13(5), 803–10.

# CHAPTER 3

# Simplifying the complexity of interpersonal emotion dynamics with regression graphics

*Jonathan E. Butner, Alexander O. Crenshaw, Ascher K. Munion, Alexander Wong, and Brian R. W. Baucom*

Dynamical systems models are being used with increasing frequency for characterizing intra- and interpersonal emotion dynamics in dyadic relationships (e.g., Butler & Randall, 2013; Butner et al., 2017; Scherer, 2009, see Chapter 2 for a review of relevant methodological approaches). Yet, having confidence in the application and interpretation of dynamical systems models remains a challenge. There are a number of excellent tutorials that provide step-by-step guidance in estimating models (e.g., Boker & Laurenceau, 2006; Butner et al., 2017; Perry et al., 2017), but many fewer resources for (1) evaluating the statistical assumptions of dynamical systems models and (2) representing and interpreting model results. The primary aim of this chapter is to provide simple, graphical methods to address these two challenges.

As an illustration, we examine the dynamics of a dyad's heart rate (HR) data collected while they discussed an area of conflict in their relationship for ten minutes. In our examination, we aim to understand how each partner's previous HR is related to the actor and their partner's HR at the next timepoint – an autoregressive relationship. The implementation of this model is based on a homeostatic view of affective, interpersonal processes (e.g., Butler & Gross, 2009). This views each partner's affect as constantly changing (e.g., Scherer, 2009), and the homeostatic aspect of the model emphasizes the factors that influence how quickly each partner can return to their baseline level when they are perturbed from their baseline. The model allows for examination of intrapersonal regulation (i.e., to what extent is a partner's ability to return to baseline linked to their previous state) and of interpersonal regulation (i.e., to what extent is a person's ability to return to baseline linked to the partner's previous state).

Prior to model estimation, HR values were aggregated to every second ($N_{\text{Husband}} = 594$; $N_{\text{Wife}} = 593$). We will be focusing on a single bivariate time series. However, all the techniques can also be expanded to multiple time series appropriate for multilevel modeling approaches and can further be expanded beyond two simultaneous equations to any number. Further, we provide R syntax for creating each of the visualizations of the model dynamics in the appendix.

## Conceptual overview

In this chapter, we take an agnostic stance about the merits of different models of emotion and instead suggest that the statistical characterization of interpersonal emotion processes can be reduced to a straightforward conceptual question: how is one person's emotional state related to another person's emotional state over time? We root this question within dynamical systems theory (DST), a conceptual framework for understanding patterns of change that emerge over time (e.g., Thelen & Smith, 1996; Vallacher & Nowak, 1994). DST views an individual's emotions as representing interpersonal affective regulation of the superordinate dyad and context in which the dyad resides. For example, different patterns of interpersonal regulation might be observed if a dyad has an argument in the privacy of their home as compared to an argument in public. When we observe variance in affect over time, that variance then represents the way affect changes over time as a function of all elements of the system (individuals, dyad, and context).

DST assumes that the many interacting parts of the system generate stable temporal patterns, which should be observable in what we choose to measure. DST recasts the meaning of error now as a function of the disruptional influences of parts we do not measure on the parts which we do measure, instead of just imprecision of measurement. These assumptions are based on systems always encountering inductions of change, even when we observe no change in our measured variables. Individuals consume coffee, work out, hold hands, and encounter work conflicts, all of which can influence emotion. These changes in the system are understood to arise from many different sources at many different timescales, some of which are represented in any given DST model (e.g., the partner) and some of which are not (e.g., coffee consumption). The changes over time that are represented in the model are characterized by a temporal pattern (i.e., the results of the DST model) that is stable despite the constant inductions of change.

Aspects of the system that are not represented in the model are referred to as *random perturbations*. In measuring the HR for members of a dyad, we expect each partner to display a temporal pattern that is a by-product of the entire system of variables contributing to HR over time. We would also constantly observe deviations from that temporal pattern. The deviations are a function of the many perturbations as the system continues to maintain the temporal patterns in a stable fashion. Thus, model error can be understood in terms of unmeasured variables from a DST perspective.

Applying DST to the study of interpersonal affective processes implies some assumptions about the nature of how emotions change. These assumptions can be reduced to three core suppositions: (1) each person's current emotional state is related to their own and the other person's subsequent emotional state, (2) the pattern of how the two people's emotional states unfold over time is a product of the interdependence of the dyad, and (3) under most circumstances, we are examining processes that have settled into a set of stable patterns of change in affect over time. That is, the stability of a pattern through time is integral to the pattern itself.

DST models then attempt to decompose the stable patterns over time into a description of the patterns themselves and the stability of those patterns in the presence of perturbations. This decomposition is very similar to the way that a polynomial regression model decomposes a complex association between the outcome and predictors (e.g., an inverted U-shaped association) into separate predictors (e.g., linear and quadratic regression parameters). DST decomposes temporal variation in two or more outcomes (e.g., changes in both partner's HR over time) into multiple parameter estimates to characterize complex forms of change over time. Within the interpersonal context, the patterns and their stability are inherently a by-product of both members of the dyad (and the context). Linkages across partners, represented as the ability of a characteristic of one person to be able to predict that of another, are interpreted as immediate driving relationships commonly called *coupling* relationships. Importantly, these linkages should not be interpreted as causal evidence in that a lack of a relationship is as much caused by the characteristics of the partnership under DST as the presence of a relationship. Instead these linkages are merely indicative of immediate future relationship behavior. Within the interpersonal context, these linkages are frequently the primary foci, and much of this chapter will be about identifying their existence. However, they should not be interpreted in isolation and therefore we will also cover other features of dynamics more generally.

These three core suppositions of DST models capture a wide range of interpersonal emotion processes including *reactivity* and *regulation*. We operationalize *reactivity* (positive and negative) to refer to the change in emotional state from one time point to the next following the introduction of some kind of stimulus or event that perturbs the dyadic emotional system. Examples of these kinds of stimuli or events include occurrences shared by both members of a dyad, such as a comment from one person to the other or watching a movie together, as well as occurrences only experienced by one member of a dyad, such as having a bad day at work or feeling ill. We operationalize *regulation* to refer to a homeostatic process where a system returns to a pattern whenever it is perturbed from that pattern. What is unique about DST is that it conceptualizes regulation as a dyadic process where both members of the dyad are seen as influencing homeostatic patterns.

Numerous interpersonal emotion processes in addition to reactivity and regulation can be modeled using a DST approach. Examples within interpersonal emotion processes include empathy (Preston & Hofelich, 2012), responsivity (Butler, 2011), intimacy (Boker & Laurenceau, 2006), and autonomic regulation (Helm et al., 2012). The challenge facing researchers at present is not whether a DST-based analytic approach can be used to model interpersonal emotion processes, but rather how to evaluate the appropriateness of any given DST model for a conceptual question. Further, it is necessary to understand and clearly communicate the implications of the results of a DST model for interpersonal emotion theory in the context of the decisions made in choosing a model. In the next section, we address the first challenge with an emphasis on evaluating the appropriateness of a given model from a statistical perspective, and we address the second challenge in the subsequent section.

## Assumptions of dynamical systems models for dyadic regulatory processes

There are assumptions about the properties of DST models that need to be evaluated in the service of determining the stability and potential bias in model results. Evaluating these assumptions can also aid researchers in selecting amongst different DST models. Most commonly, DST models for interpersonal emotion processes can be thought of as a series of simultaneous linear regressions applied to time series, and by extension, the assumptions can be conceptualized in terms of the assumptions of linear regression.[1]

Researchers in psychology and related affective science fields commonly use a series of simultaneous regressions for quantifying the associations between two variables measured at multiple time points. These models are often referred to using numerous terms including

[1] A regression-based approach to DST is only one approach, though probably the most common (since many techniques can be depicted as expansions of regression). Alternate approaches would accrue different assumptions.

repeated-measures Actor-Partner Interdependence Models (e.g., Cook & Kenny, 2005), Cross-Lagged Panel Models (e.g., Kenny et al., 2006; see Chapters 5 and 8 for examples), and Time-Series Panel Models (Ramseyer et al., 2014). These familiar models are *first order* DST models. First order means that these models describe the rate of change in the raw value of a variable from one time point to the next. If the raw value of an observation is thought of as its position on the scale of measurement of the variable, the rate of change from one moment to the next is analogous to velocity. Velocity is quantified using the first derivative, which is where the term first order change comes from.

In DST models, first order change can be characterized in numerous ways. The series of equations herein are a linear discrete change model representation of the illustrative example (HR from a heterosexual dyad every second over a ten-minute period). We will use p1 and p2 to represent the two partners (though later figures will use Husband and Wife to assist in separating axes on figures). The outcome in this model is the discrete change in partner 1's HR (Eq. 3.1) or partner 2's HR (Eq. 3.2) from one second (time = $t$) to the next second (time = $t + 1$):

$$(HR_{p1@t+1} - HR_{p1@t}) = b_0 + b_1 HR_{p1@t} + b_2 HR_{p2@t} + e_{p1} \qquad (3.1)$$

$$(HR_{p2@t+1} - HR_{p2@t}) = b_3 + b_4 HR_{p1@t} + b_5 HR_{p2@t} + e_{p2} \qquad (3.2)$$

We build on the list of assumptions for linear regression models advanced by Cohen et al. (2003). Table 3.1 presents the assumptions of standard linear regression in the left column and the six assumptions of DST models for interpersonal emotion processes in the right column (the last three DST assumptions are combined under assumptions about residuals). In presenting the assumptions of standard linear regression models and DST models separately we mean to demonstrate how knowledge of linear regression models can be expanded upon for use with DST models.

## Assumptions about measurement of variables

As is true of standard regression models, DST models assume that the values of measured variables do not include measurement error. This assumption is very important for DST models because rather than being interested in modeling variance about the mean, we are interested in modeling variance through time. Modeling variance through time means that we not only need to be able to measure the relative position of a variable on its scale but also to precisely quantify rapid temporal fluctuations in the relative position of a variable on its scale. Further, the goal is to relate those rapid temporal fluctuations to rapid

52 Butner et al.

Table 3.1. *Assumptions of standard linear regression (left) and DST models (right)*

| Categories | Standard Linear Regression | DST Models |
|---|---|---|
| Assumptions about Measurement of Variables | Variables have no measurement error | Variables have no measurement error |
| Assumptions about Variables Included in the Model | All necessary variables *must* be included | All necessary *variables do not have to* be included |
| Assumptions about Associations between Variables | *One* linear association exists between variables | *Multiple* linear associations can exist between variables |
| Assumptions about Residuals | Normality of residuals, Constant variance of residuals, Independence of residuals | Normality of residuals, Constant variance of residuals, Independence of residuals |

temporal fluctuations of another variable. For this reason, it is highly desirable to use measures with high internal reliability and sensitivity to change over time when constructing DST models. This pattern of high internal reliability and sensitivity to change over time suggests that measurements of internal consistency reliability are particularly important, but should be examined within an intraindividual context. Such procedures can be done through reliability calculations common in multilevel models where there are multiple indicators and multiple time points (see Raudenbush & Bryk, 2002).

**Assumptions about variables included in the model**

Assumptions about which variables should be included in a given model have to do with the ability to interpret an association between a predictor and an outcome as representing a unique association between those two variables that cannot otherwise be accounted for by another variable. The uniqueness of the association between a predictor and the outcome is very important in standard linear regression, and the assumption in standard linear regression is therefore that all necessary variables are included in the model to ensure correct partialling.

In contrast, in DST models the emphasis is on representing the temporal patterning of the latent system through time, and some of the variables can inherently depict more about the system than just their direct relationships. This logic is best represented through Takens' theorem (1981; and Casdagli et al., 1991 expansion to open systems), which shows that there is redundant information in the qualities of the entire system in just some of the variables in the system. For example, the partner's HR generates a stable temporal pattern as a function of the individual, the dyad, and the context. However, we can observe this temporal pattern from observing just this one partner. That is, the partner's HR contains information about the whole system, including variables that helped stabilize and perturb the partner such as the other partner's HR (and vice versa). Even if other variables that impact the system are not measured, their influence on the system is nonetheless represented in the dynamics of the observed variable(s).

The application of Takens' (1981) theorem is applicable to the extent to which the measured variables are central (or related) variables for creating the temporal pattern of interest. Since we focus on the latent system through time, Takens' (1981) theorem suggests that we can capture the dynamics of the latent system based on a reduced set of variables, while maintaining understanding of the stability of the system under assumed perturbations. As with the assumption for regression on the inclusion of variables, there is no known method for testing this assumption.

## Assumptions about associations between variables

### *Selecting an order of change*

The nature of the associations between predictors and the outcome(s) is assumed to be the same in both standard linear regression and DST models. Namely, a linear association between predictor and outcome is assumed to characterize the nature of the association between the two variables. In standard linear regression models, violations of this assumption occur when the association is nonlinear in nature, such as having a natural asymptote, curvilinearity (wherein the relationship is different between higher and lower levels of the predictors), nonmonotonicity (curvilinear with multiple points of inflection), or interactions with other variables. These nonlinear associations are typically addressed by transformations of the predictor and/or outcome, by constructing a polynomial regression model (i.e., including higher order powers of a predictor), or by building the appropriate interaction terms.

In DST models a similar notion applies, but because the focus is on modeling the temporal patterning of the system this assumption requires a different issue to be addressed first: the proper level of derivatives one should examine. For example, first order equations are capable of producing oscillatory trajectories as a by-product of the relations amongst two or more simultaneous equations – a nonlinear trajectory through time. Equations 3.1 and 3.2 are an example of a pair of first order equations (recall that the order of change refers to the level of the derivative treated as the outcome or implied by the equation). However, a single second order equation is also capable of producing oscillatory trajectories and therefore the relations amongst two second order equations instead focus on the associations of the cycles rather than their construction.

In DST models associations may exist at any order of derivatives. Further, multiple associations can exist simultaneously. Choosing to examine any one order, such as the first order equations presented earlier, is akin to choosing a focal length on a microscope wherein specific qualities of the dynamics are being highlighted and assuming that the other levels do not violate the assumptions being made to examine the current one. For example, examining first order relationships of interpersonal emotion processes assumes that the oscillatory nature of emotion does not alter the form of the relationships we are examining, nor induce problems with residuals. As of yet, there is no clear way to determine the proper levels of derivatives one should examine.

*Intra- and interpersonal associations*

Once an order of change has been chosen it is important to evaluate the linearity assumption with regard to the remainder of the simultaneous equations, namely the associations between the predictors (i.e., partner 1's and partner 2's HR during the previous second) and the outcomes (i.e., partner 1's and partner 2's HR during the current second). Nonlinearity in associations takes on special meaning in DST. Specifically, DST models group trajectories around locations where no change would be predicted, known as *setpoints* (Butner et al., 2014). Linear equation forms inherently only have a single setpoint that is fixed. For Eqs 3.1 and 3.2, this setpoint is a combined value of partner 1 and partner 2's HR for the dyad (an HR value for partner 1 and a different HR value for partner 2) and depending upon the coefficients, the model implies trajectories that converge toward the setpoint in some dimension(s), move away from it in others, and also possibly cycle around it.

Nonlinear equation forms can potentially have more than one setpoint: more than one location where change in all outcomes is predicted to be zero. Therefore nonlinear equation forms can potentially have multiple groupings of trajectories where a dyad may be moving in and out of the groupings over time. For example, for the combined dyad HR, we might observe a setpoint when both individuals have a high HR wherein they cycle around the value as each individual induces changes in the other to cope with some stressful event. We might imagine a second setpoint at lower HR values wherein both maintain low levels. Further, these setpoints can be moderated by other variables. For example, there could be a third setpoint at high HR for one person and low for the other, but this point only exists when the dyad is separate and thus not communicating (see Butner et al., 2017 for an example of this pattern in combined HR values from ambulatory HR). Examining scatterplots of higher order derivatives with lower order derivatives can assess these forms of nonlinear associations.

## Assumptions about residuals

A final set of assumptions is related to residuals. Assumptions about residuals in DST models are very similar to assumptions about residuals in standard linear regression models. For both types of models, we assume that residuals are independent (i.e., not related to one another), normally distributed, and homoskedastic (i.e., constant in variance across the range of the outcome). These assumptions are all relatively flexible in that they are model dependent, relative to the data. That is, given the correct model, these assumptions will be met.

Of these three assumptions, violating the independence of residuals assumption is most problematic in that any degree of dependency is known to drive extreme levels of alpha inflation. Further, DST models are often structured around multiple forms of potential dependencies. For example, regression is commonly used with cross-sectional data while DST applications are used with data collected over time. Further, in the case of simultaneous regression equations, dependency can exist between the dependent variables – the change in partner 1 and partner 2's HR. Regression has long been known as an acceptable time series approach as long as no dependency remains in the residuals. Essentially, the temporal dependency existent in the time series structure and couple dependency in the changes due to being part of the same couple are reconstructed through the DST model. However, if any dependency remains, the model is not adequate and needs to be modified to take this into account. For example, the two equations should be modeled simultaneously in a fashion that can include an error covariance amongst the DVs or one should consider equivalent multilevel models or Structural Equation Models to account for multiple time series. This can be assessed through calculating the intraclass correlation on the residuals themselves in regards to the various potential dependencies.

In regards to normality and homoskedasticity, the same methods used to evaluate these assumptions in standard regression models can also be used to evaluate these assumptions for DST models. More specifically, normality of the distribution of residuals and homoskedasticity can both be visually evaluated using regression diagnostic plots (Q-Q plots for normality and residuals versus fitted values for homoskedasticity). Cohen et al. (2003) is an excellent resource for additional details about these procedures.

## Summary

The assumptions of linear DST models build directly on those for standard regression models. Some assumptions, such as variables being measured with no measurement error, are more closely tied to study design and data collection than to DST modeling. Others, such as normality, constant variance, and independence of residuals, can be evaluated with standard regression diagnostics and are not unique to DST models per se – rather, they are assumptions of linear models more generally. Perhaps the most important assumption of DST models is that multiple linear associations can exist between the variables. The reason that this assumption is so important is that it is closely tied to selecting the order of change to be modeled. If an inappropriate order of change is modeled, it could lead to spurious conclusions (e.g., no evidence of interpersonal regulatory processes based on a first order model of change when coupling exists in second order change). We strongly encourage drawing on substantive theory and existing empirical evidence in selecting the order of change. In the absence of these two sources, we recommend examination of at least two orders of change to evaluate the consistency of the substantive interpretation (i.e., is there evidence of significant coupling or not?) across models.

## Graphical methods for interpreting and communicating DST results

We now turn to the example dyad's data. We will primarily focus on first order change akin to Eqs 3.1 and 3.2. If other derivative orders were examined instead, the procedure would be the same, but with the new outcomes and an expanded set of derivatives (it is common to test all lower order derivatives as predictors). Our approach will primarily be graphical, first examining the time series themselves, followed by focusing on intraindividual dynamics, and then interindividual ones. As mentioned earlier, the primary focus in interpersonal emotion dynamics is frequently on the interindividual dynamics within the dyad, but the interpersonal is intertwined with the intrapersonal in DST and therefore a staged approach is appropriate.

### *Time series plots*

Visual examination of the discrete change outcome variables should come before building the rest of the model represented in Eqs 3.1 and 3.2. Figure 3.1 shows the time series of the husband's and wife's HR over the ten-minute period. This plot serves a similar function for DST models

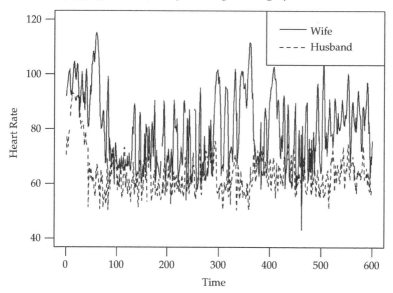

Figure 3.1. Time series of husband and wife heart rates every second during a ten-minute argument within a laboratory

as a histogram does for standard regression models, in that it allows for visual inspection of the source of variance that is of interest. In standard regression models, variance about the mean is of primary interest and a histogram is used to examine this variance by plotting the range of scores of the variable on the horizontal axis and the frequency of each score or bins of scores on the vertical axis. In DST models, variance over time is of primary interest so HR is displayed on the vertical axis and time is displayed on the horizontal axis. The ups and downs we observe in both partner's HRs are the discrete change that is represented by the outcome variables in Eqs 3.1 and 3.2.

In DST, the observed changes are inherently assumed to be a combination of the temporal patterning and the constant perturbations of which the temporal patterning is overcoming to maintain stability. This plot is useful for evaluating two aspects of the two HR time series: (1) are the raw HR values within a reasonable range and (2) are the discrete changes (i.e., changes from one time point to the next) within a reasonable range? We can examine the range of values to assess the first, and the continuity of the HR signal and change in magnitude of observation to observation to assess the second.

**Interpretation of Figure 3.1.** Visual inspection reveals that husband HR varies between the low 50s and mid-90s and wife HR varies between the low 60s and approximately 115. Both of these HR ranges are biologically plausible, though the distance between the minimum and maximum values for each time series is larger than the value of HR change typically reported in most studies of relationship conflict. This greater range is likely related to the small time window of 1 second over which HR was measured. What is of concern is the single, very low value of wife HR that occurs at approximately 460 seconds. This value, and the magnitude of change from the previous value, suggests that it is an artifact that should be corrected prior to analysis (e.g., Jennings et al., 1981).

## Individual relationships

Figure 3.2 shows the first order discrete change in HR on the vertical axis for wife (upper panel) and husband (lower panel) as a function of that partner's own current HR on the horizontal axis as a way to examine

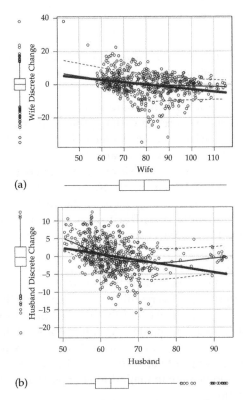

Figure 3.2. Scatterplots of discrete change in heart rates (HR) on the Y-axis and current value on the X-axis. Wife HR is the upper panel, husband HR is the lower panel

each individual independently. The thick black line is the best fitting OLS line and the thin black line is a Lowess smoother. For both partners, the OLS line is negative. Also note that both thin black Lowess lines, on the other hand, look quadratic (though for different reasons). These figures are particularly useful for identifying the homeostatic nature of the system and the linearity of associations.

**Setpoints.** As noted earlier, systems models are most easily understood relative to where they imply no change, the setpoints. For both figures we want to identify these setpoints – the HR value where the regression line crosses the horizontal axis at the origin (i.e., when change in HR equals zero). The best fitting OLS line (thick black) for each can only cross once, hence the fact that linear equations can only ever imply a single dynamic. For the wife, the setpoint is approximately 80 BPM and for the husband it is around 65 BPM.

**Homeostasis.** The slopes at the setpoint(s) indicate how trajectories are being grouped together. The negative direction of the thick black OLS slopes indicates that these values are functioning as homeostatic setpoints (known as *attractors* in systems parlance). A homeostatic setpoint is a point to which the system returns over time. The interpretation of these negative slopes as homeostatic setpoints can be understood by tracing through what happens over time given a starting value of HR. Imagine that the wife had a HR lower than 80 BPM. The best fitting straight line suggests that her HR would increase over time – positive change. Now imagine her HR is above 80 BPM. The slope would imply negative change decreasing toward that homeostatic setpoint. Regardless of the starting value, her HR would return to the homeostatic setpoint of 80 BPM, and the steeper the slope, the faster the return occurs.[2]

**Nonlinear relationships.** Returning to evaluation of the linearity assumption, the thin black Lowess smoothed line suggests that the association between previous value of HR and change is nonlinear for both partners in that the lines curve in a consistent manner. Inspection of these potential sources of non-linearity is required to determine whether it is a problematic violation of assumptions and/or if it is informative about the nature of the temporal dynamics. For example, this nonlinear association could indicate that there could be more than one homeostatic setpoint value and that the strength of attraction may vary throughout

---

[2] The interpretation of the slope of current value predicting its own change has historically been confusing. Contrary to expectations, it is not that at higher values one increases slower or decreases faster. Instead, we must always identify the setpoint because the interpretation will differ above and below that point. In this case, being above the setpoint implies moving down toward it and being below implies moving up toward it. This can imply trajectories, but it also unites temporal patterning and perturbations within a single equation representation.

the data. To identify the circumstance one must examine the curved line for the number of times it crosses the horizontal line at the origin (no change). Each time it crosses is a unique setpoint, and each setpoint can group trajectories differently depending upon the slope at that setpoint. Further, the number of setpoints, their locations, and their strengths can change when moderated by interactions with other variables, and after partialling out other associations (Butner et al., 2014).

**Interpreting the nonlinearity in Figure 3.2.** The quadratic line for the husband crosses the horizontal axis of zero change twice (the second time at a HR of around 95) and the slope of the thin black Lowess smoothed line at this second HR value is positive. While negative slopes indicate attracting setpoints, positive slopes indicate repelling setpoints. This is a setpoint value at which, when it is approached, the husband moves away. In contrast, the nonlinear association for the wife appears to be driven by a possible outlier to the left end of the Figure. If we removed that one data point, the quadratic relationship would go away; just like any regression model, issues of sampling and outliers influence DST models. This collection of observations can be interpreted as indicating that the linearity assumption for the wife will likely be met after removing the outlier while the husband potentially requires a nonlinear equation form to account for the multiple setpoints.

## Modeling the dyad

We now consider both partners simultaneously to parallel Eqs 3.1 and 3.2. Table 3.2 presents the results of the two regressions that comprise our DST model. Recall that in each regression, the change in one partner's HR from one second to the next was regressed onto that actor's HR during the previous second and the partner's HR during the previous second. We begin our interpretation by stepping through each component of the regressions.

**The intercepts.** The intercepts in the two regressions represent the homeostatic setpoint for the system. However, because the outcome of our regressions is change in HR rather than actual HR, it is difficult to

Table 3.2. *Unstandardized regression coefficients (standard errors) from linear discrete change model*

| Outcome | Intercept B (SE B) | Actor B (SE B) | Partner B (SE B) |
|---|---|---|---|
| Change in Husband HR | 10.30 (1.67) | −0.17 (0.02) | 0.01 (0.01) |
| Change in Wife HR | 7.13 (2.65) | −0.15 (0.02) | 0.07 (0.04) |

directly interpret these values, as they are the predicted change when HR is zero (meaningless without centering). The intercepts carry key information for the setpoint which can be computed by multiplying the intercept by negative one and dividing that quantity by the partner's actor effect in our linear dynamic (e.g., partner 1 setpoint = $-1 * b_0/b_1$) case.

A dyadic extension of a kernel density plot (KDP) dramatically simplifies the interpretation of the system's homeostatic setpoint(s). A KDP is similar to the figure that would be produced in a histogram with very small bins in that it represents the relative frequency of a given score on the vertical axis for a range of values of the variable, which are represented on the horizontal axis. Similar to the thin black Lowess smoothed lines in Figure 3.2, a KDP presents values that have been smoothed by the selection of a kernel.[3] Figure 3.3 is a KDP for both husband and wife HR where the relative frequency of a pair of HR values is represented in a topographical representation. In this representation, higher "peaks" indicate more likely values of the data and therefore the peaks coincide relatively close to the setpoints.

**Interpretation of the KDP for setpoint identification.** The pronounced peak of the KDP occurs at approximately 61 BPM for the husband and 67 BPM for the wife. This is the coordinate of values to which the system is drawn over time and is the same set of values as the leftmost point at which the thin black Lowess smoothed lines cross the horizontal axis in Figure 3.2a and 3.2b. The KDP also highlights the wide range of HR values for which the change in wife's HR is close to the horizontal axis in Figure 3.2a. This range of values represents the homeostatic range and is visible as the large plateau in the vertical axis (between 70 and 85 HR for the wife) of Figure 3.3. The plateau implies lots of movement around the setpoint, or movement of the setpoint itself, in that the stability of HR may be relatively weak or some other variable may relate to moving around the setpoint itself. Finally, there is also a small island of values where both husband HR and wife HR are high (Wife HR ~100, Husband HR ~90) that corresponds to the second point at which change in husband HR crosses the horizontal axis in Figure 3.2b.

**Adding in change.** The KDP can be elaborated to add visualizations that represent actor and partner effects in both regressions to begin our interpretation of the full model. Figure 3.4[4] overlays a vector for each

---

[3] A kernel is a smoother designed to emulate integration for identifying area under the curve (in a zero to one scaling). It is ideal for giving some sense of the probability density function from finite data (Cohen et al., 2003). As with Lowess smoothers, there are multiple functions that each emphasize certain data features over others.

[4] These plots are often easier to read by shortening the arrows proportionality or adding a jitter to values (if lots of points are at the same cartesian coordinate in the data).

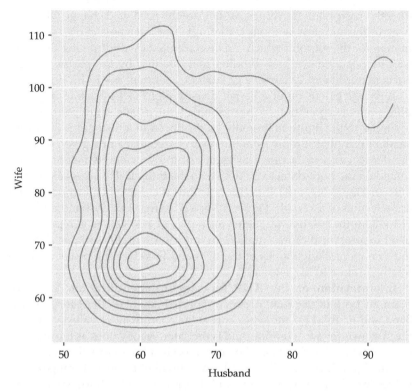

Figure 3.3. KDP of husband and wife HR. The topographical lines indicate higher frequencies of data occurring at those coordinates which show where the data collected over time

change in coordinates of HR; each vector begins with where the husband HR and wife HR coordinate at time $= t$. The arrow indicates the next coordinate value of husband HR, wife HR at time $= t + 1$. Finally, the length of each vector represents how fast the system changes in the region of HR values. This observed vector plot can be thought of as the descriptive for all the qualities we are attempting to quantify with Eqs 3.1 and 3.2.

The interpretation of vector plots is best understood in terms of identifying the direction and length of arrows relative to the local setpoints. One must first identify the local setpoint (The peaks in the KDP) and then ask what the arrows are doing relative to that point. Moving toward the point is consistent with the actor effects from Eqs 3.1 and 3.2 wherein the behavior is homeostatic (away is instead repulsive). The length of the arrows are indicative of stability of this homeostatic point in that longer arrows suggest a stronger homeostasis (farther away should also always

Vector Plot

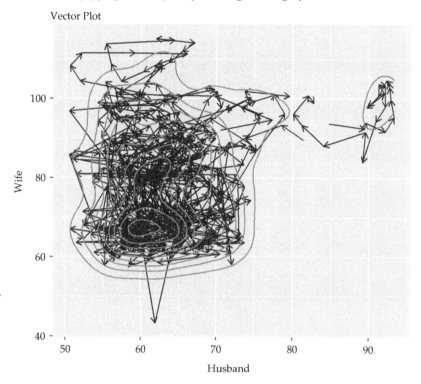

Figure 3.4. Observed vector plot of HR overlaid on a KDP

be longer than those close to the setpoint since the setpoint represents a point of no change in the system if perturbations did not exist) and will correspond to larger magnitude actor effects in Eqs 3.1 and 3.2.

On the other hand, the extent to which arrows move around the setpoint rather than just toward it is a function of the immediate linkages between partners that would be observed in the partner effects from Eqs 3.1 and 3.2; change in one partner is carrying over to the other partner. These coupling relationships indicate immediate prediction of one partner on the other, suggesting that one partner is helping stabilize or destabilize the other partner when perturbed (one partner is perturbed which the prediction suggests carries over to the other partner).

**Interpreting some exemplar areas of** Figures 3.4 and 3.5. The density of the arrows makes it difficult to get a clear sense of the dynamics. We will resolve this issue in the next set of figures. For now, there are a couple of insights in Figure 3.4. Notice that in the upper left quadrant (high wife HR and low husband HR) we have two nearly identical loops for the dyadic system. These loops represent oscillations in both HRs

64   *Butner et al.*

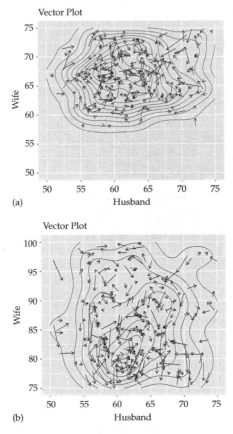

Figure 3.5. Observed vector plot and kernel density overlaid for just the dense regions of the data of low wife and low husband HR (a) and midwife and low husband HR (b). All changes were divided by five to better visualize the arrows

simultaneously, a by-product of coupling between partners as a function of the partner effects. In contrast, examine the far right island (high HR for both partners). Here the arrows approach the island and move around within it before departing – a by-product of the actor effects instead.

To understand these interpretations, we must evaluate the arrows relative to the relevant setpoints. For the cycle in the upper left, the setpoint would reside in the middle of the cycle, the point at which the data cycles around (there is no data at the setpoint in this case). For the island in the upper right, the setpoint would be in the upper right of the island where many of the arrows converge. Once this setpoint is identified, one must ask what the prominent behavior is relative to this point. Moving toward the setpoint (like the upper right island) is a tendency for homeostasis, captured by the actor effects amongst the coefficients. Cycles, on the other hand, move around the setpoint creating angular movement; when one partner is high, it predicts a change in the other partner creating vectors that are neither toward nor away from the setpoint.[5] More common interpersonal behavior will show both movement toward the setpoint and angular behavior around the setpoint. See Perry et al. (2017) for a more detailed discussion of graphical interpretation of actor and partner effects in vector plots.

To get a better sense of the dynamics in the regions with the bulk of the vectors, Figure 3.5 shows just those dense regions, zoomed in, where the values of change (the arrow lengths) have been proportionally reduced by five. By shortening the arrows, it is easier to see what each vector is doing, relative to the setpoints. To help identify those setpoints, we have overlaid the KDP.

For the portion of Figure 3.5 where the wife's HR is under 75, there appears to be a dense location where the husband's HR is slightly under 60, though it seems to extend to 65 (this is the same one we saw earlier in Figure 3.2b where it could be two setpoints, one with wiggle room, or that there might be another variable sliding the setpoint around). As before, we can examine the arrows around them relative to these points to get a sense of the interpersonal dynamics. In this case, the dominant behavior seems to be to move in and away from the setpoints with some angular behavior that seems to flow over the far right side of the peak. The same can also be said for the region where the wife's HR is above 75 – most of the arrows move toward or away from the highest density point, with a smaller subset moving at some angle relative to it. That is, the dominant behavior of the dyad is homeostatic, but not necessarily showing linkages between the two partner's HR values. A similar pattern would likely emerge if we modeled both partners' distance from home at the end of the workday. If both of their work days end at the same time, they would both leave for home at the same time and the rate at which they got closer to home would be a function of the specific road each

---

[5] There are exceptions to this, though the exceptions will cause problems for the statistical models as much as the regression graphics procedures. Specifically, to analyze this dyad level data, we would build two simultaneous equations: one examining the change in partner 1's heart rate and one examining the change in partner 2's heart rate. However, we could instead observe a high degree of synchrony in the dyad such that the partners are synonymous. In this case, you will observe the approach toward the setpoint, rather than necessarily angular behavior around the setpoint. However, all the approach vectors should be relatively diagonal to the horizontal and vertical axes. You can observe a little of this in the final approach to the upper right island in that all the motion is on the diagonal. What is unclear in the upper right island is if this is synchrony or merely due to a dearth of data occurrences around those heart rates.

was on and not a function of how close the other was from home. Both are a case of two individuals changing at the same time and doing so in a way that is unrelated to the other even though they return to a shared setpoint.

**A graphical model of the predicted equations.** We can take the equations from Table 3.2 and generate a vector plot akin to a prediction plot from regression. Like a prediction plot, it is inferential rather than observed (Figures 3.4 and 3.5 were observed). Creating a grid of points for a combination of HR values is the first step to generating this plot. Each point becomes the beginning of an arrow showing the predicted change in HR values. Figure 3.6 is thus an inferred vector plot and we have overlaid the same KDP to identify where data was primarily observed.

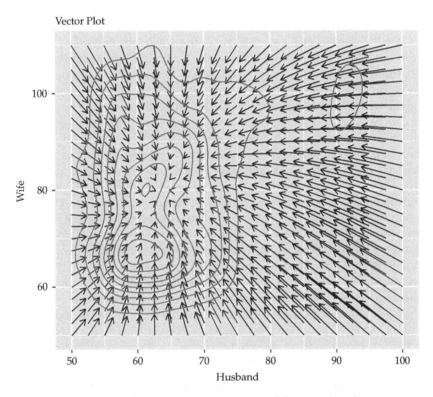

Figure 3.6. Inferred vector plot generated from testing the equations on the data

Note: As with regression planes, inferred vector plots go to positive and negative infinity and should be interpreted within the range of the data (illustrated here with the kernel density overlaid).

**Interpretation of Figure 3.6.** Notice that all of the behavior is relative to the primary homeostatic setpoint (i.e., the peak) in the KDP (the equations were linear and therefore could only represent a single setpoint, resulting in an amalgam of the various setpoints from the observed data). All the arrows indicate movement toward the setpoint and not around the setpoint. This lack of angularity is consistent with neither of the partner coefficients reaching significance at alpha $= 0.05$ (see Table 3.2). If the partners were coupled, instead the vectors would show swirling motion around the setpoint. That is, our linear equations extract what most of the observed arrows are doing relative to the amalgam setpoint.

**Examining nonlinearity.** Figure 3.6 showed that the linear equations created a single setpoint. However, when we observed the changes individually (for the husband in Figure 3.2), the thin black Lowess smoother suggested more than one setpoint and the plateau and island in the KDP (Figure 3.3) supported this possibility. We therefore desire to free up the linear assumption and allow for more than one setpoint while maintaining some degree of inferential statistics. Equation-wise constructing a nonlinear equation form would do this. Graphically, we can do so through exploratory means by creating the equivalent of the Lowess smoother, but for the two simultaneous equations.

Figure 3.7 is a Lowess-based vector plot overlaid on the KDP. Lowess smoothers also carry standard errors throughout the data window. We have therefore also shaded the vectors based on if the change would be different from zero on neither (dark gray), either axis of change (medium gray), or both axes of change (light gray). We did this by creating a 95% confidence interval around zero and indicating if the Lowess smoothed estimate of change was outside this range. There are two circumstances where we would fail to see change in both directions (represented by the dark gray): it is a setpoint in the data, or we lack enough data to distinguish the vector length from zero. Looking for nonzero vector lengths surrounding that point can differentiate these two circumstances. If an area is surrounded by nonzero (medium gray or light gray) vectors, then it is likely a setpoint (and should show some correspondence with the KDP). If instead there are clusters of vectors – especially longer ones – that are statistically indistinguishable from zero, there is likely insufficient data in those ranges of HR.

**Interpretation of Figure 3.7.** Notice that there are multiple setpoints (places where the vectors would have a length of zero, but also surrounded by nonzero vectors). Specifically, there is one setpoint that corresponds to each of the two peaks observed in the KDP (Figure 3.3) in lower HR for both partners. Further, there are different dynamics corresponding to each setpoint and a very interesting "river" of dark gray: a band of lack

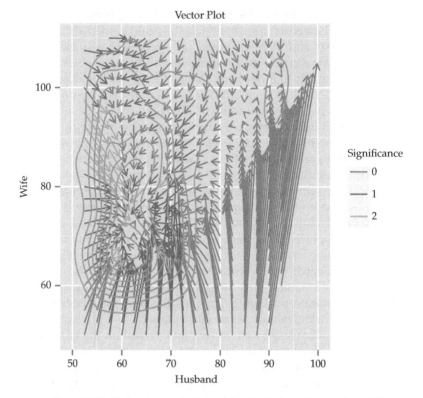

Figure 3.7.  Lowess-based vector plot shaded on the number of dimensions of change would be different from zero

Note: Dark gray indicates neither vector direction was significantly different from zero, medium gray indicates one of the vector directions was significantly different from zero. Light gray indicates both directions were significant from zero. Setpoints will appear dark gray with medium gray and light gray vectors encircling them. Other dark gray vectors do not have data to support them inferentially.

of change in the wife's HR. Our linear dynamic model implied by the two equations in Figure 3.6 primarily highlighted the attractor dynamics of the lower left setpoint (though the location of the setpoint from Figure 3.6 is more of an amalgamation of two setpoints in Figure 3.7). Further, the setpoints discussed from the observed vector plot in Figure 3.4 do not have enough data to support them (the island in the upper right). This is implicit in all the arrows in the region being non-differentiable from zero or not showing the observed dynamic (the cycles in the upper left). We discuss the three remaining dynamics in turn (dynamics around each of the two setpoints, and the river).

Dynamics around the lower left setpoint (wife HR ~ 70; husband HR ~ 63) are most consistent with the estimated equations in Table 3.2 and the predicted vector plot in Figure 3.6. Relative to this setpoint, the vast majority of arrows are showing movement toward the setpoint akin to homeostatic behavior where the relationship between the two individuals results in just their own behavior predicting changes. That is, the partner dynamics is such that when things occur that perturb their HR from this setpoint, we do not observe its influences carrying over to the partner (it is as if each partner's HR was in isolation). Further, this homeostatic pattern is one of the stronger ones in that the nonzero vectors feeding into the setpoint are some of the longer ones over the entire domain of HR values and relatively equivalent in terms of the two partners (vector length in wife HR is about the same at vector length in husband when equidistant from the setpoint; this is consistent with the actor coefficients being relatively close in that both HR values are on the same metric). This would suggest a more stable pattern where any perturbations are short-lived.

However, this pattern is not purely just actor effects in that if you look to the lower right of the setpoint the arrows imply a curved approach toward the setpoint. That is, some of the behavior is angular consistent with there being some coupling between the partners. Specifically, it is when the wife has a particularly low HR and the husband has a slightly higher HR that we see some carryover prediction suggestive that perturbations in this region carry over between partners. This is far from the dominant pattern, however.

The second setpoint is slightly higher in wife's HR, separated by the small border of nonzero vectors between them (the bottom end of the river that corresponds to the other peak in the KDP). Vectors around this setpoint all approach it in terms of lowering the wife's HR (we do not see vectors going up to the setpoint, only down to it) and the ones below flow to the other setpoint. That is, there is a limited way (akin to a trail) in which this other setpoint tends to be approached, specifically when the wife has a higher HR. These arrows, however, still primarily approach straight toward the setpoint, again suggestive of a homeostatic pattern just at this slightly elevated wife's HR value.

The river implies one of two possible interpretations. The first is that for this second setpoint, the wife's HR is very weakly homeostatic. Perturbations that would increase the wife's HR can move wife's HR around quite a bit (this is not true for the husband, though these vectors generally look shorter than those to the lower setpoint for the husband too implying that it is also relatively less stable). This interpretation would also suggest some coupling between the partners exists for this dynamic since the entire river is part of the same setpoint flow and the vectors near where we had observed the cycles in the upper left are angular relative to the setpoint. That is, when the wife has a particularly high HR within the range of this setpoint, we do observe carryover between partners.

Having multiple setpoints or having places in the vector plot that show some angular movement, but only sometimes relative to a setpoint, suggests that the interpersonal nature of HR for this dyad only exists some of the time. When this "some of the time" has to do with different regions of the vector plot, we can say that it is *phase dependent*, that the dynamic is dependent upon some special combination of factors within the system of simultaneous changes. However, common interpersonal models will fail to capture this property, only depicting the dynamics observed in Figure 3.6.

Alternatively, the river of no change could suggest that the setpoint moves as a function of some other variables that are part of the system. That is, there is another variable that we need to include to capture the interpersonal emotion dynamics, the value of which may more precisely determine the wife's setpoint. Further, there may be some values in which the stability would change (different vector lengths surrounding it) and even coupling could be observed (at some levels the vectors might imply angular movement). In the next section, we explain different reasons for why a linear dynamic model would fail.

## Nonstationarity, nonlinearity, and moderation-like behavior

As mentioned earlier, linear dynamic models have a single setpoint and behavior relative to that setpoint. As is the case here, we can instead have some nonlinear representation and there are a limited number of reasons for the nonlinearities from a systems perspective. From a modeling perspective, they come down to three primary circumstances.

*Some other variable differentiates the system dynamics.* In this case, some other variable functions in a moderation-like relationship in that as this other variable changes, so do the features of the dynamic. This is one possible explanation for the river in that some other variable moves the setpoint and alters the dynamics around that setpoint (e.g., stress). It is also a possible explanation for the two stable setpoints in that only one of them may be stable at a time. For example, when stress is high, it is possible that only the wife's higher HR is stable and when it is low only the wife's lower HR is stable. This approach can be taken into account by adding in other variables with interactions on the actor and partner effects. A main effect alone without an interaction can move a setpoint, but the dynamics around the moving setpoint remain unchanged.

*The system is multistable.* There can be more than one temporal dynamic when all else is equal. In this case, the dyad can potentially move between different dynamics over time as one gets perturbed from one area to another (the area where the arrows all flow into the same setpoint is known as the *basin* for that dynamic). For example, it could be that both setpoints are always there and whether the dyad is in one or the other has to do with where they had been before. An event (perturbation) to lower the wife's HR when in the upper homeostatic setpoint could be enough to move them to the lower one. The relationships have not changed, but the dyad has been moved to the other basin due to influences from other parts of the system that we did not measure. Multistability can only be captured through some form of nonlinear equation form. Polynomials are a reasonable approach (Butner et al., 2014b). Exploratory approaches, such as mixture modeling, may also be able to differentiate multiple basins of attraction (Butner et al., 2017).

*There are important dynamics not being taken into account at the current level of examination.* Each level of derivatives can be thought to highlight certain types of dynamics properties and treat the others as less important. It is possible that those other levels can have a substantial impact. For example, we have focused entirely on first order dynamics where coupling creates cycles. Instead, it could be that HR cycles regardless. Such cycles would still have setpoints, but coupling between partners would create vector patterns that appear akin to a Celtic knot (where different stages of the cycles would carry over to different stages of the partner's cycles) instead. This would end up making noisy looking coupled equations in the best of circumstances and could appear to have no coupling at all when only looking at first order equations. Examining second order equations also make assumptions as to the other levels. Specifically, second order equations assume that the setpoint is at a value of zero while first order equations allow for a nonzero setpoint. The extent to which the setpoint for cycles is nonzero can bias estimates of second order equations (this is commonly accounted for by first detrending the data). Thus, the ideal circumstance is to consider many equation levels.

## Conclusion

DST models allow for characterizing and quantifying complex, multi-variable, multi-faceted interpersonal emotion processes using a series of simultaneous equations that can be estimated using familiar regression-based methods. DST models have tremendous potential for advancing the study of interpersonal emotion processes, and, at the same time, we think that it is incumbent on the field to ensure that these models are thoughtfully implemented and correctly interpreted. It is our hope that the methods presented in this chapter will facilitate efforts to do just that, and will also assist researchers who are new to DST models in having greater confidence in their modeling decisions and clarity about the implications of their findings for refining interpersonal emotion theory.

## Appendix: R code for figures

### Figure 2

```
require(car)
scatterplot(data=data1,wife_cha~wife)
scatterplot(data=data1,husband_cha~husband)
```

### Figure 3

```
require(ggplot2)
ggplot(data1,aes(x=husband,y=wife))+geom_density-
2d()+ylab("Wife")+xlab("Husband")
```

### Figure 4

```
require(grid)
ggplot(data=data1,aes(x=husband,y=wife))+geom_segment
(aes(xend=husband+husband_cha,yend=wife+wife_
cha),arrow=arrow(length=unit(.2,"cm")))+
labs(list(title="VectorPlot",y="Wife",x="Husband"))+
geom_density2d()
```

### Figure 5

```
data1$husband_char<-(data1$husband_lead-data1$husband)/5
data1$wife_char<-(data1$wife_lead - data1$wife)/5

ggplot(data=data1,aes(x=husband,y=wife))+geom_segment
(aes(xend=husband+husband_char,yend=wife+wife_
char),arrow=arrow(length=unit(.2,"cm")))+
labs(list(title="VectorPlot",y="Wife",x="Husband"))+
geom_density2d()+xlim(50,75)+ylim(50,75)

ggplot(data=data1,aes(x=husband,y=wife))+geom_segment
(aes(xend=husband+husband_char,yend=wife+wife_
char),arrow=arrow(length=unit(.2,"cm")))+
labs(list(title="VectorPlot",y="Wife",x="Husband"))+
geom_density2d()+xlim(50,75)+ylim(75,100)
```

**Figure 6**

```
loess1<-loess(data=data1,hr_w_cln_cha~hr_w_cln+hr_h_cln,
  span=.5)
loess2<-loess(data=data1,hr_h_cln_cha~hr_w_cln+hr_h_cln,
  span=.5)
hr_w_cln <- seq(50,110,2.5)
hr_h_cln<-seq(50,110,2.5)
temp <- data.frame(expand.grid(hr_w_cln,hr_h_cln))
names(temp)<-c("hr_w_cln","hr_h_cln")
temp$pred1<-predict(loess1,newdata=temp,se=FALSE)
temp$pred2<-predict(loess2,newdata=temp,se=FALSE)
temp$sig<-temp1_pred1$sig + temp2_pred2$sig
ggplot(data=temp,aes(x=hr_h_cln,y=hr_w_cln))+geom_
segment(aes(xend=hr_h_cln+pred2,yend=hr_w_cln+
pred1),arrow=arrow(length=unit(.2,"cm")))+
labs(list(title="VectorPlot",x="Wife",y="Husband"))+
geom_density2d(data=data1,aes(x=hr_h_cln,y=hr_w_
cln))+xlim(50,100)+ylim(50,110)
```

## References

Boker, S. M., & Laurenceau, J. P. (2006). Dynamical systems modeling: an application to the regulation of intimacy and disclosure in marriage. In T. A. Walls & J. L. Schafer (Eds.) *Models for Intensive Longitudinal Data* (pp. 195–218). New York, NY: Oxford University Press.

Butler, E. A. (2011). Temporal interpersonal emotion systems the "TIES" that form relationships. *Personality and Social Psychology Review*, 15(4), 367–93.

Butler, E. A., & Gross, J. J. (2009). Emotion and emotion regulation: integrating individual and social levels of analysis. *Emotion Review*, 1(1), 86–7.

Butler, E. A., & Randall, A. K. (2013). Emotional coregulation in close relationships. *Emotion Review*, 5, 202–10.

Butner, J. E., Behrends, A. A., & Baucom, B. R. (2017). Mapping co-regulation in social relations through exploratory topology analysis. In R. R. Vallacher, S. J. Read, & A. Nowak's (Eds.) *Computational Social Psychology*. New York, NY: Psychology Press.

Butner, J. E., Gagnon, K. T., Geuss, M. N., Lessard, D. A., & Story, T. N. (2014). Utilizing topology to generate and test theories of change. *Psychological Methods*, 20(1), 1.

Casdagli, M., Eubank, S., Farmer, J. D., & Gibson, J. (1991). State space reconstruction in the presence of noise. *Physica D: Nonlinear Phenomena*, 51(1), 52–98.

Cohen, J., Cohen, P., West, S. G., & Aiken, L. S. (2003). *Applied Multiple Regression/ Correlation Analysis for the Behavioral Sciences*. Mahwah, NJ: Routledge.

Cook, W. L., & Kenny, D. A. (2005). The actor-partner interdependence model: a model of bidirectional effects in developmental studies. *International Journal of Behavioral Development*, 29, 101–9.

Helm, J. L., Sbarra, D., & Ferrer, E. (2012). Assessing cross-partner associations in physiological responses via coupled oscillator models. *Emotion*, 12(4), 748.

Jennings, J. R., Bberg, W. K., Hutcheson, J. S., et al. (1981). Publication guidelines for heart rate studies in man. *Psychophysiology*, 18, 226–31.

Kenny, D. A., Kashy, D. A., & Cook, W. L. (2006). *Dyadic Data Analysis*. New York, NY: Guilford.

Perry, N. S., Baucom, K. J. W., Bourne, S., et al. (2017). Graphic methods for interpreting longitudinal dyadic patterns from repeated-measures actor-partner interdependence models. *Journal of Family Psychology*. doi:10.1037/fam0000293

Preston, S. D., & Hofelich, A. J. (2012). The many faces of empathy: parsing empathic phenomena through a proximate, dynamic-systems view of representing the other in the self. *Emotion Review*, 4, 24–33.

Ramseyer, F., Kupper, Z., Caspar, F., Znoj, H., & Tschacher, W. (2014). Time-series panel analysis (TSPA): multivariate modeling of temporal associations in psychotherapy process. *Journal of Consulting and Clinical Psychology*, 82, 828.

Raudenbush, S. W., & Bryk, A. S. (2002). *Hierarchical Linear Models: Applications and Data Analysis Methods* (Volume 1). Thousand Oaks, CA: Sage.

Scherer, K. R. (2009) The dynamic architecture of emotion: evidence for the component process model. *Cognition and Emotion* 23(7), 1307–51.

Takens, F. (1981). Detecting strange attractors in turbulence. In *Dynamical Systems and Turbulence, Warwick 1980* (pp. 366–81). Berlin Heidelberg: Springer.

Thelen, E., & Smith, L. B. (1996). *A Dynamic Systems Approach to the Development of Cognition and Action*. Cambridge, MA: MIT Press.

Vallacher, R. R., & Nowak, A. E. (1994). *Dynamical Systems in Social Psychology*. San Diego, CA: Academic Press.

CHAPTER 4

# Methodological approaches to studying interpersonal emotion dynamics

*Jessica P. Lougheed and Tom Hollenstein*

Relationships can be conceptualized as self-organizing temporal inter-personal emotion systems (TIES) that emerge from emotion dynamics in interpersonal interactions (e.g., conflicts, planning events; Butler, 2011). In this chapter, we conceptualize interpersonal emotion dynamics as real-time temporal interdependencies (e.g., linkages, synchrony, contingent responses) between interaction partners' domains of emotion (e.g., physiology, expressions, and experience; Butler, 2011; see Chapter 1 for a conceptual overview). It is necessary to examine real-time dynamics – how emotions unfold in specific contexts – to understand close relationships and their associations with psychosocial adjustment (e.g., mental health; Butler, 2011; Schoebi & Randall, 2015). There are several methodological considerations in the study of interpersonal emotion dynamics, such as the selection of a study design for eliciting dynamics, and the time scale (e.g., second-to-second, day-to-day) at which to measure emotion dynamics. First, we describe methodological approaches for eliciting interpersonal emotion dynamics. Then, we review methods for measuring real-time interpersonal emotion dynamics via physiological arousal, emotional experience, and behavioral expression.

### Designs for eliciting interpersonal emotion dynamics

A broad range of designs can be used to elicit interpersonal emotion dynamics (see Table 4.1 for overview), and the decision to use any method will depend on research questions and practical limitations. Methods for eliciting and observing interpersonal emotion dynamics can be broadly categorized as either naturalistic designs, which involve observing emotion dynamics *in situ*, or dyadic interaction tasks, which involve instructing participants to complete specific tasks.

Table 4.1. *Study designs for examining interpersonal emotion dynamics*

| Study design | Strengths | Limitations | Selected references |
| --- | --- | --- | --- |
| Naturalistic designs (e.g., participant observation, dyadic experience sampling) | High ecological validity | Interpersonal dynamics of interest may not occur within observation period | Cuperman and Ickes (2009) Driver and Gottman (2004) Konvalinka et al. (2011) Sels et al. (2016) Stifter and Rovine (2015) Wang and Repetti (2014) |
| Dyadic interaction tasks (e.g., discussions, complete a task) | Greater control over participant behavior than naturalistic designs increases likelihood that dynamics of interest will be observed May have higher ecological validity than experimental designs | Lower ecological validity than naturalistic designs | Adams et al. (1995) Campos et al. (2015) Fosco and Grych (2013) Granic and Lamey (2002) Ha et al. (2014) Helm et al. (2014) Hollenstein and Lewis (2006) Levenson and Gottman (1983) Lougheed and Hollenstein (2016) Lunkenheimer et al. (2013) Randall et al. (2013) Reed et al. (2013) Sadler et al. (2009) Schoebi et al. (2012) |
| Experimental designs (including random assignment to experimental groups) | Highest level of control over participant behavior allows direct observation of dynamics of interest | Lower ecological validity than both dyadic interaction tasks and naturalistic designs | Boker et al. (2009) Butler et al. (2006) Heatherton and Vohs (2000) Hostinar et al. (2015) Lougheed et al. (2016b) |

## Naturalistic designs

The main objective of naturalistic designs is to obtain a high degree of ecological validity. In their purest form, naturalistic designs involve simply observing (e.g., via field notes or video or audio recordings) interpersonal dynamics *in situ*, with emotions emerging over the course of naturally occurring interpersonal interactions. However, such unstructured *in situ* observations may not always yield information of interest to researchers' questions (Dishion & Granic, 2004). For example, setting up video cameras in the home of cohabiting romantic partners may not result in data on emotion dynamics during conflict resolution if interpersonal conflicts do not occur during the observation period.

The canonical example of a naturalistic design in the study of interpersonal emotion dynamics comes from Gottman and colleagues' work using an apartment laboratory to observe couples' interactions for extended periods of time (e.g., Driver & Gottman, 2004). The apartment laboratory was equipped with video cameras, and participants were filmed for twelve hours per day and were instructed to "spend the day as they would at home" (Driver & Gottman, 2004). Researchers can observe a close approximation of participants' day-to-day interpersonal dynamics by obtaining lengthy samples of unstructured interactions. A procedure with a similar goal but with a much shorter observation period is the unstructured dyadic interaction task (e.g., Cuperman & Ickes, 2009). In one example of an unstructured dyadic interaction task, participants were covertly recorded in a waiting-room scenario (Cuperman & Ickes, 2009) in which dyads were led to believe that the experimenter forgot to bring necessary study materials into the observation room and then left the participants uninstructed for a period of six minutes. An advantage of these two naturalistic designs is that they provide ecological validity by not structuring participant behavior in any way, although researchers are cautioned that participant behaviors in both unfamiliar contexts (e.g., apartment and waiting room) may not be representative of their typical day-to-day behaviors because the contexts are unfamiliar.

Recently, Wang and Repetti (2014) improved upon the ecological validity of the Driver and Gottman (2004) study by intensively video-recording spousal interactions in the spouses' own homes to obtain a "fly-on-the-wall" perspective of emotional support dynamics (e.g., solicitations for and offers of support). Husbands and wives were recorded by separate hand-held cameras that followed them throughout several sessions over four days, resulting in naturalistic accounts of spousal dynamics both when they were together and events that occurred when spouses were apart (Wang & Repetti, 2014). This approach enabled an examination of dynamics that may be less likely to occur naturalistically in a structured setting, such as spontaneous solicitations and offers of emotional support between partners (Wang & Repetti, 2014).

Researchers can also take advantage of day-to-day or life events that are likely to elicit dynamics of interest to their research questions. One example is to videotape infants and their primary caregivers during routine appointments to the family physician to receive inoculations (e.g., Stifter & Rovine, 2015). Such appointments are typically distressing to infants, and thus provide opportunities to observe dynamics as caregivers soothe their infant (Stifter & Rovine, 2015). Other events that could be advantageously used in naturalistic designs include: stressful events (e.g., first day of school, the delivery of a medical diagnosis, sports games, fine arts performances) or rituals (e.g., emotional synchronization between performers in a fire-walking ritual and their relatives observing the ritual; Konvalinka et al., 2011), and major life transitions such as divorce (e.g., examining interpersonal dynamics during divorce mediation appointments). A naturalistic approach for examining dynamics at larger time scales (e.g., daily, weekly, monthly) is dyadic experience sampling, which involves participants self-reporting on emotions and interpersonal dynamics via a mobile device throughout their day-to-day lives (see section on Measuring Interpersonal Emotion Dynamics for more information; Randall & Schoebi, 2015; Sels et al., 2016).

Taken together, the main strength of naturalistic designs is their ecological validity. Researchers may consider using such designs when their research questions depend on examining behaviors that are most likely to be elicited in unstructured conditions (e.g., rapport among strangers in a waiting-room scenario, spontaneous bids for support from romantic partners) compared to designs that involve instructing participants to behave in some way (see next section on dyadic interaction tasks). Challenges of naturalistic designs relate to the difficulty of obtaining samples of the behavior of interest in a completely uncontrolled environment. Although the goal of naturalistic designs is for researchers to have minimal to no influence on study conditions, researchers could record as much information about the study setting as possible (e.g., location, participant characteristics) to control for such features statistically. Alternatively, challenges of naturalistic designs can be overcome by providing a minimal amount of structure to interpersonal interactions, which will be discussed next.

### Dyadic interaction tasks

Dyadic interaction tasks involve eliciting interpersonal emotion dynamics through structured tasks, often in a laboratory setting. Common elements include asking participants to discuss specific topics or to complete specific tasks. The extent of structure given to dyadic interaction tasks can range from minimal (e.g., instructing participants to discuss the events of the day) to extensive (e.g., instructing participants to solve a problem together). Researchers should consider the trade-offs between maintaining greater ecological validity with less structure and increasing the likelihood of observing the dynamics of interest with greater structure – these trade-offs should be considered in relation to the goals of the study and what the research questions are. For example, if researchers are primarily interested in examining interpersonal emotion dynamics during conflict resolution, a study design that provides some structure (e.g., by asking participants to discuss an area of conflict) and increases the likelihood that participants will engage in the behaviors of interest might be preferable to a study design that provides minimal structure (e.g., observing participant interactions in a completely unstructured setting).

**Discussion tasks.** One design that is common in dyadic interaction tasks is to ask participants to discuss a specific topic in a laboratory or home setting. Example topics include asking participants to discuss areas of conflict in their relationship (e.g., Granic & Lamey, 2002), the events of the day (e.g., Levenson & Gottman, 1983) or a past relationship (e.g., Campos et al., 2015); asking one partner to bring up an issue they would like to change in order to elicit support (e.g., Schoebi et al., 2012); discussing health behaviors (e.g., Randall et al., 2013; Reed et al., 2013); recalling past events that hold emotional significance (e.g., Adams et al., 1995; Campos et al., 2015); or fun, positive tasks that involve brainstorming and imagination (e.g., how to spend the winnings of a lottery; e.g., Hollenstein & Lewis, 2006). An extension of dyadic interaction tasks is to include a perturbation of some kind – some kind of event intended to "shake up" the dyadic interaction to see how participants respond. For example, Granic and Lamey (2002) instructed parents and their children to discuss a topic of conflict within their relationship for six minutes. Four minutes into the conflict discussion, an experimenter knocked on the door of the observation room and reminded participants that they had two minutes remaining to resolve the discussion (Granic & Lamey, 2002). Examinations of the interpersonal emotion dynamics both pre- and post-perturbation showed that only the interpersonal dynamics post-perturbation distinguished subtypes of children's externalizing problems (i.e., aggression with or without comorbid internalizing problems; Granic & Lamey, 2002). Designs using such within-discussion perturbations can elicit different behavioral patterns (e.g., increased or decreased stress, adjustments to changing goals of the task) depending on the form of the perturbation. Some generalizable forms of perturbations include: changing the guidelines partway through the interactions, introducing an incentive or challenge that was not present at the beginning of the interaction, and experimenter feedback partway through the interaction.

It is also common to examine interpersonal emotion dynamics in a series of dyadic interaction tasks to examine differences between contexts. Such designs may vary the valence of the emotion elicitation task (positive or negative) in any number of ways, but common patterns include ABC (neutral, positive, negative; e.g., Helm et al., 2014) and ABA (positive, negative, positive; e.g., Hollenstein & Lewis, 2006) designs. The goals of such comparisons can vary. For example, researchers might be interested in examining interpersonal emotion dynamics in different contexts (e.g., conflict versus support; discussing shared worries versus mutual excitement). In such cases, the order of the tasks may not be especially important, although a common consideration is if the elicitation of emotions will have carry-over effects that introduce an unintended element into the study design. Researchers who wish to minimize the influence of carry-over effects should consider randomizing the task order and controlling for it in analyses.

Some research questions may involve ordering tasks to maximize carry-over effects, such as when research questions are related to interpersonal emotion dynamics during "repair" or "recovery" (i.e., how difficult it is for dyads to experience positive emotions after a negative interaction). Researchers interested in emotional repair have used an ABA design by first having participants discuss a positive or fun topic such as brainstorming a dream vacation, then having a conflict discussion, and finishing with a second positive brainstorming topic (Granic & Lamey, 2002; Hollenstein & Lewis, 2006). Recently, we extended such designs in two ways with the Emotional Rollercoaster task (Lougheed & Hollenstein, 2016). First, because it is common for dyadic interaction tasks to elicit a broad range of positively or negatively valenced emotions, we designed the Emotional Rollercoaster task to elicit specific positive (e.g., happy/excited, proud, grateful) and negative (e.g., sad/worried, frustrated/annoyed) emotions by instructing dyads to have a series of five 3-minute discussions with each other about strong emotions they felt toward each other. Second, we used an ABABA design to elicit multiple reversals between positive and negative emotions to more fully examine the interpersonal dynamics involved in switching between emotional contexts. We found that dyads who showed moderate levels of emotional flexibility – measured by shifts between emotional states and the range of emotions expressed during interactions – tended to have better psychosocial adjustment than dyads who had low flexibility (Lougheed & Hollenstein, 2016). The Emotional Rollercoaster task is among the first to elicit specific positive and negative interpersonal emotion dynamics, and this task will be useful in a range of samples such as with romantic partners, friends, and other parent–child relationships, and in samples of different ages from late childhood through older adulthood. The Emotional Rollercoaster task is also flexible in that the order of the discussion topics can be modified according to specific research questions. For example, researchers could counterbalance the order of the discussion topics to examine emotion dynamics in discrete emotion contexts.

**Other tasks.** Dyadic interaction tasks can also involve participants completing a challenge or problem-solving task. For example, participants can be instructed to work together to deduce the personality of an unknown individual based on responses to the thematic apperception test (Sadler et al., 2009). An ambiguous task with no clear goal or correct outcome allows for a range of emotion-related dynamics in terms of dominance and compliance between dyadic partners (Sadler et al., 2009).

Dynamics can also be observed during an activity such as eating a meal (e.g., Patterson, 1982) or while playing a game (e.g., Fosco & Grych, 2013) in either a laboratory or home environment. The choice of activity will depend on the dynamics of interest. For example, parent–child dynamics during challenging situations can be observed by recording dyads during a task that is designed to be beyond the child's skill level, or by instructing parents to guide their children to clean up from a preceding free-play session (Lunkenheimer et al., 2013). Positive emotions and competitive behaviors can be elicited by asking participants to play a game with each other (Fosco & Grych, 2013).

*Experimental designs*

Experimental designs offer the highest degree of control over interpersonal interactions. In studies of dyadic interactions, one or both partners may be randomly assigned to experimental conditions to examine the effects of specific manipulations (e.g., the use of emotion regulation strategies) on interpersonal emotion dynamics. In one study, dyads watched an upsetting film clip to elicit negative emotions, and then one partner was randomly assigned to either suppress (mask the expression of emotion) or reappraise (view the negative film clip from a more positive perspective) their emotions during a discussion about the film clip with their interaction partner (Butler et al., 2006). An experimental design for comparing dynamics between different types of relationship partners is to elicit stress in one dyadic partner and then observe support dynamics in randomly assigned interactions with either a close relationship partner (e.g., parents) or strangers following the stress elicitation (Hostinar et al., 2015). Interpersonal dynamics can also be manipulated experimentally by priming one or both interaction partners to have a specific attitude prior to a dyadic interaction (e.g., Heatherton & Vohs, 2000) or by manipulating the level of physical closeness between partners during social stress (e.g., Lougheed et al., 2016b).

Recent technological advances are permitting even more nuanced control of interpersonal dynamics with computer-mediated social interactions. One example involves having participants interact with each other via videoconference, in which one participant is a confederate whose facial expressions, head movements, and vocal qualities are subtly modified over the course of the videoconference by manipulation of an avatar based on the confederate's real-time behaviors and expressions (Boker et al., 2009). The use of such computer-mediated interactions enables researchers to examine the specific qualities of dyadic interactions (e.g., mirroring of expressivity and postures) that are related to outcomes such as perceived rapport.

*Summary*

There are numerous designs for observing interpersonal dynamics, ranging from naturalistic observations to tightly controlled experimental manipulations. Any one design has both benefits and drawbacks, and researchers must carefully consider their research questions when designing a study. The choice of study design will influence how interpersonal emotion dynamics can be measured, and measurement (reviewed in the following section) should therefore also be factored in to methodological decisions.

## Measuring interpersonal emotion dynamics

Across the various research designs described above, there are myriad ways to measure interpersonal emotion dynamics. Because we are interested in dynamics, change must be detected; hence, measurement of at least one time series is necessary. Most of the time, the measures of two or more series are used to capture either non-directional (e.g., synchrony, coupling) or directional (e.g., reciprocity, transmission, contagion) influences of one series (e.g., one person's emotions over time) on another (Butler, 2011). For designs in which two or more series have been measured, temporal synchrony is a necessary measurement characteristic – all time series (e.g., derived from video recordings of more than one camera or multiple channels of physiological sensors) require the same zero point or time stamp. Although measures that provide continuous values (e.g., skin conductance) are most desirable for many statistical approaches, the use of ordinal or categorical variables (e.g., affect coding) may be necessary when constructs do not map well theoretically onto continuous conceptualizations, such as discrete emotions. In the subsequent sections, we review dynamic measurement within three primary domains of the emotion system: physiological arousal, self-reported experience, and behavioral expressions. The description of analytical techniques for interpersonal dynamics is beyond the scope of this chapter (see Chapters 2 and 3), however, we will end this section with a description of methods for deriving indices of interpersonal dynamics that can be used in later statistical analyses.

## Measuring dynamics of the emotion system

**Physiological arousal.** Currently, measurement of the autonomic nervous system is the predominant psychophysiological domain in interpersonal emotional dynamics (see Chapter 6).[1] The autonomic system has two branches, the sympathetic nervous system (SNS) that is responsible for the upregulation of arousal and the flight or fight response, and the parasympathetic nervous system (PNS) that is responsible for maintaining calm and steady levels of arousal as well as long-term bodily functions (e.g., reproduction, immune response). Measures of SNS (e.g., skin conductance), PNS (e.g., respiratory sinus arrhythmia), or SNS/PNS combinations (e.g., heart rate) are natural, dynamic time series that, when measured during verified emotion elicitation designs, are indicative of emotional processes. The choice of which to use is a balance of the research question and the characteristics of the measure.

Heart rate (HR) in beats per minute is the most straightforward and easily understandable measure. However, the interbeat interval (IBI), or milliseconds between heartbeats, is often considered a better measure from which to derive dynamic indices of variability. Moreover, because it reflects a combination of SNS and PNS activation, it is never clear whether increased HR is an index of greater SNS arousal, PNS regulation, or both. Instead, SNS arousal is easily measured with skin conductance (SCR) or galvanic skin response (GSR). SCR/GSR measures are easily obtained and provide smooth measurement without interfering high frequency noise. Most importantly, these SNS measures are very responsive to both sudden and slow changes in arousal. There are many examples of studies that have used SCR or GSR to show dyadic synchrony (e.g., see Timmons et al., 2015 for a review) or arousal transmission (e.g., Lougheed et al., 2016b).

---

[1] In the future, emotions within interpersonal interactions may be dynamically measurable and ecologically valid with neuroimaging techniques and blood or salivary assays.

Respiratory sinus arrhythmia (RSA), or the difference between HR during respiratory inhalation and exhalation, is an index of the influence of the vagus nerve (i.e., the PNS) on the heart. RSA is derived from the IBI time series (and sometimes respiration rate) information. As such, it requires a minimum amount of HR information to get a reliable estimate. When used for interpersonal dynamics research, this means that the RSA series must be of a longer time scale. For example, Helm et al. (2014) used 30-second epochs to estimate RSA values of adult romantic partners. As such, RSA dynamics are not at a "real-time" scale but slightly slower; thus, interpersonal linkages with other real-time measures cannot be synchronous and these measures are not sensitive to emotional changes that typically occur on the order of seconds. However, Gates et al. (2015) present a very exciting extension of this approach by using a moving 32-second window to calculate an RSA time series. By calculating RSA within each window in sequence (0-32s, 1-33s, 2-34s, etc.), a second-by-second time series was created to show that greater RSA linkage between spouses was related to greater conflict. This technique still does not allow for synchrony analyses with other series, but it does enable an examination of the RSA synchrony of Person 1 with Person 2.

**Emotional experience.** Typically, self-reported emotional experience comes from static measures (e.g., questionnaires delivered at a single time point), yet there are a few methods to obtain dynamic self-report time series. The first uses a dynamic input device such as a dial or joystick to obtain participants' assessments of their own emotional state and/or the emotional state of their interaction partners. Most often, this input is recorded as voltage through a psychophysiological recording channel but stand-alone devices are also available (see Randall et al., 2013). There is a short list of variations on this technique. Since one of the earliest and most well-known interaction studies with a self-report rating dial (Gottman & Levenson, 1985), most studies used video-cued recall. Much like an observational coder, self-raters watch their video and indicate their feelings *at the time of the interaction* using polarized scales such as negative-positive (Gottman & Levenson, 1985). Occasionally, participants have been asked to report on two dimensions. For example, Butler et al. (2014b) had couples report on the valence (negative to positive) and engagement (protective buffering to full engagement) they experienced during health-related disagreements. Because this is a recall method, cued by behavior observed on video, analysts should consider the time lags shared or not shared with time series in other domains. Third-party trained observers are likely to be applying changes to the stream of codes at about the same lag as self-ratings, whereas there may be some delay between psychophysiological changes and self-report recall. Although there have been no systematic examinations of what is a typical lag, some studies of intra-individual concordance have used maximum cross-correlations within ±6 to 10 second windows (e.g., Butler et al., 2014a). Consistent with unpublished explorations in our own data, these studies found a wide distribution of lags for the maximum within-person correlations across self-report, observer report, and psychophysiology. Thus, it is likely that there are untested moderators that could explain these individual differences in timing.

The second method for interpersonal emotional experience measurement is dyadic experience sampling (ESM) or ecological momentary assessment (EMA). Although these do not measure real-time dynamics that can be synchronized with most other interpersonal time series, the dynamics occur at a longer time scales of days or weeks (e.g., Randall & Schoebi, 2015). Moreover, because the sampling is intermittent (e.g., ten times a day for two weeks), the intervals between measurement points may or may not be consistent. Nevertheless, ESM and EMA have provided a bridge from the lab to the real world to understand what people are actually doing in their day-to-day lives. Some studies have obtained samples from couples across the same time period (Laurenceau et al., 2005). Other studies used experience-contingent sampling for which participants provide a report for every social interaction that they have during the day. For example, Côté and Moskowitz (1998) examined the dimensions of dominance-submission, pleasant-unpleasant, and agreeable-quarrelsome in relation to personality traits. With advances in technology making both video-cued recall and ESM/EMA more affordable and user-friendly, interpersonal emotion dynamics research will have even greater opportunities in the future for dynamically measuring self-reported emotions.

**Behavioral expression.** By far the most common type of measure, observational coding of emotions has been the mainstay of interpersonal dynamics research. Advances in observational software have rendered frequency counts of behaviors or the use of multi-second time bins (e.g., observer ratings at 30-second intervals) obsolete. To retain full information about behavioral streams and to enable even basic time series analysis of coupled dynamics, real-time coding is the gold standard. The goal is to come as close as possible to the format of a physiological time series, which has dozens if not hundreds of values per second.

The primary method for achieving the real-time goal is through the application of a mutually exclusive and exhaustive set of behavioral codes to each dyad member. That is, Person 1 and Person 2 each have a complete record of their own behavior. Observational software typically records on the order of hundredths of a second, and we have found in our work that reliability and validity appear to be optimal at 1 second (1 Hz). Often, codes of interpersonal emotions are nominal (e.g., anger, humor), as with the much-used Specific Affect Coding System (SPAFF; Gottman et al., 1995). While these measures allow some event-based analyses (e.g., multilevel survival analysis; Lougheed et al., 2015, 2016a) or, as we discuss below, state space grid derivation of measures, they do not provide continuous ordinal or ratio scales. There are two ways around this issue. First, Gottman and colleagues arranged affect categories in a quasi-ordinal sequence based on a combination of valence and intensity: contempt was a −4, sadness a −1, interest a +2, affection a +4, and neutral a 0 (e.g., Gottman et al., 1999). Through this quantification, series created from SPAFF or other coding systems are then amenable to dynamic analysis.

The second way to obtain continuous measures from behavioral coding is to have observers apply a numerical scale rating a specific behavior. Like Butler et al. (2014b) study's self-rating, this could be two streams, one of valence and the other of engagement. In our own lab, we have developed the Shame Code (De France et al., 2017) system for which observers use multiple viewing passes to provide binary ratings on 7 dimensions (0 = behavior is absent and 1 = behavior is present). Thus, we obtain 7 binary time series, in columns, that can be combined (summed) across every time unit, in rows, to create an overall score indicating real time shame expressions (De France et al., 2017). This binary summing approach has pragmatic advantages as coders do not need to make priority decisions of which behavioral code to apply when two seem present. For this reason, training is less onerous and coding can be completed more efficiently.

### Deriving dynamic measures with state space grids

Just obtaining a time series that captures some aspect of an interpersonal interaction is most often not sufficient for analysis. Data need to be cleaned, reformatted, or transformed. An intervening step between raw measurement and study results is exploratory data analysis and the derivation of variables. State space grids (SSGs) are well-suited for this task, especially with interpersonal interaction data. Here we provide a brief review of this technique, but interested readers can read a comprehensive review (Hollenstein, 2013) or download the free SSG software (www.statespacegrids.org).

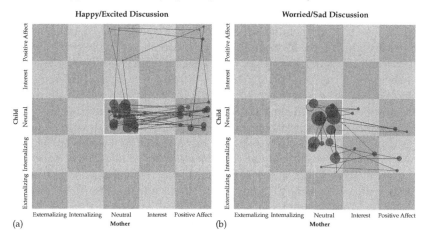

Figure 4.1. State space grids of a mother–daughter dyad in two different emotion contexts: a discussion about times they felt happy and/or excited toward each other (a), and a discussion about times they felt worried and/or sad toward each other (b)

Dyads function as dynamic systems, which are complex systems characterized by time dependence among system elements (Butler, 2011). In dynamic systems, higher-order system characteristics emerge from temporal associations among lower-order components, and in turn, these higher-order characteristics constrain the dynamics among lower-order components. Within a relationship system, each person's emotions are linked in time to their partners' emotions (Butler, 2011); hence the combination of each member's time series is not simply additive but made up of *dyadic states*. Higher-order characteristics of the dyad, such as relationship quality, emerge from lower-order moment-to-moment interpersonal emotion dynamics (Granic, 2005). One way to represent a dyadic system is on a state space, the intersection of both dyad member's possible states, with a trajectory tracing the sequence of observed states. Figure 4.1 shows example SSGs of a mother-daughter dyad in two different emotional contexts. The mother's states are represented along the $x$-axis, and the daughter's states are represented along the $y$-axis. Each cell represents a combination of mother-daughter affect, with all possible combinations represented by the grid. Plot points indicate dyadic affect events, with larger plot points indicating a longer duration of each dyadic affect event. Dyadic affect events that occurred sequentially are connected by lines between plot points. Figure 4.1 shows that, other than mutually neutral states, the dyad showed primarily neutral/positive affect states during the Happy/Excited discussion, whereas the same dyad showed a combination of maternal neutral/positive affect and daughter neutral/negative affect during the Worried/Sad discussion.

Several kinds of measures can be extracted from SSGs. First, measures of the overall dynamics can be obtained through indices of the range of states (Cells), that range controlling for duration in each cell (Dispersion), the number of state changes (Transitions), how "stuck" the trajectory gets (Average Mean Durations), or the predictability of the sequence of states (Entropy). In parent–child research, these measures have been related to psychosocial well-being in infants (Sravish et al., 2013), toddlers (Lunkenheimer et al., 2013), early childhood (Hollenstein et al., 2004), older children (Granic & Lamey, 2002), and adolescents (Lougheed & Hollenstein, 2016; van der Giessen et al., 2013).

A second kind of SSG measure focuses on a subset of the state space, either a cell or region of cells. From each cell or region, measures of frequency, duration, mean duration, time of first entry, time of last exit, and time until return can all be obtained as an index of the system's attractors (absorbing states). These attractors can be theoretically important states (e.g., mutual hostility) or empirically derived for each dyad to establish the location of their attractor(s) in the state space. In this way, the dynamics of a dyadic trajectory can be translated into quantities that can be used in subsequent statistical analyses.

A final variation we will cover here is the use of lagged time series with SSGs, described through an example. In the Butler et al. (2014b) study, the time series were ordinal integers, ranging from −2 to +2 for negative-positive and protect-engage dimensions. We then created change variables for time $t$ to $t + 1$ and $t + 1$ to $t + 2$ and used those lagged variables as dimensions on the SSGs. Now we could create SSGs such as the husband's change in engagement from time $t$ to $t + 1$ on the $x$-axis and the wife's change in valence from time $t + 1$ to $t + 2$. Cells in such an SSG then represent a three-step sequence (e.g., one cell represented husband increasing engagement by 1 unit followed by wife's increasing positivity by 2 units). With these SSGs we were able to specify regions of cells that, if occupied by the couple's trajectory, shared the same meaning based on combinations of increasing and/or decreasing values. In general, this lagged arrangement of data on SSGs allows the derived descriptive measures to capture meaningful sequences in the interpersonal dynamics.

Taken together, there are numerous ways to measure interpersonal emotion dynamics. Researchers typically obtain two time series of the measure of interest (i.e., physiological arousal, self-reported experience, behavioral expressions), one from each person, to model interpersonal dynamics statistically (e.g., Butler, 2011; Hollenstein, 2013; Laurenceau et al., 2005; Stifter & Rovine, 2015). Important considerations include if the measures of interest are compatible with the study design (e.g., measures that involve the placement of physiological sensors may not be appropriate in naturalistic designs), and if the resulting measures will be appropriate for the desired statistical modeling.

## Conclusion

Numerous methodological approaches can be taken in the study of inter-personal emotion dynamics – the temporal interdependencies between interaction partners' emotions – across myriad dyad types. The wealth of approaches available to researchers indicate that several issues should be considered at the design stage of any study, such as the ideal design to measure the dynamics of interest, and the use of measures for statistical models. It is an exciting time to be a researcher of interpersonal dynamics, as sophisticated methods and technologies are becoming increasingly accessible to behavioral scientists.

## References

Adams, S., Kuebli, J., Boyle, P. A., & Fivush, R. (1995). Gender differences in parent-child conversations about past emotions: a longitudinal investigation. *Sex Roles*, 33(5–6), 309–23.

Boker, S. M., Cohn, J. F., Theobald, B.-J., et al. (2009). Effects of damping head movement and facial expression in dyadic conversation using real-time facial expression tracking and synthesized avatars. *Philosophical Transactions of the Royal Society of London B: Biological Sciences*, 364(1535), 3485–95.

Butler, E. A. (2011). Temporal interpersonal emotion systems: the "TIES" that form relationships. *Personality and Social Psychology Review*, 15(4), 367–93.

Butler, E., Gross, J., & Barnard, K. (2014a). Testing the effects of suppression and reappraisal on emotional concordance using a multivariate multilevel model. *Biological Psychology*, 98, 6–18.

Butler, E. A., Hollenstein, T., Shoham, V., & Rohrbaugh, M. J. (2014b). A dynamic state-space analysis of interpersonal emotion regulation in couples who smoke. *Journal of Social and Personal Relationships*, 31(7), 907–27.

Butler, E. A., Wilhelm, F. H., & Gross, J. J. (2006). Respiratory sinus arrhythmia, emotion, and emotion regulation during social interaction. *Psychophysiology*, 43(6), 612–22.

Campos, B., Schoebi, D., Gonzaga, G. C., Gable, S. L., & Keltner, D. (2015). Attuned to the positive? Awareness and responsiveness to others' positive emotion experience and display. *Motivation and Emotion*, 39(5), 780–94.

Côté, S., & Moskowitz, D. S. (1998). On the dynamic covariation between inter-personal behavior and affect: prediction from neuroticism, extraversion, and agreeableness. *Journal of Personality and Social Psychology*, 75(4), 1032–46.

Cuperman, R., & Ickes, W. (2009). Big five predictors of behavior and perceptions in initial dyadic interactions: personality similarity helps extraverts and introverts, but hurts "disagreeables". *Journal of Personality and Social Psychology, 97*(4), 667–84.

De France, K., Lanteigne, D., Glozman, J., & Hollenstein, T. (2017). A new measure of the expression of shame: the shame code. *Journal of Child and Family Studies, 26*(3), 769–80.

Dishion, T. J., & Granic, I. (2004). Naturalistic observation of relationship processes. In S. N. Haynes & E. M. Heiby (Eds.), *Comprehensive Handbook of Psychological Assessment: Behavioral Assessment* (Vol. 3, p. 143). Hoboken, NJ: John Wiley & Sons.

Driver, J. L., & Gottman, J. M. (2004). Daily marital interactions and positive affect during marital conflict among newlywed couples. *Family Process, 43*(3), 301–14.

Fosco, G. M., & Grych, J. H. (2013). Capturing the family context of emotion regulation: a family systems model comparison approach. *Journal of Family Issues, 34*(4), 557–78.

Gates, K. M., Gatzke-Kopp, L. M., Sandsten, M., & Blandon, A. Y. (2015). Estimating time-varying RSA to examine psychophysiological linkage of marital dyads. *Psychophysiology, 52*(8), 1059–65.

Gottman, J. M., & Levenson, R. W. (1985). A valid procedure for obtaining self-report of affect in marital interaction. *Journal of Consulting and Clinical Psychology, 53*(2), 151–60.

Gottman, J. M., McCoy, K., Coan, J., & Collier, H. (1995). *The Specific Affect Coding System (SPAFF) for observing emotional communication in marital and family interaction.* Mahwah, NJ: Erlbaum.

Gottman, J., Swanson, C., & Murray, J. (1999). The mathematics of marital conflict: Dynamic mathematical nonlinear modeling of newlywed marital interaction. *Journal of Family Psychology, 13*(1), 3-19.

Granic, I. (2005). Timing is everything: developmental psychopathology from a dynamic systems perspective. *Developmental Review, 25*(3), 386–407. doi:10.1016/j.dr.2005.10.005

Granic, I., & Lamey, A. V. (2002). Combining dynamic systems and multivariate analyses to compare the mother–child interactions of externalizing subtypes. *Journal of Abnormal Child Psychology, 30*(3), 265–83.

Ha, T., Dishion, T. J., Overbeek, G., Burk, W. J., & Engels, R. C. (2014). The blues of adolescent romance: Observed affective interactions in adolescent romantic relationships associated with depressive symptoms. *Journal of Abnormal Child Psychology, 42*(4), 551–62. doi:10.1007/s10802-013-9808-y

Heatherton, T. F., & Vohs, K. D. (2000). Interpersonal evaluations following threats to self: role of self-esteem. *Journal of Personality and Social Psychology, 78*(4), 725–36.

Helm, J. L., Sbarra, D. A., & Ferrer, E. (2014). Coregulation of respiratory sinus arrhythmia in adult romantic partners. *Emotion, 14*(3), 522–31.

Hollenstein, T. (2013). *State space grids: depicting dynamics across development.* New York, NY: Springer.

Hollenstein, T., Granic, I., Stoolmiller, M., & Snyder, J. (2004). Rigidity in parent–child interactions and the development of externalizing and internalizing behavior in early childhood. *Journal of Abnormal Child Psychology*, 32(6), 595–607.

Hollenstein, T., & Lewis, M. D. (2006). A state space analysis of emotion and flexibility in parent–child interactions. *Emotion*, 6(4), 656–62.

Hostinar, C. E., Johnson, A. E., & Gunnar, M. R. (2015). Parent support is less effective in buffering cortisol stress reactivity for adolescents compared to children. *Developmental Science*, 18(2), 281–97.

Konvalinka, I., Xygalatas, D., Bulbulia, J., et al. (2011). Synchronized arousal between performers and related spectators in a fire-walking ritual. *Proceedings of the National Academy of Sciences of the United States of America*, 108(20), 8514–19.

Laurenceau, J.-P., Barrett, L. F., & Rovine, M. J. (2005). The interpersonal process model of intimacy in marriage: a daily-diary and multilevel modeling approach. *Journal of Family Psychology*, 19(2), 314–23.

Levenson, R. W., & Gottman, J. M. (1983). Marital interaction: physiological linkage and affective exchange. *Journal of Personality and Social Psychology*, 45(3), 587–97.

Lougheed, J. P., Craig, W. M., Pepler, D., et al. (2016a). Maternal and peer regulation of adolescent emotion: associations with depressive symptoms. *Journal of Abnormal Child Psychology*, 44(5), 963–74.

Lougheed, J. P., & Hollenstein, T. (2016). Socioemotional flexibility in mother-daughter dyads: riding the emotional rollercoaster across positive and negative contexts. *Emotion*, 16(5), 620–33.

Lougheed, J. P., Hollenstein, T., Lichtwarck-Aschoff, A., & Granic, I. (2015). Maternal regulation of child affect in externalizing and typically-developing children. *Journal of Family Psychology*, 29(1), 10–19.

Lougheed, J. P., Koval, P., & Hollenstein, T. (2016b). Sharing the burden: the interpersonal regulation of emotional arousal in mother–daughter dyads. *Emotion*, 16(1), 83–93.

Lunkenheimer, E. S., Albrecht, E. C., & Kemp, C. J. (2013). Dyadic flexibility in early parent–child interactions: relations with maternal depressive symptoms and child negativity and behaviour problems. *Infant and Child Development*, 22(3), 250–69.

Patterson, G. R. (1982). *Coercive Family Process* (Vol. 3). Eugene, OR: Castalia Publishing Company.

Randall, A. K., Post, J. H., Reed, R. G., & Butler, E. A. (2013). Cooperating with your romantic partner: associations with interpersonal emotional coordination. *Journal of Social and Personal Relationships*, 30, 1072–95.

Randall, A. K., & Schoebi, D. (2015). Lean on me: susceptibility to partner affect attenuates psychological distress over a 12-month period. *Emotion*, 15(2), 201–10.

Reed, R. G., Randall, A. K., Post, J. H., & Butler, E. A. (2013). Partner influence and in-phase versus anti-phase physiological linkage in romantic couples. *International Journal of Psychophysiology*, 88(3), 309–16.

92     *Jessica P. Lougheed and Tom Hollenstein*

Sadler, P., Ethier, N., Gunn, G. R., Duong, D., & Woody, E. (2009). Are we on the same wavelength? Interpersonal complementarity as shared cyclical patterns during interactions. *Journal of Personality and Social Psychology*, 97(6), 1005–20.

Schoebi, D., & Randall, A. K. (2015). Emotional dynamics in intimate relationships. *Emotion Review*, 7(4), 342–348.

Schoebi, D., Way, B. M., Karney, B. R., & Bradbury, T. N. (2012). Genetic moderation of sensitivity to positive and negative affect in marriage. *Emotion*, 12(2), 208.

Sels, L., Ceulemans, E., Bulteel, K., & Kuppens, P. (2016). Emotional interdependence and well-being in close relationships. *Frontiers in Psychology*, 7(283), 1–13.

Sravish, A. V., Tronick, E., Hollenstein, T., & Beeghly, M. (2013). Dyadic flexibility during the face-to-face still-face paradigm: a dynamic systems analysis of its temporal organization. *Infant Behavior & Development*, 36(3), 432–7.

Stifter, C. A., & Rovine, M. (2015). Modeling dyadic processes using hidden markov models: a time series approach to mother–infant interactions during infant immunization. *Infant and Child Development*, 24(3), 298–321.

Timmons, A. C., Margolin, G., & Saxbe, D. E. (2015). Physiological linkage in couples and its implications for individual and interpersonal functioning: a literature review. *Journal of Family Psychology*, 29(5), 720.

van der Giessen, D., Branje, S. J. T., Frijns, T., & Meeus, W. H. J. (2013). Dyadic variability in mother-adolescent interactions: developmental trajectories and associations with psychosocial functioning. *Journal of Youth and Adolescence*, 42(1), 96–108.

Wang, S., & Repetti, R. L. (2014). Psychological well-being and job stress predict marital support interactions: a naturalistic observational study of dual-earner couples in their homes. *Journal of Personality and Social Psychology*, 107(5), 864–78.

# CHAPTER 5

# Biochemical contributions to interpersonal emotion dynamics

*Baldwin M. Way and Alexis Keaveney*

A central theme of this book is that psychology's traditional focus on emotion as an intrapersonal process overlooks the rich, dynamic nature of emotion. Studying an isolated person sitting in a laboratory watching an emotion-inducing film does not capture the full palette of human emotional experience. As discussed in other chapters of this book, there has been a recent flourishing of psychological research into the interpersonal aspects of emotion that clearly demonstrates humans are fundamentally social animals and our emotional states ebb and flow primarily based on interactions with others.

In many ways the fields studying the chemical components of neurotransmission – neuropharmacology, biochemistry, and psychiatry – have followed the same trajectory as the psychological study of emotion. For example, experimental studies on the emotional effects of psychopharmacological agents (e.g., Prozac) have largely examined individuals performing tasks in the laboratory by themselves. The standard paradigm involves participants reporting to the laboratory, being administered a psychoactive drug such as an antidepressant, and then, after the drug has entered the brain, responding to emotional stimuli on the computer such as facial expressions of different emotions. Similarly, in clinical studies of psychopharmacological drugs, the patient's overall emotional changes resulting from drug treatment have traditionally been assessed without reference to the interpersonal or situational factors that may have elicited them. Only recently has the relationship between biochemical signaling and emotion in an interpersonal context begun to be explored. It is important to gain a better understanding of the interrelationship between emotions and biochemistry in multiple contexts, because biochemicals are the pathways by which emotions can influence risk for health outcomes like cardiovascular disease, depression, and cancer.

In this chapter, we review the role of the serotonin and immune systems in modulating emotional reactivity. By necessity, the bulk of this evidence is drawn from the studies of emotion in an intrapersonal context. However, this review will pay particular attention to several examples where these systems have been studied in an interpersonal context. Intriguingly, findings from this nascent literature underscore the importance of studying biochemical influences in the interpersonal context because it appears this context can change the direction of the relationship between a biochemical and particular emotional responses when compared with the direction of effects seen in studies of intrapersonal emotion.

## The association between intrapersonal emotion and biochemistry

A widely held view of the relationship between biochemical systems and emotion in psychiatry is that there is a correspondence between an emotional state and a particular biochemical system (Cloninger, 1987). This perspective is reflected in colloquial terminology. The selective serotonin reuptake inhibitors (e.g., Prozac) are called "anti-depressants" because they are purported to reduce the emotional state of depression. Anxiolytics (e.g., Valium) are so named because they reduce the emotional state of anxiety. Similarly, cortisol is often conceived of as the "stress hormone" and oxytocin as the "cuddle chemical." In many ways this is akin to the *basic emotions perspective* (Ekman, 1992) in psychology where there are specific emotions such as fear or happiness that are generated by specific brain circuits that elicit associated subjective experiences, patterns of autonomic activity, and behavioral tendencies. For example, fear is associated with elevation of autonomic arousal, avoidant behaviors, and a psychological experience of being afraid. When extended to the biochemical level, the implication is that there are specific biochemicals involved in regulating activity within the neural circuitry underlying a particular basic emotion. The implication is that different levels of a biochemical will lead to differences in a particular emotional response (Cloninger, 1987). This model does not appear to hold in all situations described in this chapter, particularly interpersonal contexts, which will be highlighted in the conclusion.

## Serotonin and susceptibility to partner emotion

Susceptibility to a partner's emotion is a form of emotion exchange between romantic partners where an individual's emotion at one time point is influenced by his or her partner's emotion at a prior time point

(Schoebi, 2008). For example, in a study of multiple structured interactions between couples over the first eight years of marriage, a participant's positive emotion after the discussions was influenced by his or her partner's positive emotion prior to the discussion (Schoebi et al., 2012). This susceptibility to a partner's positive emotion is important because it appears to be associated with symptoms of mental health. In a study of couples who reported their emotion multiple times per day for a period of ten days, the degree to which an individual was susceptible to the partner's positive emotion predicted lower levels of depressive symptomatology twelve months later (Randall & Schoebi, 2015).

Multiple individual psychological differences can influence the degree of susceptibility to partner emotion. One example of susceptibility to partner emotion comes from an experience sampling study of couples transitioning from individual activities to being together. For husbands who were high in perspective taking proclivity, their emotion after reunion on a dimension from sad to upbeat was influenced by their partner's emotion on this same sad to upbeat dimension (Schoebi, 2008).

Individual differences in susceptibility to partner emotion appear to extend to the biochemical level as well. The most pertinent evidence has come from studies on the serotonin system using a genetic approach. One of the better studied genetic variants in psychiatry is a genetic polymorphism (5-HTTLPR) in the promoter region of the serotonin transporter gene (*SCL6A4*). The reason the serotonin transporter gene has been the focus of so much research is that serotonin reuptake inhibitors (e.g., Prozac) act on the serotonin transporter to exert their clinical effect (Owens et al., 2001). Due to the location of this polymorphism within the serotonin transporter gene, it would be expected to affect the amount of expression of the serotonin transporter. In peripheral cells (lymphocytes), it does indeed appear that the 5-HTTLPR impacts the amount of serotonin transporter produced by the gene (Lesch et al., 1996). At this site, there are two primary alleles: the short allele and the long allele. Every individual has two alleles in one of three different possible combinations (i.e., short/short; short/long; or long/long). In terms of the functional effect of the 5-HTTLPR, one of the seminal studies in the area indicated that individuals with the short allele, particularly those with two copies of the short allele, were at greater risk of becoming depressed when exposed to negative life events (Caspi et al., 2003).[1] This suggested that the short allele confers greater reactivity or sensitivity to negative events.

---

[1] This finding has been replicated in several meta-analyses (e.g., Sharpley et al., 2014) but not by others (Culverhouse et al., 2017). In line with this chapter's theme, perhaps contextual influences influence the association between genotype and phenotype.

The increased reactivity to stressors of individuals with the short allele has also been seen in laboratory psychological stress paradigms assessing cortisol response (Miller et al., 2013; Way et al., 2016; Way & Taylor, 2010a).

In the study of couples during the first eight years of their marriage by Schoebi and colleagues described above, variation in the 5-HTTLPR was associated with the degree of susceptibility to partner emotion over the course of multiple structured couple interactions (including both supportive and conflictual interactions (Schoebi et al., 2012). Thus, it would appear that individual genetic differences and, by extension, biochemical differences, can be added to the list of factors that influence interpersonal emotion dynamics.

In this study, according to reports of positive emotion after the interaction, spouses with the short allele were more responsive to their partner's positive emotion during the course of the interaction than individuals with two copies of the long allele (i.e., long/long individuals). This suggests that the short allele facilitates detection of positive emotional signals or heightens the reaction to them. Thus, the 5-HTTLPR not only influences reactivity to negative events and emotions, but positive ones as well. In other words, rather than influencing reactivity to a particular valence of stimuli, it appears to influence general reactivity to both positive and negative stimuli. Those with the short allele appear to be more sensitive to emotional stimuli in general. This is reflective of a larger process known as differential susceptibility that was first noted in the developmental literature (Belsky, 1997) and has now been extended to the genetics literature (Belsky & Pluess, 2009; Way & Gurbaxani, 2008; Way & Taylor, 2010b). Many other examples have been documented. For example, a recent meta-analysis of developmental studies showed that children with the short allele were more impacted by both negative and positive environments than children with the two copies of the long allele (van Ijzendoorn et al., 2012). Additional support for the differential susceptibility model has also been found among individual's engaging in a couples conflict discussion where the 5-HTTLPR moderated the relationship between discussion related emotion and later relationship satisfaction (Haase et al., 2013). For those with two copies of the short allele relative to those with the long allele, the more positive one's emotional response, the greater the increase in one's relationship satisfaction. Conversely, the more negative the emotional response amongst short/short individuals, the greater the decline in relationship satisfaction over time. Thus, it appears the 5-HTTLPR is influencing a general sensitivity to the environment, particularly the emotional environment, more than a particular valence of emotion.

This study of the 5-HTTLPR and susceptibility to partner emotion (Schoebi et al., 2012) also showed that individuals with the short allele were more responsive to the partner's negative affect, as one would expect according to the differential susceptibility model. However, the direction of effect was not congruent between partners. When one spouse was anxious prior to the interaction, spouses with the short allele were more responsive. They showed greater reductions in negative emotion, specifically angry or dominant emotion (irritable, hostile, upset) in response to their partner's anxiety. For the short allele carriers, that one spouses' heightened negative emotion led to a reduction in the other spouses' negative emotion suggests a complex process is occurring. The opposite direction of response between the two spouses is most likely due to the interpersonal context. When one's close other is distressed, it can be relationship promoting to reduce one's anger toward them. Such a pattern of responses is unlikely to have occurred in a standard intrapersonal laboratory paradigm (e.g., viewing facial expressions of an anonymous person) and highlights the importance of studying emotion dynamics in an interpersonal context.

This latter finding also helps to generate hypotheses about the component processes by which the 5-HTTLPR, and the serotonin system more generally, influence information processing to differentially modulate susceptibility to interpersonal emotion. First, the 5-HTTLPR could be affecting attentional deployment to social signals conveying emotion. For example, short allele carriers show an attentional bias toward angry faces (Pérez-Edgar et al., 2010). Thus, short allele carriers may be able to better decode and therefore respond to their partner's emotional cues. Alternatively, if the 5-HTTLPR is not heightening responsivity by attentional processes, it could be amplifying the significance given to the emotional stimulus from the partner. It is unclear whether this significance is computed before or after the incorporation of the situationally relevant information that it is one's partner who is showing anxiety and thus one should reduce one's anger. The opposite direction of affect change between partners would appear to rule out emotion contagion as a mechanism (Hatfield et al., 1994), because this generally involves the same direction of change in emotion between sender and perceiver. Future research will be needed to delineate between these explanations and others. However, because such genetic effects are fundamentally correlational in nature and small in effect size, they need to be validated with experimental pharmacology approaches.

*Pharmacological evidence for differential susceptibility*

Because the 5-HTTLPR is believed to influence expression of the serotonin transporter, pharmacological agents such as serotonin transporter inhibitors (e.g., Prozac) should lead to responses that look like individuals with the 5-HTTLPR long allele. We are not aware of a study that has examined the effects of serotonin reuptake inhibitors on susceptibility to partner emotion in a romantic relationship context. However, the afore-mentioned effects of the 5-HTTLPR are consistent with other research on intrapersonal emotions and clinical observations of sensitivity to the environment. Most of the following studies are not time-lagged like in studies of susceptibility to partner emotion, so they may involve slightly different processes, but nonetheless are informative. For example, clini-cians have long noted that one side effect of selective serotonin reuptake inhibitors is that they lead to a blunting of emotion, eliciting a response akin to individuals with the 5-HTTLPR long allele. Obviously, one of the main reasons these drugs are prescribed and have achieved such a high rate of use is that they reduce negative emotion. Hence the common name "antidepressant." But, less known is that these drugs can reduce positive emotion as well. In a qualitative study of interviews of individ-uals chronically using serotonin reuptake inhibitors, the authors noted, "Most participants reported that the intensity of positive emotions was 'dampened down' or 'toned down', such that participants did not expe-rience the same emotional 'lift' or 'high'" (Price et al., 2009). With respect to social situations, the authors also noted "many participants described reduced enjoyment of, for example, social situations ... [and] felt reduced love or affection towards others and, in particular, reduced attraction towards their partner or reduced feelings of love or pride towards their family." This blunting of positivity in a social context along with the bet-ter documented blunting of negativity is consistent with both differential susceptibility as well as the previously discussed relationship between 5-HTTLPR and responses to partner emotion.

There also is experimental evidence to support the serotoninergic blunting of positive emotion, which may be a component of differential susceptibility to another person's emotion. Subchronic (seven days) SSRI administration blunted the neural response to eating chocolate in regions involved in reward processing (McCabe et al., 2010) and acute SSRI administration blunted the heart rate response to looking at positive, arousing images (Kemp & Nathan, 2004). In a meta-analysis of neuroim-aging studies of antidepressants, these drugs were found to reduce activ-ity in reward circuits (i.e., nucleus accumbens, medial prefrontal cortex) in healthy subjects (Ma, 2015). It should be noted that antidepressants appear to have different effects in depressed patients who may have a dysfunctional serotonin system.

The degree to which the emotional blunting seen in these antidepres-sant studies is the same as seen in the previously described couples stud-ies of the 5-HTTLPR is an open question and underscores the need for further studies into the psychological mechanisms. Because administering antidepressants involves significant ethical and procedural hurdles (e.g., psychiatrist's interview), our laboratory has pursued a different approach to identifying potential mechanisms contributing to differential susceptibility. In particular, our lab has focused on using acetaminophen to alter emotional reactivity. In animal models, an acute dose of acetaminophen (also called paracetamol) increases brain levels of serotonin within an hour to a level comparable to those seen after a serotonin reuptake inhibitor (Pini et al., 1996). Acetaminophen also has effects on other biochemical systems,[2] in particular the immune system (discussed later). We describe here our studies on acetaminophen in an intrapersonal context as they form a platform for future studies in an interpersonal context.

In two separate samples of healthy young adults, we found that an acute dose of acetaminophen (1,000 mg; the dose for a headache) acted in a differentially susceptible manner. Participants rated how much emotion they perceived in a set of both positive (e.g., babies, erotic images) and negative (e.g., feces, mutilations) emotional images. Acetaminophen reduced the extremity of ratings for both positive and negative images, having a slightly greater effect on blunting responses to positive images (Durso et al., 2015). The drug did not impact judgments of the extremity of nonemotional stimuli (the degree of a color in the images). Generalizing broadly from this example of differential susceptibility, it suggests that differential susceptibility arises as a result of more extreme responses to emotional stimuli, but not other forms of stimuli.

## Biochemical influences on empathy

We have also studied the effects of acetaminophen on empathy. Surprisingly, the empathy and interpersonal emotion literatures have little overlap (Wondra & Ellsworth, 2015), yet components of the empathic response to others are likely to be involved in interpersonal emotional processes. In two separate double-blind, placebo-controlled studies, an acute dose of acetaminophen (1,000 mg) reduced the personal distress and empathic concern over reading about another suffering a physically painful or socially painful experience (Mischkowski et al., 2016). Across the studies, the effect sizes for acetaminophen were greater for personal distress, e.g., "I feel uncomfortable" and empathic concern, e.g., "I feel

---

[2] At first glance, acetaminophen may not appear to be as clean a biochemical manipulation as the administration of a serotonin reuptake inhibitor. It should be noted that even though the class of drugs is called "selective" serotonin reuptake inhibitors, they have effects on other biochemical pathways as well (Owens et al., 2001).

sympathetic" – Hedge's g = 0.47 and 0.45, respectively – than for perception of the target's suffering, e.g., "How much pain do you think this
person is experiencing?" – Hedge's g = 0.23. This may indicate acetaminophen affects one's emotion-driven response to another's pain more so
than a more cognitively driven understanding of that person's pain.

In a follow-up replication and extension, acetaminophen also blunted
personal distress and empathic concern for an individual undergoing an
actual experience of rejection so the effects were not just limited to narra-
tive descriptions. Furthermore, acetaminophen also blunted emotional
empathy for positive events such as reading about another's wedding
proposal (Mischkowski, Crocker, & Way, unpublished results). In this
latter study, participants also rated the positive and negative scenarios
using the same ratings as were used to rate the emotional images in the
previously discussed acetaminophen study. The effects of acetaminophen on the empathy responses were over and above the effect of these
ratings of emotional extremity, suggesting that acetaminophen may be
reducing empathy by additional means other than just the blunting of
emotion. These effects of acetaminophen on empathy are likely to have
effects in interpersonal contexts. If one is less reactive to a partner's
pain, one may offer less responsive support to one's partner. If one is
less reactive to a partner's joys, one may fail to engage in capitalization,
or the sharing, celebration of, and building upon successes. Both support and capitalization are critically important to relationship thriving
(Feeney & Collins, 2015), and thus blunted empathy may have serious
consequences for relationship dynamics.

The biochemical pathway(s) underlying this reduction in empathy by
acetaminophen is unclear. One obvious candidate is the serotonin system. In a study of moral dilemmas where those high in trait empathy
were less likely to endorse hypothetical actions that involved personal
harm to others, acute administration of a serotonin reuptake inhibitor
seemed to amplify the aversiveness of harming others, presumably
because the other is represented with greater saliency and this signal
is amplified by serotonin (Crockett et al., 2010). This is consistent with
genetic data that found two copies of the 5-HTTLPR short allele are associated with greater psychological distress to watching empathy inducing
videos and also greater physiological reactivity on an index reflecting
primarily sympathetic nervous system activation (Gyurak et al., 2013).
These studies suggest that the serotonin system is indeed involved in
empathy, but don't clearly delineate whether it is higher or lower levels
of serotonin that increase empathy due to the unspecified relationship
between genetic variation and biochemical data.

Another approach to answering the role of serotonin in empathy is to study the effects of the "hug drug" methylenedioxymethamphetamine (MDMA), which goes by the street name ecstasy. MDMA leads to elevation of serotonin levels one or two orders of magnitude greater than a selective serotonin reuptake inhibitor (Mechan et al., 2002). MDMA increased emotional empathy, particularly for positive situations, but had no effect on cognitive empathy (Hysek et al., 2014; Schmid et al., 2014). In a different study, MDMA again raised emotional empathy, but did not impact performance on the Reading the Mind in the Eyes Test (Baron-Cohen et al., 2001), a frequently used measure that purportedly assesses cognitive empathy. Thus, according to multiple methods, the serotonin system appears to be involved in affective empathy and thus when extended to the interpersonal context may impact interpersonal emotional dynamics by affecting the degree to which one partner feels the distress or joys of the other partner. More speculatively, serotonin may even be involved in the perception of the responsiveness of a partner, as MDMA increased the degree to which one felt understood and regarded by the research assistant after a structured social interaction (Wardle & de Wit, 2014).

Overall, it seems clear that the serotonin system is impacting responses to others that are relevant to susceptibility to partner emotion. What is less clear is the mechanism by which it is doing so. On the one hand, the data from selective serotonin reuptake inhibitors and acetaminophen (in so far as it is increasing central serotonin levels) suggest serotonin is blunting the components of the emotional response that leads to empathy. On the other hand, the evidence from the MDMA studies indicates that serotonin is amplifying affiliative signals from others. Perhaps, there is a dose dependence of the effect, with the extremely high levels of serotonin release following MDMA leading to an amplification of the emotional signal that is transmitted and the more moderate increase in serotonin associated with serotonin reuptake inhibitors and acetaminophen leading to a blunting of the emotional signal that is transmitted.

With respect to acetaminophen, an alternative possibility is that its effects on empathy are mediated more by the immune system than the serotonin system. Acetaminophen is not traditionally viewed as an anti-inflammatory like ibuprofen or aspirin due to its lack of effects on inflammation in the periphery (Graham et al., 2013). However, it has been known since the 1970s that acetaminophen acts in the brain like aspirin and ibuprofen to inhibit the production of molecules activated by inflammation, the prostaglandins (Vane, 1971).

## Inflammation as a potential moderator of interpersonal emotion dynamics

Inflammation reflects activation of the immune system and can be triggered not only by pathogens such as bacteria or viruses, but also by psychological stress. For example, greater hostility during a couples conflict discussion is associated with greater increases in pro-inflammatory cytokines (Kiecolt-Glaser et al., 2005). Although the bulk of research has focused on how such increases in inflammation triggered by marital conflict may be a critical factor by which marriage can impact health (Kiecolt-Glaser & Newton, 2001), there has been less investigation into the role of inflammation on emotional responding and particularly emotional dynamics in couples. Inflammation may contribute to the transmission of emotion between partners because peripheral activation of the immune system can signal the brain and increase the production of prostaglandins (Dantzer et al., 2008). Again, as with the data from the serotonin system, we initially borrow from studies of intrapersonal emotion that are likely to be relevant to the interpersonal context as well.

### *Inflammation's effect on intrapersonal emotion*

In human samples, research has primarily focused on the effects of inflammation on intrapersonal mood, emotional processing, and reactivity. Clinical studies have shown that depressed patients tend to have higher levels of pro-inflammatory cytokines and other markers of inflammation than controls (Howren et al., 2009). Multiple theorists have proposed a causal role for pro-inflammatory cytokines in depression (Dantzer et al., 2008; Raison et al., 2006). For example, pharmacological therapies that increase inflammatory cytokines for immune related dysfunctions trigger clinical depressive episodes in about half of patients (Capuron & Miller, 2004). These findings would suggest that cytokines can augment negative reactions to stimuli.

Experimentally manipulated inflammation in healthy participants also reliably affects mood and reactivity. One way to experimentally induce inflammation is to inject participants with endotoxin, which mimics a bacterial infection and leads to robust increases in pro-inflammatory cytokines. As would be expected based on the aforementioned correlational data, endotoxin increased anxiety (Grigoleit et al., 2011) and depressed mood (Eisenberger et al., 2010b; Moieni et al., 2015). Low-dose endotoxin also selectively impaired memory for negative emotional stimuli (Grigoleit et al., 2011). Participants injected with low-dose endotoxin showed reduced memory for emotional images presented 24 hours earlier, but there was no effect on memory for nonemotional images. With respect to positively valenced stimuli, endotoxin reduced reactivity in the ventral striatum, an area associated with reward processing, to monetary reward cues (Eisenberger et al., 2010a). Overall, the work in on intrapersonal emotion in humans suggests inflammation generally lowers positive and increases negative emotion.

*Inflammation's effect in interpersonal situations*

Recent work has begun to examine the effects of inflammation on emotion and mood within more interpersonal contexts. For instance, experimentally induced inflammation by endotoxin injection led to increases in feelings of social disconnection (Eisenberger et al., 2010b). For women, endotoxin also increases neural reactivity in the dorsal anterior cingulate cortex and anterior insula to experiences of social rejection (Eisenberger et al., 2009), suggesting the inflammation makes this a more aversive experience for them. Higher levels of measured pro-inflammatory cytokines in bereaved women are also associated with increased neural reactivity during a grief elicitation task (O'Connor et al., 2009), suggesting that inflammation increases how responsive one is to emotionally evocative tasks. With respect to threat, those injected with endotoxin showed increased amygdala reactivity to social threat (Inagaki et al., 2012). This effect was specific to images of social threat to which humans are evolutionarily prepared to respond (e.g., fear faces), with no effect of inflammation on reactivity to other forms of threat (e.g., gun images).

One study found that experimentally induced inflammation via endotoxin reduced performance on a purported measure of cognitive empathy, the Reading the Mind in the Eyes Test, even when controlling for self-reported confusion, although this study was limited by the lack of a control task to determine effects of endotoxin on motivation and cognitive ability (Moieni et al., 2015). Nonetheless, these findings do suggest that reductions in the ability to mentalize about others could impact interpersonal emotion dynamics in close relationships.

Based on the above evidence, inflammation may heighten responses to negative stimuli and decrease responses to positive stimuli, having a valence-consistent effect. However, this may be due to insufficient attention to the social context. If one has high levels of inflammation due to an illness (e.g., the flu), it could potentially be adaptive to seek out support from close others. Thus, the significance of such individuals might be heightened. Accordingly, endotoxin increased the self-reported desire to be around a highly supportive other and increased ventral striatum reactivity in response to viewing images of a supportive other (Inagaki et al., 2015). This suggests that inflammation could potentially moderate both negative as well as positive emotions in an interpersonal interaction.

Altogether, there is considerable evidence to suggest inflammation plays a role in emotion in interpersonal contexts. An intriguing goal for future research will be to determine if inflammation may contribute to reciprocal effects for partners. For example, as mentioned earlier, conflictual discussions between couples can lead to elevated inflammation. This elevated inflammation may heighten reactivity to this social threat (Inagaki et al., 2012), which could perpetuate the conflict and then further increase inflammation in both members of the couple. This process may induce a downward spiral of emotional transmission within couples.

## Conclusion

As we have described here, study of interpersonal emotion is not merely just the transplanting of principles derived from intrapersonal emotions to the interpersonal context. There are two differences between these contexts that are worth highlighting. The first is that when shifting from the intrapersonal to the interpersonal context, the interaction partner is generally the main stimulus eliciting the emotion and is likely to have different importance to the respondent, particularly in the case of romantic relationships. We discussed examples in both the serotonin and inflammation sections where responding to a known and valued other led to opposite associations between the biochemical effect and the behavioral effect than was the case for an unknown other typical of intrapersonal emotion studies. Thus, the sensitivity of the 5-HTTLPR short allele confers greater negative emotion in response to negative events, but in the interpersonal context can elicit greater reductions in negative emotion when a partner is experiencing negative emotion. Similarly, inflammation can lead one to avoid strangers, but also approach loved ones. Thus, there is not a simple 1:1 relationship between a chemical and a behavioral outcome. This perspective would have more in common with appraisal (Smith & Ellsworth, 1985) or constructivist models of emotion (Barrett, 2013) where information processing about the situation is a critical determinant of the nature of the emotion experience. As there becomes greater incorporation of pharmacological manipulations and biochemical measurements in studies of interpersonal emotion dynamics, future research will likely uncover further examples of contextually variable responses. Eventually it is hoped that this will lead to a systematic taxonomy of how different interpersonal factors alter the relationship between specific biochemical systems and behavior as well as psychological experience.

A second area where the interpersonal context is different from the intrapersonal is that interpersonal interactions are dynamic; there is a give and take, a back and forth, to the social interaction across multiple channels – verbal, behavioral, and physiological. It is highly likely that there are reciprocal biochemical influences as well. In other words, receiving a drug might impact not only an individual, but also his interactions with others. This, in turn, could affect their biochemistry so that one person taking a drug can influence another's behavior and biochemistry. There is intriguing evidence that oxytocin levels are influenced in this manner by interpersonal interactions (for a recent review: Uchino & Way, 2017). In other words, person A's oxytocin levels impact person B's oxytocin levels, which feedback to affect person A's oxytocin levels. This could be the potential building blocks of interpersonal biochemical regulation. As described in the conclusion to the section on inflammation, inflammatory processes may be having a similar effect leading to a downward spiral where conflict elicits increases in inflammation, which leads to further biasing of information processing in a manner that fosters irritability or depression and that can lead to further conflict. Thus, studying the reciprocal influences between interpersonal interactions and biochemistry is likely to lead to a better understanding of how social stressors and social support impact health. Social relationships are one of the most powerful influences on our health (Holt-Lunstad et al., 2010), yet the processes by which this occurs are poorly specified and have not been empirically demonstrated. Interpersonal emotional transmission is likely to be a key component of these health effects and altered neurotransmission is likely to be the key means by which these social influences are transduced into the physiological processes that cause disease. With improved understanding of the relationship between interpersonal interactions and biochemistry, it is hoped that psychological therapies can be better targeted to impact the underlying biochemistry and thereby improve therapeutic response.

## References

Baron-Cohen, S., Wheelwright, S., Hill, J., Raste, Y., & Plumb, I. (2001). The "Reading the Mind in the Eyes" test revised version: a study with normal adults, and adults with Asperger syndrome or high-functioning autism. *Journal of Child Psychology and Psychiatry*, 42(2), 241–51.

Barrett, L. F. (2013). Psychological construction: the Darwinian approach to the science of emotion. *Emotion Review*, 5(4), 379–89.

Belsky, J. (1997). Variation in susceptibility to environmental influence: an evolutionary argument. *Psychological Inquiry*, 8(3), 182–6.

Belsky, J., & Pluess, M. (2009). Beyond diathesis stress: differential susceptibility to environmental influences. *Psychological Bulletin*, 135(6), 885–908.

Capuron, L., & Miller, A. H. (2004). Cytokines and psychopathology: lessons from interferon-alpha. *Biological Psychiatry*, 56(11), 819–24.

Caspi, A., Sugden, K., Moffitt, T. E., et al. (2003). Influence of life stress on depression: moderation by a polymorphism in the 5-HTT gene. *Science*, 301(5631), 386–9.

Cloninger, C. R. (1987). A systematic method for clinical description and classification of personality variants: a proposal. *Archives of General Psychiatry*, 44(6), 573–88.

Crockett, M. J., Clark, L., Hauser, M. D., & Robbins, T. W. (2010). Serotonin selectively influences moral judgment and behavior through effects on harm aversion. *Proceedings of the National Academy of Sciences*, 107(40), 17433–8.

Culverhouse, R. C., Saccone, N. L., Horton, A. C., et al. (2018). Collaborative meta-analysis finds no evidence of a strong interaction between stress and 5-HTTLPR genotype contributing to the development of depression. *Molecular Psychiatry*. 23, 133–42

Dantzer, R., O'Connor, J. C., Freund, G. G., Johnson, R. W., & Kelley, K. W. (2008). From inflammation to sickness and depression: when the immune system subjugates the brain. *Nature Reviews Neuroscience*, 9(1), 46–56.

Durso, G. R. O., Luttrell, A., & Way, B. M. (2015). Over-the-counter relief from pains and pleasures alike: acetaminophen blunts evaluation sensitivity to both negative and positive stimuli. *Psychological Science*, 26(6), 750–8.

Eisenberger, N. I., Inagaki, T. K., Rameson, L. T., Mashal, N. M., & Irwin, M. R. (2009). An fMRI study of cytokine-induced depressed mood and social pain: the role of sex differences. *Neuroimage*, 47(3), 881–90.

Eisenberger, N. I., Berkman, E. T., Inagaki, T. K., et al. (2010). Inflammation-induced anhedonia: endotoxin reduces ventral striatum responses to reward. *Biological Psychiatry*, 68(8), 748–54.

Eisenberger, N. I., Inagaki, T. K., Mashal, N. M., & Irwin, M. R. (2010). Inflammation and social experience: an inflammatory challenge induces feelings of social disconnection in addition to depressed mood. *Brain, Behavior, and Immunity*, 24(4), 558–63.

Ekman, P. (1992). An argument for basic emotions. *Cognition & Emotion*, 6(3–4), 169–200.

Feeney, B. C., & Collins, N. L. (2015). A new look at social support: a theoretical perspective on thriving through relationships. *Personality and Social Psychology Review*, 19, 113–47.

Graham, G. G., Davies, M. J., Day, R. O., Mohamudally, A., & Scott, K. F. (2013). The modern pharmacology of paracetamol: therapeutic actions, mechanism of action, metabolism, toxicity and recent pharmacological findings. *Inflammopharmacology*, 21(3), 201–32.

Grigoleit, J.-S., Kullmann, J. S., Wolf, O. T., et al. (2011). Dose-dependent effects of endotoxin on neurobehavioral functions in humans. *PloS One*, 6(12), e28330.

Gyurak, A., Haase, C. M., Sze, J., et al. (2013). The effect of the serotonin transporter polymorphism (5-HTTLPR) on empathic and self-conscious emotional reactivity. *Emotion*, 13(1), 25–35.

Haase, C. M., Saslow, L. R., Bloch, L., et al. (2013). The 5-HTTLPR polymorphism in the serotonin transporter gene moderates the association between emotional behavior and changes in marital satisfaction over time. *Emotion*, 13(6), 1068–79.

Hatfield, E., Cacioppo, J. T., & Rapson, R. L. (1994). *Emotional contagion*. New York, NY: Cambridge University Press.

Holt-Lunstad, J., Smith, T. B., & Layton, J. B. (2010). Social relationships and mortality risk: a meta-analytic review. *PLoS medicine*, 7(7), e1000316.

Howren, M. B., Lamkin, D. M., & Suls, J. (2009). Associations of depression with C-reactive protein, IL-1, and IL-6: a meta-analysis. *Psychosomatic Medicine*, 71(2), 171–86.

Hysek, C. M., Schmid, Y., Simmler, L. D., et al. (2014). MDMA enhances emotional empathy and prosocial behavior. *Social Cognitive and Affective Neuroscience*, 9(11), 1645–52.

Inagaki, T. K., Muscatell, K. A., Irwin, M. R., Cole, S. W., & Eisenberger, N. I. (2012). Inflammation selectively enhances amygdala activity to socially threatening images. *Neuroimage*, 59(4), 3222–6.

Inagaki, T. K., Muscatell, K. A., Irwin, M. R., et al. (2015). The role of the ventral striatum in inflammatory-induced approach toward support figures. *Brain, Behavior, and Immunity*, 44, 247–52.

Kemp, A. H., & Nathan, P. J. (2004). Acute augmentation of serotonin suppresses cardiovascular responses to emotional valence. *The International Journal of Neuropsychopharmacology*, 7(1), 65–70.

Kiecolt-Glaser, J. K., Loving, T. J., Stowell, J. R., et al. (2005). Hostile marital interactions, proinflammatory cytokine production, and wound healing. *Archives of General Psychiatry*, 62(12), 1377–84.

Kiecolt-Glaser, J. K., & Newton, T. L. (2001). Marriage and health: his and hers. *Psychological Bulletin*, 127(4), 472–503.

Lesch, K. P., Bengel, D., Heils, A., et al. (1996). Association of anxiety-related traits with a polymorphism in the serotonin transporter gene regulatory region. *Science*, 274(5292), 1527–31.

Ma, Y. (2015). Neuropsychological mechanism underlying antidepressant effect: a systematic meta-analysis. *Molecular Psychiatry*, 20(3), 311–19.

McCabe, C., Mishor, Z., Cowen, P. J., & Harmer, C. J. (2010). Diminished neural processing of aversive and rewarding stimuli during selective serotonin reuptake inhibitor treatment. *Biological Psychiatry*, 67(5), 439–45.

Mechan, A. O., Esteban, B., O'Shea, E., et al. (2002). The pharmacology of the acute hyperthermic response that follows administration of 3, 4-methylenedioxymethamphetamine (MDMA,'ecstasy') to rats. *British Journal of Pharmacology*, 135(1), 170–80.

Miller, R., Wankerl, M., Stalder, T., Kirschbaum, C., & Alexander, N. (2013). The serotonin transporter gene-linked polymorphic region (5-HTTLPR) and cortisol stress reactivity: a meta-analysis. *Molecular Psychiatry*, 18(9), 1018–24.

Mischkowski, D., Crocker, J., & Way, B. M. (2016). From painkiller to empathy killer: acetaminophen (paracetamol) reduces empathy for pain. *Social Cognitive and Affective Neuroscience*, 11(9), 1345–53.

Moieni, M., Irwin, M. R., Jevtic, I., Breen, E. C., & Eisenberger, N. I. (2015). Inflammation impairs social cognitive processing: a randomized controlled trial of endotoxin. *Brain, Behavior, and Immunity*, 48, 132–8.

O'Connor, M.-F., Irwin, M. R., & Wellisch, D. K. (2009). When grief heats up: pro-inflammatory cytokines predict regional brain activation. *NeuroImage*, 47(3), 891–96.

Owens, M. J., Knight, D. L., & Nemeroff, C. B. (2001). Second-generation SSRIs: human monoamine transporter binding profile of escitalopram and R-fluoxetine. *Biological Psychiatry*, 50(5), 345–50.

Pérez-Edgar, K., Bar-Haim, Y., McDermott, J. M., et al. (2010). Variations in the serotonin-transporter gene are associated with attention bias patterns to positive and negative emotion faces. *Biological Psychology*, 83(3), 269–71.

Pini, L. A., Sandrini, M., & Vitale, G. (1996). The antinociceptive action of paracetamol is associated with changes in the serotonergic system in the rat brain. *European Journal of Pharmacology*, 308(1), 31–40.

Price, J., Cole, V., & Goodwin, G. M. (2009). Emotional side-effects of selective serotonin reuptake inhibitors: qualitative study. *The British Journal of Psychiatry*, 195(3), 211–17.

Raison, C. L., Capuron, L., & Miller, A. H. (2006). Cytokines sing the blues: inflammation and the pathogenesis of depression. *Trends in Immunology*, 27(1), 24–31.

Randall, A. K., & Schoebi, D. (2015). Lean on me: susceptibility to partner affect attenuates psychological distress over a 12-month period. *Emotion*, 15(2), 201–10.

Schmid, Y., Hysek, C. M., Simmler, L. D., et al. (2014). Differential effects of MDMA and methylphenidate on social cognition. *Journal of Psychopharmacology*, 28(9), 847–56.

Schoebi, D. (2008). The coregulation of daily affect in marital relationships. *Journal of Family Psychology*, 22(4), 595–604.

Schoebi, D., Way, B. M., Karney, B. R., & Bradbury, T. N. (2012). Genetic moderation of sensitivity to positive and negative affect in marriage. *Emotion*, 12(2), 208–12.

Sharpley, C. F., Palanisamy, S. K. A., Glyde, N. S., Dillingham, P. W., & Agnew, L. L. (2014). An update on the interaction between the serotonin transporter promoter variant (5-HTTLPR), stress and depression, plus an exploration of non-confirming findings. *Behavioural Brain Research*, 273, 89–105.

Smith, C. A., & Ellsworth, P. C. (1985). Patterns of cognitive appraisal in emotion. *Journal of Personality and Social Psychology*, 48(4), 813.

Uchino, B. N., & Way, B. M. (2017). Integrative pathways linking close family ties to health: a neurochemical perspective. *The American Psychologist*, 72(6), 590–600.

van Ijzendoorn, M. H., Belsky, J., & Bakermans-Kranenburg, M. J. (2012). Serotonin transporter genotype 5HTTLPR as a marker of differential susceptibility? A meta-analysis of child and adolescent gene-by-environment studies. *Translational Psychiatry*, 2, e147.

Vane, J. R. (1971). Inhibition of prostaglandin synthesis as a mechanism of action for aspirin-like drugs. *Nature: New Biology*, 231(25), 232–5.

Wardle, M. C., & de Wit, H. (2014). MDMA alters emotional processing and facilitates positive social interaction. *Psychopharmacology*, 231(21), 4219–29.

Way, B. M., Brown, K. W., Quaglia, J., McCain, N., & Taylor, S. E. (2016). Nonsynonymous HTR2C polymorphism predicts cortisol response to psychosocial stress II: evidence from two samples. *Psychoneuroendocrinology*, 70, 142–51.

Way, B. M., & Gurbaxani, B. M. (2008). A genetics primer for social health research. *Social and Personality Psychology Compass*, 2(2), 785–816.

Way, B. M., & Taylor, S. E. (2010a). The serotonin transporter promoter polymorphism is associated with cortisol response to psychosocial stress. *Biological Psychiatry*, 67(5), 487–92.

(2010b). Social influences on health: is serotonin a critical mediator? *Psychosomatic Medicine*, 72(2), 107–12.

Wondra, J. D., & Ellsworth, P. C. (2015). An appraisal theory of empathy and other vicarious emotional experiences. *Psychological Review*, 122(3), 411–28.

CHAPTER 6

# Physiological correlates associated with interpersonal emotion dynamics

*Darby Saxbe, Hannah Khoddam, Geoffrey W. Corner, Sarah A. Stoycos, and Mona Khaled*

Close relationships are known to influence life-long health: high-quality relationships buffer stress and improve longevity, whereas social isolation is a significant risk factor for all-cause mortality (Cohen, 2004). Interpersonal emotion dynamics, which reflect relationship characteristics between people in the moment and also shape relationship quality over time, may contribute to these long-term health outcomes through their influences on physiology. We define interpersonal emotion dynamics here as the process by which emotion emerges and is reshaped by social interaction within dyads or groups (see Chapter 1 for a conceptual overview). How do interpersonal emotion dynamics get "under the skin"? One potential pathway is through the impact of short-term social interaction and longer-term characteristics of social relationships – such as relationship quality – on the body's endocrine and autonomic nervous systems. Increasing evidence from our laboratory and others suggests that not only do relationship contexts influence physiology, but also that close relationship partners can directly influence each other's physiology, in much the same way that partners can influence each other's emotional states.

## Close relationships and physiology: introduction and theoretical overview

Orson Welles's quote – "We're born alone, we live alone, and we die alone" – is memorable, but fundamentally untrue. At birth, we emerge into a web of social relationships that shape our mind and body across the life span. Rather than "born alone," children enter the world already embedded in a social context. And given that newborns require intensive parental help in order to eat, move, and communicate, our very first experiences of life are interdependent.

Developmental researchers have observed that parents and children show "biobehavioral synchrony" (Feldman, 2012, p. 42): coordination of gaze, touch, vocalization, affect, and arousal. Coordinated infant-caregiver interactions may provide scaffolding to help children build their own self-regulatory capacities. For example, a sensitive parent might return an infant's smile, escalating the give-and-take of positive emotion, or adopt a look of concern when the infant becomes over-aroused and distressed. Parents of more securely attached infants appear to show stronger coordination during face-to-face interactions, as characterized by more reciprocal and responsive exchanges (Isabella & Belsky, 1991). Parent–child contact appears to have physiological as well as emotional and behavioral components. For example, infant thermoregulation and the regulation of sleep and appetite are informed by parental proximity.

Extending work on interpersonal physiological coordination beyond early childhood, Hofer (1994) developed the theory of "relationships as regulators," arguing that close relationships serve as hidden regulators of physiology beyond infancy and through adulthood. Hofer focused on the sequelae of spousal bereavement (sleep problems, endocrine and immune changes), which may reflect not only psychological response to loss, but physiological or biological changes brought on by a cohabitating "co-regulator" whose routines and rhythms help to entrain the chrono-biological clock.

Consistent with Hofer's framework, Beckes and Coan (2011)'s Social Baseline Theory (SBT) suggests that groups show homeostatic regulation of emotion and behavior, with individuals coordinating with each other to maintain optimal group-level setpoints. SBT is based on the principle of "economy of action": organisms must take in more energy than they consume. Being with others, according to SBT, is less energetically costly than being alone because groups can distribute the load of responding to the environment (e.g., vigilantly scanning for threats or for resources) and cooperate to accomplish shared goals. This framework suggests that psychology's traditional focus on the individual as the unit of analysis should be complemented by research on the study of dynamic exchanges within groups. Although SBT was not developed with a focus on physiology, the theory's assumptions may translate well into understanding how stress response systems fluctuate and become dynamically adjusted within groups.

Building on the theories described above, this chapter will review research on the physiological correlates of interpersonal emotion dynamics, with a particular focus on physiological linkage within dyads such as adult couples and parent–child pairs. Within-dyad linkage has been described using multiple terms, including coregulation, covariation, synchrony, attunement, and stress contagion. Each of these terms imply different statistical approaches, for example concurrent versus time-lagged analyses, but the literature has tended to use them fairly interchangeably (see Butler, 2011, for reviews of the statistical considerations involved). Following Timmons et al. (2015), we prefer the more general term "linkage" to describe the overarching phenomenon of within-couple associations in physiology. This chapter provides a broad overview of physiological systems associated with interpersonal emotion dynamics for researchers who may not focus primarily on physiology. We focus primarily on the HPA axis as that has been the main focus of our lab's research, but also discuss research on the autonomic nervous system (ANS), oxytocin, and testosterone. We focus on these systems because each appears responsive to social cues (e.g., they show fluctuations during interpersonal interaction) and each appears to show some degree of within-dyad linkage. After introducing each system, we first describe evidence for the influence of social context on that system, and then describe evidence for within-dyad linkage within that system.

## Physiological systems linked to interpersonal dynamics

### The hypothalamic-pituitary-adrenal (HPA) axis

The HPA axis, a major neuroendocrine system within the body, has multiple functions including the regulation of digestion and metabolism, sleep, and the immune system, and is best known to psychologists because of its role in the stress response. When a threat or stressor is detected, the hypothalamus of the brain secretes corticotropin releasing hormone (CRH), which then stimulates the pituitary gland to produce adrenocorticotropic hormone (ACTH), which signals the release of cortisol, a glucocorticoid hormone, from the adrenal glands. Cortisol then acts on the brain as part of a feedback loop to inhibit the hypothalamus and the pituitary gland. Cortisol influences the availability of glucose in the body (increased stress leads to increased cortisol, which makes it easier for the body to access quick energy in order to mobilize a fight or flight responses) and suppresses the activity of the metabolically costly immune system.

In addition to cortisol's role in the acute stress response, the hormone also has a circadian rhythm, or diurnal slope. Cortisol levels initially rise sharply in the first 30–45 minutes after awakening (the Cortisol Awakening Response, or CAR), and then decline steadily across the day. A steep diurnal slope – in which cortisol levels are significantly lower at bedtime than during the morning hours – appears to be a marker of the body's successful adaptation to everyday demands; flattened slopes, in which cortisol levels start low and fail to drop across the day, have been observed in individuals reporting high chronic stress, burnout, chronic fatigue, and post-traumatic stress disorder (Kumari et al., 2011).

The HPA axis is a plausible target for the study of social relationships and emotions, for a number of reasons. First, cortisol appears to be responsive to momentary stressors, particularly social stressors such as a social evaluative threat (Dickerson & Kemeny, 2001), while the presence of supportive others may buffer or dampen cortisol responses (Kirschbaum et al., 1995). Also, cortisol can be measured relatively non-invasively and repeatedly across a relatively short time frame, allowing for its use in ecologically valid contexts such as during social interactions (e.g., couples conflict or support; Kiecolt-Glaser & Newton, 2001). As such, cortisol may reflect interpersonal emotion dynamics.

**Close relationships and the HPA axis.** The HPA axis represents a potential pathway through which close relationships may affect health. Within couples, relationship dissatisfaction and other problems have been associated with dysregulated patterns of diurnal cortisol, including lower waking levels (Floyd & Riforgiate, 2008) and higher total daily output (Ditzen et al., 2008; Vedhara et al., 2006). Additionally, poor relationship functioning (assessed by measures of insecure attachment, poor spousal relationship quality, and low sociability) and high home and work demands were associated with lower morning cortisol and flatter diurnal cortisol slopes in a study of women with young children (Adam & Gunnar, 2001). Conversely, dual-income couples who reported greater intimacy and relationship quality showed lower overall cortisol excretion across the day (Ditzen et al., 2008).

In a sample of 30 cohabitating, married, dual-earner couples with children who participated in UCLA's Center for the Everyday Lives of Families (CELF) study, we found that, among women, greater relationship satisfaction was associated with a steeper cortisol slope and moderated within-person associations between evening cortisol levels and both afternoon workload ratings and afternoon cortisol (Saxbe et al., 2008). More satisfied wives showed stronger basal cortisol cycles and greater physiological recovery from particularly busy workdays. This finding dovetails with epidemiological research suggesting that, while marriage carries an overall health benefit for men, women may be more sensitive to the quality of the relationship (Kiecolt-Glaser & Newton, 2001). In a follow-up study using the same sample, we found that women's open-ended descriptions of their home environment were also linked with diurnal slopes of cortisol, such that women who talked more about clutter and unfinished home projects had flattened slopes and increased levels of depressed mood across the day (Saxbe & Repetti, 2010). These studies suggest that that the everyday social context informs HPA axis rhythms. Associations between relationship characteristics and HPA axis patterns are most likely driven by social interaction and interpersonal emotion dynamics within couples and families. In the following section, we describe evidence for direct HPA axis linkage within couples.

**HPA axis linkage within close relationships.** In addition to being influenced physiologically by the close relationship context, partners may directly influence each other's physiology, resulting in physiological linkage between partners. We first explored this phenomenon in the sample of 30 CELF couples described above by examining salivary cortisol and mood states collected multiple times per day over several days. We found that partners' cortisol and negative mood levels were positively associated at each timepoint (Saxbe & Repetti, 2010). In other words, if a husband had higher-than-usual cortisol or negative mood at a particular sampling timepoint (adjusting for his own mean level of cortisol/mood and the sampling time of day), his wife was likely to have higher-than-usual cortisol or negative mood at that same timepoint. Couples who were more strongly linked in their momentary negative mood states also had more strongly linked cortisol levels. Marital satisfaction moderated this association: distressed couples showed stronger linkage in both cortisol and negative mood.

This evidence that marital satisfaction weakened linkage may initially seem counterintuitive: shouldn't couples who are more physiologically similar to each other show better relationship quality? The SBT notion of a homeostatic social baseline provides a useful counter-explanatory framework. Couples biologically adapt to each other as part of cohabitation and intimacy, but within a well-functioning relationship, partners help to buffer each other's stress states. Given that momentary cortisol elevations themselves may reflect a system that is out of balance, high levels of linkage in stress hormones may reflect a system that is tipping toward shared over- or under-activation in a process of "co-dysregulation." Physiological linkage in cortisol offers an example of interpersonal emotion dynamics. For example, it might reflect couples' negative affect reciprocity (Levenson & Gottman, 1983), or reactivity to each other's negative states, and may characterize couples with difficulty modulating negative emotions. Our finding that couples show HPA axis linkage in daily life, and that this linkage appears stronger in distressed relationships, has now been replicated by other researchers as well as within our lab (e.g., Liu et al., 2013; Papp et al., 2013; Saxbe et al., 2015).

More research is needed to elucidate which aspects of relationship distress might translate into stronger HPA linkage, for example whether contexts like relationship conflict or high daily stress foster intensified HPA linkage within couples. In turn, this has long-term implications for individual and relational well-being.

## *The autonomic nervous system (ANS)*

There are two primary components of the ANS: the sympathetic nervous system (SNS) and the parasympathetic nervous system (PSNS), and both have been associated with interpersonal emotion dynamics. Arousal of the SNS is associated with a "fight or flight" response that promotes mobilization when threatened (Jansen et al., 1995). Although this response is adaptive in the face of imminent threat, chronic activation of this system threatens cardiovascular health (Curtis & O'Keefe, 2002; Smith & Ruiz, 2002). The PSNS is responsible for "rest and digest" processes, storing and conserving energy and regulating bodily responses during periods of rest (McCorry, 2007). There are multiple indices of ANS activity, including heart rate and skin conductance. Below, we review several of the most commonly used indices of ANS activity and then discuss associations between these indices and interpersonal emotion dynamics within couples.

**Heart rate and heart rate variability.** Heart rate is typically measured through the use of an electrocardiogram (ECG), which involves the placement of electrodes on the body to measure the time between heart beats as indicated by the intervals between R-waves (i.e., R-R or interbeat intervals), or peaks in electrical activity captured by an ECG (Porges & Byrne, 1992). Heart rate is regulated by both the sympathetic and parasympathetic components of the ANS through the sinoatrial node. The SNS is responsible for increases in heart rate through norepinephrine released by the accelerans nerve, while the PSNS is responsible for decreases in heart rate through acetylcholine released by the vagus nerve (Schmidt-Nielsen, 1997). In addition to studying raw heart rate, researchers also examine heart rate variability (HRV), or the amount of variation in the time interval between beats of the heart. HRV can be further divided into high and low frequency components (Porges, 2007). The high frequency component (HF-HRV) is also known as respiratory sinus arrhythmia (RSA) and is largely or entirely influenced by PSNS or vagus nerve activity (Eckberg, 1997), commonly referred to as vagal tone. The term "RSA" refers to HRV as influenced by breathing patterns. In the context of interpersonal emotion dynamics, tonic, baseline, or "resting" RSA is typically used as a trait-like measure of the capacity for regulatory cardiac control (Porges, 2007; Smith et al., 2011).

**Skin conductance.** Skin conductance is measured by monitoring voltage on the volar surface, usually the surface of the skin on one's hand, which naturally varies in a wave-like rhythm (Lykken & Venables, 1973) and changes as a result of the activation of sweat glands innervated by the SNS. Thus, unlike measuring heart rate or HRV, capturing skin conductance response (SCR) is believed to isolate SNS activity. In psychophysiological studies, skin conductance is referred to by several different names that can represent somewhat different concepts, including electrodermal activity (EDA), galvanic skin response (GSR), and simply skin conductance or SCR. The average skin conductance level at a resting or baseline state is referred to as tonic skin conductance (Lykken & Venables, 1973).

**Interpersonal emotion dynamics and the ANS: the physiology of couples' interactions.** Many studies have explored ANS activity in the context of couples' discussions. During conflict, partners typically show an increase in heart rate (Robles & Kiecolt-Glaser, 2003), which appears to reflect physiological arousal in response to stressful interaction. Heart rate reactivity to conflict has been shown to be more profound for husbands when they demonstrate higher cynical hostility (Smith & Brown, 1983), and attenuated heart rate reactivity to the Trier Social Stress Test (TSST) has been shown in women who received positive partner physical contact prior to stress induction (Ditzen et al., 2007). Conversely, however, another study demonstrated that husbands who exhibit decreases in heart rate in response to a conflict discussion also showed higher levels of verbal aggression toward their wives (Gottman et al., 1995). This suggests that both hypo- and hyper-reactivity of the ANS in the context of conflict with a partner may be indicative of negative relationship functioning. Consistent with this belief, further research using a conflict paradigm with couples has demonstrated an association between conflict-related ANS reactivity and relational aggression, particularly when partners are less satisfied with their relationship (Murray-Close et al., 2012). This physiological response is associated with both emotional reactivity and aggressive behavior (Scarpa & Raine, 1997). Again, however, under-arousal of the ANS in response to relational stressors is also sometimes associated with aggression in close relationships (Murray-Close, 2011). Additionally, a composite index of physiological arousal during a conflict discussion that included heart rate and skin conductance was found to predict declines in relationship satisfaction over the following three years (Levenson & Gottman, 1983). Therefore, it is also possible that certain profiles of physiological reactivity predispose individuals to longer-term relationship risks.

An increasing body of research has focused on HRV, particularly HF-HRV or RSA, and partner interactions. Smith et al. (2011) conceptualize baseline levels of RSA, or vagal tone, as an individual's capacity for emotional and behavioral self-regulation. Higher resting RSA is associated with higher levels of marital quality (Smith et al., 2011) and several long-term health outcomes (Thayer & Lane, 2007). Supporting the role of RSA in emotion regulation and the functioning of romantic relationships, men with greater vagal reactivity in response to a relationship description task showed greater within-couple linkage in negative emotion and in negative interactions with their partner (Diamond et al., 2011). Similarly, women show increases in RSA during conflict, followed by decreases in resting RSA, suggesting the activation and depletion of self-regulation resources (Smith et al., 2011).

**ANS linkage within close relationships.** Partners can become linked with respect to ANS activity (Timmons et al., 2015). This has been observed for heart rate (Helm et al., 2012), skin conductance (Chatel-Goldman et al., 2014), RSA (Helm et al., 2014), blood pressure (Reed et al., 2013), and a composite index of physiological activity (Levenson & Gottman, 1983). Evidence has been mixed with regard to whether this linkage reflects or contributes to positive or negative relationship functioning (Timmons et al., 2015). Helm et al. (2012) found that greater linkage in RSA was associated with higher relationship satisfaction, and Chatel-Goldman et al. (2014) found that greater linkage in skin conductance was associated with partners' greater trait empathy. Conversely, Chatel-Goldman et al. (2014) also found that the effect of physical touch on skin conductance linkage was lessened among more empathic individuals, and Levenson and Gottman (1983) found that greater linkage in a composite physiological activity index was associated with less relationship satisfaction. More neutrally, it has also been reported that greater linkage in heart rate is associated with greater linkage in affect (Ferrer & Helm, 2013). Together, these studies paint a complicated picture. The implications of couples' linkage in ANS activity likely depend on their larger relational context, how coregulation is operationalized and defined (Butler & Randall, 2013), and which specific indices of ANS activity are used. Moderators such as relationship quality and partner influence may help determine the degree of linkage. In one study, partners who had low influence on each others' health behaviors showed "anti-phase" linkage of blood pressure (changes in opposite directions), whereas partners with high influence on each other showed "in-phase" linkage of blood pressure (changes in unison) (Reed et al., 2013). Levenson and Gottman's theory of negative affect reciprocity (1983) suggest that distressed couples tend to reciprocate each other's negative emotion states and corresponding physiological arousal, which helps to escalate conflict and may exacerbate relationship distress over time.

*Oxytocin*

Oxytocin is a neuropeptide centrally synthesized in the hypothalamus, stored in the posterior pituitary gland, and then released into the blood as a hormone (MacDonald & MacDonald, 2010). Central to reproductive functions in mammals, peripheral oxytocin activates and strengthens uterine contractions during labor and birth, as well as stimulates muscle contractions for the release of breast milk (Fuchs et al., 1984; MacDonald & MacDonald, 2010). Perhaps due to oxytocin's essential role in reproduction, research has investigated oxytocin's function as a social affiliative neuropeptide. Oxytocin has been associated with prosocial behavior and mother–infant bonding in both nonhuman mammals and humans (Insel & Young, 2001), and may play a role in interpersonal emotion dynamics by promoting trust (Kosfeld et al., 2005) and positive communication behavior (Ditzen et al., 2009).

Discrepant findings regarding oxytocin as an affiliative peptide may result from different approaches to measurement (Nave et al., 2015). For example, studies of oxytocin and social behaviors have examined plasma, salivary, urinary, and cerebrospinal oxytocin; basal and reactive oxytocin; exogenously administered intranasal oxytocin; and variations in the oxytocin receptor gene. Various methods of measuring oxytocin display differing levels of the peptide, since, for example, oxytocin is expressed in plasma in a shorter amount of time than in urine (Feldman et al., 2011). Even among studies measuring plasma oxytocin, different extraction and assay methods are weakly correlated (Szeto et al., 2011). Nave et al. (2015) note that differing methodologies, lack of replication, and publication bias have yielded an inconsistent oxytocin literature rife with conflicting findings. Therefore, the findings summarized below should be interpreted with caution.

**Oxytocin and interpersonal dynamics.** In nonhuman mammals, oxytocin has been shown to promote affiliative behavior (Carter et al., 1995; Young & Wang, 2004). Similarly, in human samples, experimentally administered intranasal oxytocin has been found to increase interpersonal trust (Kosfeld et al., 2005), and positive communication behavior during couple conflict (Ditzen et al., 2009). Higher plasma and salivary oxytocin levels have also been associated with mother–infant attachment and bonding (Feldman et al., 2007; Galbally et al., 2011), as well as maternal affectionate parenting behavior and paternal stimulating parenting behavior (Gordon et al., 2010a).

Although oxytocin is generally believed to promote prosocial behavior, research on oxytocin and social affiliation has been inconsistent. Several studies indicate that oxytocin may actually reflect interpersonal distress. Higher basal plasma oxytocin in women was linked with more interpersonal problems (Turner et al., 1999). Among forty-five men and women, higher plasma oxytocin concentration was associated with greater anxious attachment in close relationships (Marazziti et al., 2006). In anxiously attached male adults, subjects who received intranasal oxytocin had more negative mental representations of their mothers than subjects who received the placebo (Bartz et al., 2010). Cyranowski et al. (2008) found that in depressed female participants, plasma oxytocin levels were positively associated with symptoms of depression, anxiety, and interpersonal dysfunction.

Additionally, Tabak et al. (2011) measured plasma oxytocin levels in a sample of thirty-five women who had experienced an interpersonal stressor such as romantic infidelity, rejection, or a break-up. Five days later, the women delivered a four-minute speech in the lab about the transgression. Task-related oxytocin reactivity (but not basal oxytocin) was positively associated with post-conflict interpersonal anxiety and participants' lack of forgiveness. In another test of the notion that oxytocin may be associated with relational distress, higher concentrations of plasma oxytocin in postmenopausal women was linked with poor relationship quality and less positive partner relations (Taylor et al., 2006). Similarly, Taylor et al. (2010) found that elevated levels of women's plasma oxytocin were associated with more romantic relationship distress. Interestingly, Tayor et al. (2010) found that men's oxytocin levels were not related to relational distress, suggesting that sex may moderate the relationship between oxytocin and interpersonal stress.

Expanding upon the evidence for sex effects on oxytocin, Feldman et al. (2011) examined plasma, salivary, and urinary oxytocin levels in 112 mothers and fathers interacting with their four- to six-month-old infants. Among mothers, but not fathers, urinary oxytocin levels were positively correlated with interactive stress during infant play, parenting stress, and anxious attachment style. However, mothers' plasma and saliva oxytocin levels were not correlated with urinary oxytocin or interpersonal distress.

**Oxytocin linkage within close relationships.** Mothers and fathers appear to show levels of plasma, salivary, and urinary oxytocin that are correlated with each other (Feldman et al., 2011; Gordon et al., 2010a). One study found that first-time parents' oxytocin levels were correlated during the first weeks after birth, and also at six months postpartum (Gordon et al., 2010a). Interestingly, both mothers and fathers' oxytocin at the first time point predicted their partners' oxytocin at six months postpartum, suggesting that couples' hormones may converge in early parenthood.

Oxytocin linkage among parents and their infants may mirror their behavioral coordination. During play, parents and infants' salivary oxytocin showed parallel increases, and behavioral synchrony moderated this hormonal linkage (Feldman et al., 2010). When parents and infants displayed high behavioral synchrony, stronger correlation of parent and infant oxytocin emerged; however, among dyads who did not display behavioral synchrony, oxytocin levels were not closely correlated. Similarly, during triadic family interactions including mother, father, and infant, mothers' and fathers' plasma oxytocin predicted synchronization of physical touch, proximity, and gaze between parents and infant (Gordon et al., 2010b).

Although not many studies have investigated oxytocin linkage within interpersonal relationships, some studies have suggested that a parent's physiology may regulate an infant's physiology through social contact, especially in cases in which social behaviors are coordinated. In one such study, experimentally administered intranasal oxytocin increased fathers' salivary oxytocin, which in turn exponentially increased infants' salivary oxytocin (Weisman et al., 2012). Fathers who received the administered oxytocin showed longer periods of gaze synchrony and physical contact with their infants. Oxytocin administration also increased fathers' RSA, which similarly increased the infants' RSA. Parents' oxytocin measured when the infant was six months old combined with parental behavior predicted the child's oxytocin at three years of age during an interaction in the home with the child's closest friend (Feldman et al., 2013). In conclusion, several studies have found evidence of linkage in oxytocin within couples and parent–child dyads. Moreover, oxytocin appears to promote behavioral coordination within families, particularly in early parenthood.

*Testosterone*

Testosterone (T), a steroid hormone, plays a key role in the development of male reproductive tissues, and promotes secondary sexual characteristics such as increased muscle, bone mass, and body hair. T is synthesized by the hypothalamic-pituitary-gonadal axis, which acts as a negative feedback loop to regulate the amount of T in the bloodstream. When T levels are low, gonadotropin releasing hormone (GnRH) is released by the hypothalamus, stimulating the pituitary gland to release follicle-stimulating hormone (FSH) and lutenizing hormone (LH), which both stimulate the testes to synthesize T (Mooradian et al., 1987).

**Testosterone and close relationships.** The role of testosterone in close relationships is complex. In general, testosterone's role in reproduction may operate within a trade-off framework, in which high testosterone leads to an advantage in competitive challenges and low testosterone leads to greater monogamy and investment in parenting. In support of this hypothesis, high T has been associated with competition and aggression, whereas low T has been associated with pair-bonding and nurturance and care of offspring (van Anders et al., 2012). Longitudinal and cross-sectional investigations of fatherhood have found lower T levels in partnered fathers and fathers who are more involved in their children's care (e.g., Burnham et al., 2003; Gettler et al., 2011; Gray et al., 2007; Wynne-Edwards, 2001). Additionally, research suggests that men who are more committed to romantic relationships also show lower T levels compared to less committed men (Alvergne et al., 2009). Taken together, these studies suggest that lower T may reflect greater investment in family relationships (Fleming et al., 2002; Gettler et al., 2011; Storey & Ziegler, 2015); T may shape interpersonal emotion dynamics by affecting motivation within different social contexts, for example asserting power and dominance in the presence of potential mates versus showing nurturing behavior toward family members.

**Testosterone linkage within close relationships.** Few studies have investigated within-couple linkage in T, and these studies have yielded mixed results. Two studies found no evidence of T linkage between partners: one of these investigated T linkage within a small sample of pregnant couples before and after the birth of the child (Berg & Wynne-Edwards, 2002), and the other measured T in new couples during an in-lab conflict discussion task (Schneiderman et al., 2014). A larger study found small positive correlations in T within 307 couples (Booth et al., 1999). Another found marginally significant correlations in T in twenty-seven heterosexual couples whose T was sampled several times prior to the birth of their child (Edelstein et al., 2015). A study from our group that reanalyzed these data from the twenty-seven couples found that fathers who show a stronger decline in T across pregnancy and stronger correlations with mothers' testosterone at each assessment, reported higher postpartum investment, commitment, and satisfaction (Saxbe et al., 2017). These were independent effects with T declines and within-dyad correlations in T measured within the same multilevel model. Although several studies have suggested that men's declines in T around the transition to parenthood are associated with greater relationship adjustment (e.g., Gettler et al., 2011), this study is the first to report that T linkage in expectant couples might also support better relationship quality postpartum.

## Conclusions and future directions

In conclusion, research suggests that interpersonal dynamics within close relationships do have physiological correlates, although these correlates vary by physiological system, by individual or couple characteristics (e.g., sex; attachment style; relationship quality), and by social context (e.g., relationship conflict; parent–child interaction). As summarized above, within-couple physiological linkage has been most reliably found for cortisol and the ANS, although several studies have also found intriguing within-dyad linkage in oxytocin and testosterone. However, all the literatures summarized above are small and preliminary in the context of understanding interpersonal emotion dynamics.

Does physiological linkage reflect "good" or "bad" overall relationship functioning? Thus far, a preponderance of studies to date have suggested that HPA axis linkage is "bad," particularly within couples, while research on other systems has been less conclusive (Timmons et al., 2015). For example, oxytocin linkage may promote more coordinated behavior within families (Feldman et al., 2010), and testosterone linkage during pregnancy was associated with greater paternal investment in the couple relationship (Saxbe et al., 2017). The meaning of linkage within a particular physiological system may depend on the larger function of that system: activation of the HPA axis and ANS may reflect stress and arousal, whereas oxytocin and testosterone both contribute to reproduction and appear to be important within a transition-to-parenthood context. Additionally, more research is needed into potential moderators of physiological linkage. For example, although relationship distress has been associated with stronger linkage, what specific aspects of distress might underlie this effect? Some distressed relationships are characterized by frequent conflict, whereas others are characterized by low affection; the former type of distressed relationship might be more likely to be characterized by HPA axis linkage, but empirical evidence is needed. Similarly, intrusive but not neglectful parenting might translate into greater parent–child linkage. The study of interpersonal emotion dynamics can inform research into linkage by identifying specific features of dyadic interaction that shape both physiology and relationship quality over time.

Also, how does physiological linkage develop and change over the life span? Longitudinal research that follows relationship partners over repeated assessments and across the lifespan may help to inform this question. Adolescents, who are reorienting from parent–child relationship to peer and romantic relationships, might also show changes in linkage that are related to their social motivation. Laws et al. (2015) followed newlyweds over the first several years of parenthood and found that cortisol linkage increased over time. The transition to parenthood might represent another important juncture where couples' hormonal linkage has evolutionary significance. And older adults may also show interesting changes in linkage when one member of the couple becomes ill and the other takes on the caregiver role. Moreover, it remains unknown how physiological linkage might contribute to long-term health outcomes and whether couples with more similar physiology also have more similar health outcomes.

The research we have reviewed focuses on close relationships, primarily adult romantic couples. There are many unanswered questions about physiological linkage within other types of social groups, such as adolescent peer and romantic relationships, classmates, roommates, and coworkers. As psychological research continues to progress beyond the study of the individual and into more dynamic mapping of the social world, our field's understanding of health and the body can continue to broaden as well.

## References

Adam, E. K., & Gunnar, M. R. (2001). Relationship functioning and home and work demands predict individual differences in diurnal cortisol patterns in women. *Psychoneuroendocrinology*, 26(2), 189–208.

Alvergne, A., Faurie, C., Raymond, M. (2009). Variation in testosterone levels and male reproductive effort: insight from a polygynous human population. *Hormones and Behavior*, 56, 491–7.

Bartz, J. A., Zaki, J., Ochsner, K. N., et al. (2010). Effects of oxytocin on recollections of maternal care and closeness. *Proceedings of the National Academy of Sciences*, 107(50), 21371–5.

Beckes, L., & Coan, J. A. (2011). Social baseline theory: The role of social proximity in emotion and economy of action. *Social and Personality Psychology Compass*, 5(12), 976–88.

Berg, S. J., & Wynne-Edwards, K. E. (2001, June). Changes in testosterone, cortisol, and estradiol levels in men becoming fathers. In *Mayo Clinic Proceedings* (Vol. 76, No. 6, pp. 582–92). Elsevier.

Booth, A., Johnson, D. R., & Granger, D. A. (1999). Testosterone and men's health. *Journal of Behavioral Medicine*, 22(1), 1–19.

Burnham, T. C., Chapman, J. F., Gray, P. B., et al. (2003). Men in committed, romantic relationships have lower testosterone. *Hormones and Behavior*, 44(2), 119–22.

Butler, E. A. (2011). Temporal interpersonal emotion systems: The "TIES" that form relationships. *Personality and Social Psychology Review*, 15(4), 367–93.

Butler, E. A., & Randall, A. K. (2013). Emotional coregulation in close relationships. *Emotion Review*, 5(2), 202–10.

Carter, C. S., Devries, A. C., & Getz, L. L. (1995). Physiological substrates of mammalian monogamy: the prairie vole model. *Neuroscience & Biobehavioral Reviews*, 19(2), 303–14.

Chatel-Goldman, J., Congedo, M., Jutten, C., & Schwartz, J. (2014). Touch increases autonomic coupling between romantic partners. *Frontiers in Behavioral Neuroscience*, 8(1), 1–12.

Cohen, S. (2004). Social relationships and health. *American Psychologist*, 59(8), 676.

Curtis B. M., & O'Keefe, J. H. (2002). Autonomic tone as a cardiovascular risk factor: the dangers of chronic fight or flight. *Mayo Clinic Proceedings*, 77(1), 45–54.

Cyranowski, J. M., Hofkens, T. L., Frank, E., et al. (2008). Evidence of dysregulated peripheral oxytocin release among depressed women. *Psychosomatic Medicine*, 70(9), 967–75.

Diamond, L. M., Hicks, A. M., & Otter-Henderson, K. D. (2011). Individual differences in vagal regulation moderate associations between daily affect and daily couple interactions. *Personality and Social Psychology Bulletin*, 37(6), 731–44.

Dickerson, S. S., & Kemeny, M. E. (2004). Acute stressors and cortisol responses: a theoretical integration and synthesis of laboratory research. *Psychological Bulletin*, 130(3), 355–95.

Ditzen, B., Hoppmann, C., & Klumb, P. (2008). Positive couple interactions and daily cortisol: On the stress-protecting role of intimacy. *Psychosomatic Medicine*, 70(8), 883–889.

Ditzen, B., Neumann, I. D., Bodenmann, G., et al. (2007). Effects of different kinds of couple interaction on cortisol and heart rate responses to stress in women. *Psychoneuroendocrinology*, 32, 565–74.

Ditzen, B., Schaer, M., Gabriel, B., et al. (2009). Intranasal oxytocin increases positive communication and reduces cortisol levels during couple conflict. *Biological Psychiatry*, 65(9), 728–31.

Eckberg, D. L. (1997). Sympathovagal balance: a critical appraisal. *Circulation*, 96(9), 3224–32.

Edelstein, R. S., Wardecker, B. M., Chopik, W. J., Moors, A. C., Shipman, E. L., & Lin, N. J. (2015). Prenatal hormones in first-time expectant parents: Longitudinal changes and within-couple correlations. *American Journal of Human Biology*, 27(3), 317–25.

Feldman, R. (2012). Parent–infant synchrony: a biobehavioral model of mutual influences in the formation of affiliative bonds. *Monographs of the Society for Research in Child Development*, 77(2), 42–51.

Feldman, R., Gordon, I., Influs, M., Gutbir, T., & Ebstein, R. P. (2013). Parental oxytocin and early caregiving jointly shape children's oxytocin response and social reciprocity. *Neuropsychopharmacology*, 38(7), 1154–62.

Feldman, R., Gordon, I., & Zagoory-Sharon, O. (2010). The cross-generation transmission of oxytocin in humans. *Hormones and Behavior*, 58, 669–76.

Feldman, R., Gordon, I., & Zagoory-Sharon, O. (2011). Maternal and paternal plasma, salivary, and urinary oxytocin and parent–infant synchrony: considering stress and affiliation components of human bonding. *Developmental Science*, 14(4), 752–61.

Feldman, R., Weller, A., Zagoory-Sharon, O., & Levine, A. (2007). Evidence for a neuroendocrinological foundation of human affiliation: plasma oxytocin levels across pregnancy and the postpartum period predict mother-infant bonding. *Psychological Science*, 18(11), 965–70.

Ferrer, E., & Helm, J. M. (2013). Dynamical systems modeling of physiological coregulation in dyadic interactions. *International Journal of Psychophysiology*, 88(3), 296–308.

Fleming, A. S., Corter, C., Stallings, J., & Steiner, M. (2002). Testosterone and prolactin are associated with emotional responses to infant cries in new fathers. *Hormones and Behavior*, 42(4), 399–413.

Floyd, K., & Riforgiate, S. (2008). Affectionate communication received from spouses predicts stress hormone levels in healthy adults. *Communication Monographs*, 75(4), 351–68.

Fuchs, A. R., Fuchs, F., Husslein, P., & Soloff, M. S. (1984). Oxytocin receptors in the human uterus during pregnancy and parturition. *American Journal of Obstetrics and Gynecology*, 150(6), 734–41.

Galbally, M., Lewis, A. J., IJzendoorn, M. V., & Permezel, M. (2011). The role of oxytocin in mother-infant relations: a systematic review of human studies. *Harvard Review of Psychiatry*, 19(1), 1–14.

Gettler, L. T., McDade, T. W., Feranil, A. B., & Kuzawa, C. W. (2011). Longitudinal evidence that fatherhood decreases testosterone in human males. *Proceedings of the National Academy of Sciences*, 108(39), 16194–9.

Gordon, I., Zagoory-Sharon, O., Leckman, J. F., & Feldman, R. (2010a). Oxytocin and the development of parenting in humans. *Biological Psychiatry*, 68(4), 377–82.

(2010b). Oxytocin, cortisol, and triadic family interactions. *Physiology & Behavior*, 101, 679–84.

Gottman, J. M., Jacobson, N. S., Rushe, R. H., et al. (1995). The relationship between heart rate reactivity, emotionally aggressive behavior, and general violence in batterers. *Journal of Family Psychology*, 9(3), 227–48.

Gray, P. B., Parkin, J. C., & Samms-Vaughan, M. E. (2007). Hormonal correlates of human paternal interactions: a hospital-based investigation in urban Jamaica. *Hormones and Behavior*, 52(4), 499–507.

Helm, J. L., Sbarra, D., & Ferrer, E. (2012). Assessing cross-partner associations in physiological responses via coupled oscillator models. *Emotion*, 12(4), 748–62.

Helm, J. L., Sbarra, D. A., & Ferrer, E. (2014). Coregulation of respiratory sinus arrhythmia in adult romantic partners. *Emotion*, 14(3), 522–31.

Hofer, M. A. (1994). Hidden regulators in attachment, separation, and loss. *Monographs of the Society for Research in Child Development*, 59(29c), 192–207.

Insel, T. R., & Young, L. J. (2001). The neurobiology of attachment. *Nature Reviews Neuroscience*, 2(2), 129–36.

Isabella, R. A., & Belsky, J. (1991). Interactional synchrony and the origins of infant mother attachment: a replication study. *Child Development*, 62(2), 373–84.

Jansen, A. S., Van Nguyen, X., Karpitskiy, V., Mettenleiter, T. C., & Loewy, A. D. (1995). Central command neurons of the sympathetic nervous system: basis of the fight-or-flight response. *Science*, 270(5236), 644–6.

Kiecolt-Glaser, J. K., & Newton, T. L. (2001). Marriage and health: His and hers. *Psychological Bulletin*, 127(4), 472–503.

Kirschbaum, C., Klauer, T., Filipp, S. H., & Hellhammer, D. H. (1995). Sex-specific effects of social support on cortisol and subjective responses to acute psychological stress. *Psychosomatic Medicine*, 57(1), 23–31.

Kosfeld, M., Heinrichs, M., Zak, P. J., Fischbacher, U., & Fehr, E. (2005). Oxytocin increases trust in humans. *Nature*, 435(7042), 673–76.

Kumari, M., Shipley, M., Stafford, M., & Kivimaki, M. (2011). Association of diurnal patterns in salivary cortisol with all-cause and cardiovascular mortality: findings from the Whitehall II study. *The Journal of Clinical Endocrinology & Metabolism*, 96(5), 1478–85.

Laws, H. B., Sayer, A. G., Pietromonaco, P. R., & Powers, S. I. (2015). Longitudinal changes in spouses' HPA responses: convergence in cortisol patterns during the early years of marriage. *Health Psychology*, 34(11), 1076–89

Levenson, R. W., & Gottman, J. M. (1983). Marital interaction: physiological linkage and affective exchange. *Journal of Personality and Social Psychology*, 45(3), 587.

Liu, S., Rovine, M. J., Cousino Klein, L., & Almeida, D. M. (2013). Synchrony of diurnal cortisol pattern in couples. *Journal of Family Psychology*, 27(4), 579–88.

Lykken, D. T., & Venables, P. H. (1971). Direct measurement of skin conductance: A proposal for standardization. *Psychophysiology*, 8(5), 656–72.

MacDonald, K., & MacDonald, T. M. (2010). The peptide that binds: a systematic review of oxytocin and its prosocial effects in humans. *Harvard Review of Psychiatry*, 18(1), 1–21.

Marazziti, D., Dell'Osso, B., Baroni, S., et al. (2006). A relationship between oxytocin and anxiety of romantic attachment. *Clinical Practice and Epidemiology in Mental Health*, 2(1), 28–34.

McCorry, L. K. (2007). Physiology of the autonomic nervous system. *American Journal of Pharmaceutical Education*, 71(4), 1–11.

Mooradian, A. D., Morley, J. E., & Korenman, S. G. (1987). Biological actions of androgens. *Endocrine Reviews*, 8(1), 1–28.

Murray-Close, D. (2011). Autonomic reactivity and romantic relational aggression among female emerging adults: moderating roles of social and cognitive risk. *International Journal of Psychophysiology*, 80(1), 28–35.

Murray-Close, D., Holland, A. S., & Roisman, G. I. (2012). Autonomic arousal and relational aggression in heterosexual dating couples. *Personal Relationships*, 19(2), 203–18.

Nave, G., Camerer, C., & McCullough, M. (2015). Does oxytocin increase trust in humans? A critical review of research. *Perspectives on Psychological Science*, 10(6), 772–89.

Papp, L. M., Pendry, P., Simon, C. D., & Adam, E. K. (2013). Spouses' cortisol associations and moderators: Testing physiological synchrony and connectedness in everyday life. *Family Process*, 52(2), 284–98.

Porges, S. W. (2007). The polyvagal perspective. *Biological Psychology*, 74(2), 116–43.

Porges, S. W., & Byrne, E. A. (1992). Research methods for measurement of heart rate and respiration. *Biological Psychology*, 34(2–3), 93–130.

Reed, R. G., Randall, A. K., Post, J. H., & Butler, E. A. (2013). Partner influence and in-phase versus anti-phase physiological linkage in romantic couples. *International Journal of Psychophysiology*, 88(3), 309–16.

Robles, T. F., & Kiecolt-Glaser, J. K. (2003). The physiology of marriage: pathways to health. *Physiology & Behavior*, 79(3), 409–16.

Saxbe, D. E., Adam, E. K., Schetter, C. D., et al. (2015). Cortisol covariation within parents of young children: moderation by relationship aggression. *Psychoneuroendocrinology*, 62, 121–8.

Saxbe, D. E., Edelstein, R. S., Lyden, H. M., et al. (2017). Fathers' decline in testosterone and synchrony with partner testosterone during pregnancy predicts greater postpartum relationship investment. *Hormones and Behavior*, 90, 39–47.

Saxbe, D. E., & Repetti, R. L. (2010). For better or worse? Coregulation of couples' cortisol levels and mood states. *Journal of Personality and Social Psychology*, 98(1), 92–103.

Saxbe, D. E., Repetti, R. L., & Nishina, A. (2008). Marital satisfaction, recovery from work, and diurnal cortisol among men and women. *Health Psychology*, 27(1), 15–25.

Scarpa, A., & Raine, A. (1997). Psychophysiology of anger and violent behavior. *The Psychiatric Clinics of North America*, 20(2), 375–94.

Schmidt-Nielsen, K. (1997). *Animal Physiology: Adaptation and Environment*. Cambridge, UK: Cambridge University Press.

Schneiderman, I., Kanat-Maymon, Y., Zagoory-Sharon, O., & Feldman, R. (2014). Mutual influences between partners' hormones shape conflict dialog and relationship duration at the initiation of romantic love. *Social Neuroscience*, 9(4), 337–51.

Smith, T. W., & Brown, P. C. (1991). Cynical hostility, attempts to exert social control, and cardiovascular reactivity in married couples. *Journal of Behavioral Medicine*, 14(6), 581–92.

Smith, T. W., Cribbet, M. R., Nealey-Moore, J. B., et al. (2011). Matters of the variable heart: respiratory sinus arrhythmia response to marital interaction and associations with marital quality. *Journal of Personality and Social Psychology*, 100(1), 103–19.

Smith, T. W., & Ruiz, J. M. (2002). Psychosocial influences on the development and course of coronary heart disease: current status and implications for research and practice. *Journal of Consulting and Clinical Psychology*, 70(3), 548–68.

Storey, A. E., & Ziegler, T. E. (2015). Primate paternal care: interactions between biology and social experience. *Hormones and Behavior*, 77, 260–71.

Szeto, A., McCabe, P. M., Nation, D. A., et al. (2011). Evaluation of enzyme immunoassay and radioimmunoassay methods for the measurement of plasma oxytocin. *Psychosomatic Medicine*, 73(5), 393.

Tabak, B. A., McCullough, M. E., Szeto, A., Mendez, A. J., & McCabe, P. M. (2011). Oxytocin indexes relational distress following interpersonal harms in women. *Psychoneuroendocrinology*, 36(1), 115–22.

Taylor, S. E., Gonzaga, G. C., Klein, L. C., et al. (2006). Relation of oxytocin to psychological stress responses and hypothalamic-pituitary-adrenocortical axis activity in older women. *Psychosomatic Medicine*, 68(2), 238–45.

Taylor, S. E., Saphire-Bernstein, S., & Seeman, T. E. (2010). Are plasma oxytocin in women and plasma vasopressin in men biomarkers of distressed pair-bond relationships? *Psychological Science*, 21(1), 3–7.

Thayer, J. F., & Lane, R. D. (2007). The role of vagal function in the risk for cardiovascular disease and mortality. *Biological Psychology*, 74(2), 224–2.

Timmons, A. C., Margolin, G., & Saxbe, D. E. (2015). Physiological linkage in couples and its implications for individual and interpersonal functioning: a literature review. *Journal of Family Psychology*, 29(5), 720–31.

Turner, R. A., Altemus, M., Enos, T., Cooper, B., & McGuinness, T. (1999). Preliminary research on plasma oxytocin in normal cycling women: investigating emotion and interpersonal distress. *Psychiatry*, 62(2), 97–113.

van Anders, S. M., Tolman, R. M., & Volling, B. L. (2012). Baby cries and nurturance affect testosterone in men. *Hormones and Behavior*, 61(1), 31–6

Vedhara, K., Miles, J. N., Sanderman, R., & Ranchor, A. V. (2006). Psychosocial factors associated with indices of cortisol production in women with breast cancer and controls. *Psychoneuroendocrinology*, 31(3), 299–311.

Weisman, O., Zagoory-Sharon, O., & Feldman, R. (2012). Oxytocin administration to parent enhances infant physiological and behavioral readiness for social engagement. *Biological Psychiatry*, 72(12), 982–9.

Wynne-Edwards, K. E. (2001). Hormonal changes in mammalian fathers. *Hormones and Behavior*, 40(2), 139–45.

Young, L. J., & Wang, Z. (2004). The neurobiology of pair bonding. *Nature Neuroscience*, 7(10), 1048–54.

CHAPTER 7

# Interpersonal emotion dynamics in families

*Rena L. Repetti and Galen D. McNeil*

Framing emotion as a phenomenon that exists within an individual facilitates the study of emotion expression and the isolation of emotion-eliciting stimuli, yet it is rare that in our daily lives we experience and process emotional content without another's input. In the laboratory, a picture of a pile of rotting garbage may trigger a facial expression of disgust. The subject's physiology or subjective experience of emotional intensity in response to the image can be measured. However, when taking out the rotting trash at home, the subject's disgust might be augmented by her child's whine that the kitchen stinks, or might shift into amusement as her child scrunches up his nose and stinks his tongue out at the smell. Though capturing a person's individual emotional response may tell us about some innate properties of emotion such as facial expressions and physiology, it is in studying emotional processes within personal relationships that we can better understand the role emotions play in our everyday lives.

Relationships with parents, children, siblings, and spouses or partners are particularly important, both because they are long-lasting and because they are often sources of the strongest social bonds and emotional experiences in one's lifetime. These two characteristics of family relationships – their persistence and power – magnify the impact that those emotion dynamics have on individual well-being and functioning (Repetti & Saxbe, in press). The study of interpersonal emotion dynamics locates the experience and expression of emotion within social interaction, instead of contained within an individual. From this perspective, emotions unfold in our daily lives as reciprocal sequences involving at least two people, as each one's emotional state is modified by the emotions and behavior of others. Although some models of interpersonal influence on emotion focus exclusively on the intentional pursuit of an

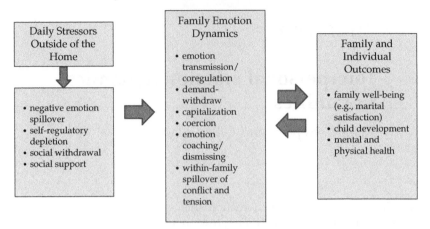

Figure 7.1. Associations among family emotion dynamics, daily stressors, and individual and family outcomes

emotion regulation goal (e.g., seeking emotional support from another), our definition does not include that constraint (cf., Zaki & Williams, 2013). We assume that many of the processes described here take place without any deliberate effort by family members. At the same time, the spread of emotion across family members is affected by experiences in the outside world. Emotion generated by events outside of the home is carried into the family and shapes day-to-day fluctuations in social and emotional behavior.

Our chapter begins with an overview of several family emotion dynamics that have been described in the psychological research literature. Most of that work uses a dyadic paradigm, focusing on marital or parent–child interactions. Some of the patterns – such as mood coregulation, emotion transmission, and spillover – involve linkage of emotion across family members. Others – such as demand-withdraw, capitalization, and emotion coaching and dismissing – describe behavioral responses to a partner's emotion expression that, in turn, influence the partner's emotion. The next major section considers how emotion in the family is affected by the members' exposure to daily stressors, and that is followed by a summary of a large body of research on links between family emotion dynamics, development, and health. Figure 7.1 presents an outline of the emotion dynamics described here and their associations with daily stressors and family and individual outcomes. The chapter concludes with recommended future directions for research.

## Emotion dynamics in the marital dyad

*Emotion transmission and mood coregulation*

Once expressed in the home, emotion rarely remains contained within the individual, rather it becomes intertwined with emotions expressed by other family members. Emotion transmission is the process through which one person's emotional state alters another's. Intensive repeated measures methods, such as daily diaries, allow researchers to track emotion frequency and directionality both within and between members of a household (Larson & Almeida, 1999). In marital relationships, this process is often bidirectional where, rather than one spouse continually influencing the other's emotional state, the partners develop a synchronous dynamic in which they regulate one another's emotional experiences. The term "coregulation" describes this dynamic in which partners experience a bidirectional linkage of emotional channels including subjective experience, expressive behavior, and autonomic physiology (Butler & Randall, 2013).

Situational factors, family characteristics, and individual differences affect the covariation of emotion and physiology between family members. Those factors include physical proximity and time spent together (Butner et al., 2007; Saxbe & Repetti, 2010; Song et al., 2008), their exposure to life stressors (Downey et al.,1999; Larson & Gillman, 1999; Thompson & Bolger, 1999), whether there are children in the family (Song et al., 2008), the spouses' marital satisfaction (Saxbe & Repetti, 2010) and whether they are coping with the same stressful event that day (Berg et al., 2011), and individual levels of interpersonal insecurity (Schoebi, 2008). Randall and Schoebi (Chapter 1) review situational, contextual, and individual variables that shape interdependent emotional changes between two partners, including family members.

In fact, much of the research highlighted in this volume centers on the study of temporal interconnections between two partners' emotions – including physiological, emotional, and behavioral indicators of emotion. This aspect of interpersonal emotion dynamics is not only at the core of the framework suggested by Randall and Schoebi (Chapter 1), but emotional covariation and emotional influencing are the key characteristics of dynamics that occur between individuals in the Sels, Ceulemans, and Kuppens' (Chapter 2) general framework. Shenhav, Hovasapian, and Campos (Chapter 9) argue that the maintenance of intimate relationships depends on emotion coordination, including transmission and synchronization processes, which then lead to convergence or divergence of the partners' emotions. Consistent with an emphasis on correlated change in partners' states, the chapters representing biological perspectives discuss the role of the serotonin system in susceptibility to partner emotion (Way & Keaveney, Chapter 5), and physiological linkages in systems such as the hypothalamic-pituitary-adrenal axis and the autonomic nervous system (Saxbe, Lyden, Corner, Stoycos, & Khaled, Chapter 6). The two methodological chapters also share this focus: one presents an overview of methods to study real time interdependencies of emotion parameters in two partners (Lougheed & Hollenstein, Chapter 4), and the other demonstrates a graphical approach to model the coupling of two partners' heart rates (Butner, Crenshaw, Munion, Wong & Baucom, Chapter 3). In addition to studies of temporal links between family members' emotions, our chapter calls attention to patterns of family interaction that are defined by the behaviors that modify another member's emotions.

## Demand/withdraw

In close relationships, a partner influences not only the emotions experienced but also the expression of those emotions. Spouses develop styles of expression in response to each other's emotions that become ingrained in the marital dynamic. One prominent sequence observed during conflictual interactions is the demand/withdraw pattern (Wile, 1981): a spouse (typically the woman in heterosexual couples) demands more emotional engagement from the other spouse, and that partner responds by withdrawing from the conflict (Christensen & Heavey, 1990). The withdrawal response further fuels the conflict and increases the wife's desire and demands for engagement, which causes the husband to continue to avoid the conflict and withdraw more. Though both partners become angry, their expression of that anger is shaped by the other's reaction. This pattern continues as couples move into later stages of life but with both husbands and wives becoming more avoidant (Holley et al., 2013). Though older couples continue to express anger in the demand/withdraw pattern, they are more likely to actively avoid conflict by changing the subject or agreeing to disagree.

Recent research on same-sex couples suggests that the demand/withdraw pattern is commonly found in gay and lesbian couples, and thus not bound to gender roles (Holley et al., 2010). These authors highlight differential power in the relationship, rather than gender, to explain the roles that the partners assume: the partner with less power uses demand behaviors to bring about desired change and the higher-powered partner responds by withdrawing in order to maintain the status quo.

*Capitalization*

In addition to escalations of anger, spouses also enhance each other's positive emotion. The sharing of positive events in one's life with a partner – known as capitalization – improves the mood of both partners. Both disclosing a positive event and being on the receiving end of a positive disclosure is pleasurable (Hicks & Diamond, 2008). The type of response a partner has to the other's positive event can further its impact of the event leading to even more positivity than the original event evoked. For example, Gable et al. (2004) found that married individuals with spouses who provide active and constructive responses to positive events experienced greater intimacy as well as greater daily relationship satisfaction and fewer daily conflicts. Capitalization provides the opportunity to relive the positive event, to hear how the other is pleased for you and to experience that partner's pride in your accomplishment (Langston, 1994).

## Emotion dynamics in the parent–child dyad

*Emotion transmission*

"Dyadic synchrony" is a style of parent–child interaction, most often used to describe mother–infant dyads, that is characterized by mutual responsiveness, the matching of affective states ("affect attunement"), and a coordinated smooth flow of affect and behavior (Harrist & Waugh, 2002). Although most studies of dyadic synchrony in parent–child dyads focus on expressions of positive emotion, there is evidence for transmission of both positive and negative emotion, including in families with school-age children and adolescents. Intensive repeated measures studies examine whether changes in an individual's mood can be predicted by a family members' mood. A number of studies using this paradigm have shown mood synchrony in mother–child dyads, including the transmission of both positive and negative emotion from mothers to their adolescent children (Downey et al., 1999; Larson & Gillman, 1999; Matjasko & Feldman, 2005). Child transmission of emotion to parents has been observed in some investigations (Larson & Richards, 1994; Parker, 2016), but not all (Larson & Gillman, 1999). Interestingly, it is not evident that parent–child emotion synchrony extends to fathers. In one study there was no emotion transmission from fathers to their adolescent children (Matjasko & Feldman, 2005). In addition to naturalistic designs, linkages in family members' emotions, behavior, and physiology are studied in laboratory settings. For example, during a family conflict task mothers' cortisol levels were predicted by their children's earlier cortisol levels, but the children's cortisol levels were predicted by their fathers' earlier cortisol; fathers' cortisol levels were predicted by their wives' cortisol (Saxbe et al., 2014).

## Parent responses to child emotion

Separate from the possibility of emotion transmission, there is no question that family members' responses help to direct and shape children's expressions of emotion in the family. Champion, Ha, and Dishion (Chapter 8) conceptualize coercion as an interpersonal emotion dynamic observed in parent–child dyads. In coercive exchanges a parent inadvertently rewards a child's aversive behavior (e.g., a temper tantrum). The child's expression of negative emotion may be maintained by positive reinforcement (e.g., the child receives attention from parent) or negative reinforcement (e.g., the parent stops demanding that the child complete a task) (Patterson, 2016). Displays of positive emotion also can be reinforced by parents' rewarding responses, such as smiles (Cole et al., 2004; Morris et al., 2007). The Center on the Everyday Lives of Families (CELF) recorded families as they went about their daily lives over the course of a week. An analysis of parent–child interactions showed that the odds of a child sustaining a spontaneous expression of positive emotion were higher if a sibling or parent was also displaying positive emotion or if a family member was touching the child (Bai et al., 2016). Parent responses to negative emotions are sometimes grouped into "coaching" behaviors, which label and validate the distressing emotions and engage children in problem-solving, versus "dismissing" behaviors, which minimize anger and sadness and view both the emotions and the circumstances that gave rise to them as conditions that should be changed quickly (Gottman et al., 1996). Dismissing responses – such as ignoring, minimizing statements, and punishment – are often viewed as detrimental to family emotion dynamics. Although some verbally dismissing responses may reinforce and exacerbate negative emotion (Anastopoulos et al., 1993; Pearl, 2009), others, such as ignoring the emotion, may encourage the development of self-soothing and coping strategies. In the CELF observational study, most child displays of negative emotion were fairly mild in intensity. In this context, the most common parent response was to ignore the expression, which increased the likelihood of the child switching to a neutral or positive expression. In contrast, verbally dismissive responses, such as critical and negative statements, prolonged the negative emotion (Sperling & Repetti, 2018).

## Within-family spillover of conflict and tension

Another emotion dynamic observed in families is a "leakage" of irritability and conflict from one dyad to another dyad. Anger, aggression and hostility between marital partners are associated with the use of more harsh discipline with children and less parental acceptance (Krishnakumar & Buehler, 2000). For example, spouses who express more verbal and nonverbal anger and hostility toward each other are also observed behaving in a less sensitive manner toward their children (Klausli & Tresch Owen, 2011). The processes that underlie these associations, sometimes referred to as within-family spillover, have been investigated by testing short-term sequential associations between the experience of conflict and tension in one dyad and behavior in the other. For example, following a conflict discussion between spouses, fathers showed less support and were more withdrawn with their sons (Kitzmann, 2000). Margolin et al. (1996) found that tensions and conflicts spilled-over from the marital dyad to the parent–child dyad both within and across days, and there was also tension spillover between parent-child and sibling dyads. Similar associations were reported in a daily diary study: adolescents were more likely to argue with their parents on days when the parents reported marital arguments (Chung et al., 2009). Both mothers and fathers in another study were more likely to report tense interactions with their children if there had been marital tension the previous day; there was also evidence of tension spillover from father–child interactions to next-day marital interactions (Almeida et al., 1999).

Consistent with the patterns described above, a recent diary study reported evidence of same-day spillover of conflict between marital and parent–child dyads in both directions: marital conflicts predicted more anger and frictional behavior with children, and parent–child conflicts predicted more anger and frictional behavior with the spouse. The effects were observed with independent reporters describing parent–child and marital interactions (e.g., child-reports of mother–child conflict predicted husband-reports of wife frictional marital behavior). In addition, the observed linkages were partially mediated by negative mood (Sears et al., 2016a). Thus, there is now a reliable body of evidence indicating that the persistence and carryover of negative emotion causes conflict to spread from one family dyad to another.

## The impact of daily stress on family emotion dynamics

Besides the stress caused by conflict with a family member, an individual's exposure to other types of stressful events can act as a force that affects their expression of emotion within the family system. We focus our discussion here on the short-term effects of common daily stressors, particularly those arising outside of the family, such as overload or distressing social interactions at work. This line of research is based on the observation that the emotional impact of a stressful event is not immediately eliminated as soon as the stressor is removed or the individual exits the situation. An emotional residue that persists can color perceptions and shape behavior in subsequent social settings. The separation – in time and in space – of the experience of the stressor from the expression of emotion in the family, helps us to understand the influence that one has on the other. As summarized below, researchers have found that stress-related emotional states generated outside of the home can be transferred into the family.

*Mediators of the daily effects of stress on family emotion dynamics*

Negative mood spillover refers to expressions of impatience, frustration, and irritability at home resulting directly from negative mood generated in a different setting, such as the workplace (Repetti et al., 2009). For example, a two-week study of low income mothers and their preschool-age children found that on days with more supervisor criticism mothers described more harsh interactions with their preschool-aged children (Gassman-Pines, 2011). Another study found that fathers of school-aged children increased their expressions of anger and use of disciplinary tactics, such as yelling and punishing, after more socially stressful days at work (Repetti, 1994). Other investigations have found increases in anger and conflict during marital interactions following high stress days at work (Schulz et al., 2004; Story & Repetti, 2006). There is even evidence that stressors exacerbate the transmission of tensions between marital and parent–child dyads. In one daily diary study, fathers were more than twice as likely to experience a spillover of tensions from interactions with their wives to interactions with their children on days when they reported other stressors, such as work overloads (Almeida et al., 1999).

The data suggest that negative moods originating outside of the home do sometimes persist when the employed family member returns home; and those spillover effects at least partially account for increases in expressions of anger with spouses and with children (Story & Repetti, 2006). Other mediators have also been examined. In a sample of newlyweds, self-regulatory depletion, including reports of fatigue and mental preoccupation, accounted for increases in negative behaviors (such as expressions of anger, impatience, criticism, blame) on high-stress days (Buck & Neff, 2012). Evidence from a 56-day daily diary study of stress and marital interaction indicated that, in addition to negative mood acting as a mediator, a spouse's fatigue and desire to be alone also accounted for increases in expressions of anger and disregard of the partner's needs on busier and more demanding days (Sears et al., 2016b).

At the same time, family members actively strive to recover from, and cope with, the lingering emotional, cognitive, and physical effects of stressors, and those efforts also change the family's emotion dynamics. For instance, social withdrawal – an overall reduction in expression of emotion and social engagement – is another common short-term response to increases in daily job stress (Story & Repetti, 2006). In one study, air traffic controllers were more emotionally and socially withdrawn from their wives and children after busier and more demanding days at the airport (work shifts marked by lower visibility and more air traffic volume; Repetti, 1989, 1994). In another study, mothers were observed speaking less and engaging in fewer caring and loving/warm behaviors with their preschoolers following more stressful days at work (Repetti & Wood, 1997). Daily stressor effects on family emotion dynamics may even carry over into the next day. In the two-week study mentioned above, supervisor criticisms were followed by declines in warm mother–child interactions on the following day (Gassman-Pines, 2011). A social withdrawal response may be a coping strategy, a way to avoid the direct expression of negative emotion generated earlier in the day.

Children's exposures to stressors at school may also shape day-to-day changes in emotion expression in the family. Children describe themselves as more demanding and difficult at home, and they report more conflict with parents, on days when they experienced more difficulties at school, such as academic or peer problems (Bai et al., 2017; Chung et al., 2011; Lehman & Repetti, 2007; Repetti, 1996; Timmons & Margolin, 2015). The impact of stressors has been primarily observed in how children perceive their family's daily emotion dynamics. Unlike the studies of parents' work stress, there is less consistent evidence when other family members are asked to describe the child's behavior. One pattern that is consistent with the adult literature is the role of negative mood as a mediator. Changes in children's depressed, anxious, and distressed mood states at least partially account for daily links between negative school events and their perceptions of family interactions (Bai et al., 2017; Chung et al., 2011; Lehman & Repetti, 2007; Timmons & Margolin, 2015).

## Long-term effects of chronic stressors on family emotion dynamics

The daily effects of stressors on emotion expression in the family may cumulate over time so that chronic stress influences more stable patterns of emotion dynamics. This phenomenon is reflected in the association between chronic job stressors and emotional qualities of the parent–child relationship; the effects may be particularly salient among fathers. For example, mothers' ratings of a more negative interpersonal atmosphere at work predicted less sensitive mother–infant and father–infant interactions 3 months later, as well as more intrusive father–infant interactions (Costigan et al., 2003). In another observational study, fathers employed in less supportive work environments were less engaged and less sensitive with their infants (Goodman et al., 2008). The effects extend to older children as well: fathers' relationships with their teenage children were less positive and more conflictive if the fathers worked longer hours and reported more role overload (Crouter et al., 2001).

There is also evidence of adaptive responses to daily stressors that have positive effects on the family. For example, a spouse may take steps to accommodate an employed partner who is experiencing chronic stress. Videos of daily family life from the CELF study showed that the wives who reported higher levels of job stress received more social support from their husbands than did the wives employed in low-stress jobs. The association was explained both by the high-stress wives soliciting more support and by their husbands making more offers of support (Wang & Repetti, 2014).

*Individual and family differences in the effects of daily stress on family emotion dynamics*

Of course, not all families are affected by stress in the same way. One study identified significant individual differences in responses to daily overload and those differences were related to both the individual's and the spouse's level of marital satisfaction. For instance, husbands with lower marital satisfaction were more likely to express anger on stressful days (Sears et al., 2016b). Other individual and family characteristics, such as levels of depression and family conflict, also act as moderators of short-term spillover effects (Repetti & Wood, 1997; Schulz et al., 2004; Story & Repetti, 2006). The CELF study uncovered two patterns of emotional behavior associated with fathers' exposure to job stress. Fathers who reported more job stress and scored high on a measure of trait neuroticism were observed expressing more negative emotion during interactions with spouses and with children; the low neuroticism-high stress fathers expressed low levels of negative emotion (Wang et al., 2011).

To summarize, stressful experiences outside of the home can have lingering effects on an individual's emotional state and be carried back into the family, where they influence interactions with other members. With chronic exposure to daily stressors, repetitions of these carryover patterns may shape more stable relationship dynamics in the family.

## Family emotion dynamics and individual functioning

Emotion dynamics are an important indicator of a family's well-being and have implications for the development and health of its members. It is not surprising that couples who express more anger, have more disagreements, or show less affection also report that they are less satisfied with their marriages (Sears et al., 2016b). The demand-withdraw pattern is linked with greater marital distress (Eldridge et al., 2007) and capitalization is associated with more relationship satisfaction (Gable et al., 2006). (See Sels, Ceulemans, & Kuppens (Chapter 2) for further discussion of the association between interpersonal emotion dynamics and both relational and psychological adjustment.)

Beyond affecting the quality of family life, certain types of emotion dynamics have an impact on children's emotional, social, and physiological development. Repeated physiological/neuroendocrine and emotional/behavioral responses to high levels of family conflict and aggression and cold, unsupportive, or neglectful relationships can, over time, give rise to heightened physiological and emotional reactivity to stress (Repetti et al., 2002). For example, chronic exposure to anger and conflict may sensitize children to anger, so that they react with greater distress, anger, anxiety, and fear. Compared to other children, they appear to be hyperprepared for threats and hyperresponsive to those threats, which may contribute to their increased physiological reactivity (Repetti et al., 2011). Emotion regulation refers to altering the trajectory of an emotion, by decreasing or increasing its magnitude or duration (Gross, 2015). The emotion modeled by parents helps to socialize the way that children regulate positive and negative emotion (Denham et al., 2014). For example, children express more positive emotion when their parents show more positive emotion expressivity (Halberstadt & Eaton, 2002; Sallquist et al., 2010), responsiveness (Davidov & Grusec, 2006), and warmth (Zhou et al., 2002).

Mental and physical health are also influenced by emotion in the family (Repetti et al., 2002). Distress and conflict in parents' marital relationships are associated with a range of adjustment problems in children; and the link between couple hostility and child mental health appears to be mediated by emotion in the parent–child dyad, specifically high levels of conflict, harshness, and hostility (Bradford et al., 2008). Some parent responses to children's expressions of anger, fear, and sadness can reinforce those emotions and contribute to risk for the development of psychopathology (Klimes-Dougan et al., 2007). An intervention that successfully taught parents strategies like identifying and empathizing with children's negative emotions resulted in a decline in children's behavior problems compared to a control group (Havighurst et al., 2010). Parents' reactions to positive emotion also matter. Less accepting and more min-imizing or disapproving responses to displays of positive emotions are associated with more symptoms of depression in adolescents (Katz et al., 2014; Yap et al., 2008). In contrast, dyadic synchrony, which includes recip-rocation of positive emotion and mutual responsiveness, is linked with fewer behavioral problems and greater social competence in children (Deater-Deckard & Petrill, 2004; Harrist & Waugh, 2002; Lunkenheimer et al., 2011).

The impact of family emotion dynamics extends to the adult members of the household too. Frequent arguments, and a spouse's hostile, insult-ing and demeaning behaviors take a toll on the physical and mental health of marital partners (Kiecolt-Glaser & Newton, 2001). A meta-analysis of both cross-sectional and prospective longitudinal studies showed that these signs of marital distress are reliably associated with a very wide range of objective indicators of a poor health, as well as heightened risk for all-cause mortality and early mortality (Robles et al., 2013). Discord with a spouse also predicts both the onset and the course of depression (Beach & Whisman, 2012; Proulx et al., 2007), and depression may medi-ate the effects that discord has on physical health (Kiecolt-Glaser et al., 2002). In a study that combined diary and longitudinal data, susceptibil-ity to a partner's emotions, as indicated by reductions in negative affect in the response to partner positive affect, predicted declines in depressive symptoms over 12 months (Randall & Schoebi, 2015).

At the same time that individuals are affected by their family's emo-tion dynamics, their mental and physical health also contribute to emo-tion expression at home. The "stress generation" model of depression describes a cycle in which symptoms of depression both create and exacerbate interpersonal problems, including in the spousal relationship (Davila et al., 1997). Therefore, it is not surprising that a history of a major depressive disorder increases risk for a more distressed marriage in the future (Kiecolt-Glaser et al., 2002). Children's problematic behaviors also act on a family's emotional climate. For example, negative emotional reactivity in children predicts increases in marital conflict (Schermerhorn et al., 2007). In one study, misbehaviors displayed by children with dis-ruptive behavior problems predicted subsequent parenting behavior more strongly than parenting predicted children's subsequent behav-ior (Pettit & Arsiwalla, 2008). Furthermore, chronic physical illness – whether in a spouse or child – and the worry and caregiving demands that it entails can also act as a stressor on families (Repetti & Saxbe, in press). In short, there is strong evidence of reciprocal linkages between the expression of emotion in a family and the psychological and physical functioning of its members.

## Promising directions for research on family emotion dynamics

A variety of research literatures in psychology contribute to our understanding of family emotion dynamics. Our review suggests that each subfield has its own favored conceptualizations of emotion, research designs, and methodologies. We advocate three strategies for future research that would leverage the power of the different theoretical and empirical approaches by combining them in multimethod studies. First, we note that there are striking differences in the way that emotion is construed and assessed in different subfields within psychology. Emotion researchers assess specific behaviors associated with distinct emotions (e.g., disgust, pride, gratitude), whereas family researchers tend to rely on self-report measures of broadly defined states of positive and negative mood. Although the designs that predominate in the two literatures differ – one largely characterized by experiments in laboratory settings, the other by correlational studies – we believe integrating a more differentiated conceptualization of emotions would strengthen the study of family emotion dynamics. For example, differentiating between sadness and anger may better explain when negative emotion transmission represents an empathic process and when it represents antagonism between partners. Future research could also assess how specific positive emotions, such as compassion and gratitude, may be transmitted between family members.

The social and emotional processes described in this chapter, such as spillover and emotion transmission, take place over seconds, minutes, or days, but as they are repeated again and again in families the patterns can become ingrained, as evidenced by their correlations with stable individual and family difference variables. Our second suggestion is to embed assessments of family emotion dynamics at multiple time points in prospective longitudinal designs in order to examine how those short-term processes become more lasting characteristics of a family. The fact that major life transitions, such as the birth of a first child, can change the emotional tone in a family suggests that some patterns may share common developmental trajectories (Campos et al., 2013). Moreover, investigations that repeatedly assess short-term processes over the course of years would advance our understanding of how family emotion dynamics gradually shape individuals and their health (Repetti et al., 2015).

The research reviewed here shows how much we can learn from observations of marital and parent–child dyads in laboratory settings and from self-reports of behavior in natural settings, particularly the use of intensive repeated measures. Our third recommendation is that these two approaches be integrated with more direct observational methods incorporated into naturalistic studies of family emotion dynamics. The CELF study, which was mentioned at several points in the chapter, illustrates how naturalistic observations can provide new perspectives on emotion dynamics in the family. The video recordings contain situations that cannot be duplicated in a laboratory and reveal nuances in behavior that cannot be captured through self-report methods. For example, an examination of diurnal patterns of spontaneous emotion expression uncovered a dip in mothers' positive emotion during the evening hours (Campos et al., 2013). Another analysis of the CELF data archive showed that, while positive and affectionate behaviors were common in parent–child reunions at the end of the work and school day, fathers – who tended to return home later than mothers – were more likely to be ignored by their children or greeted in a distracted manner (Campos et al., 2009). It is only by combining different approaches that we can begin to integrate insights based on how family members describe their behavior, how they act in controlled settings and how they behave in their everyday lives.

The emotion dynamics that characterize interactions with spouses, children, siblings, and parents are unique in a number of important ways. Patterns like emotion transmission and synchrony, demand/withdraw, capitalization, coercion, emotion coaching, and emotion dismissing are repeated with the same people in the same shared setting on a daily basis. And the impact of interactions with any single partner is magnified by spreading to other dyads, as illustrated by studies of within-family spillover of anger and conflict. Family members' lives are truly interlaced; the research reviewed in this chapter indicates that even their separate daily experiences in the outside world influence each other's emotional experience at home. It is no wonder that emotion dynamics within family systems have lifelong repercussions for the health and development of all members.

## References

Almeida, D. M., Wethington, E., & Chandler, A. L. (1999). Daily transmission of tensions between marital dyads and parent–child dyads. *Journal of Marriage and the Family*, 61(1), 49–61.

Anastopoulos, A. D., Shelton, T. L., DuPaul, G. J., & Guevremont, D. C. (1993). Parent training for attention-deficit hyperactivity disorder: Its impact on parent functioning. *Journal of Abnormal Child Psychology*, 21(5), 581–96.

Bai, S., Repetti, R. L., & Sperling, J. (2016). Children's expressions of positive emotion are sustained by smiling, touching and playing with parents and siblings: A naturalistic observational study of family life. *Developmental Psychology*, 52, 88–101.

Bai, S., Reynolds, B. M., Robles, T. F., & Repetti, R. L. (2017). Daily links between school problems and youth perceptions of interactions with parents: A diary study of school-to-home spillover. *Social Development*, 26, 813–30.

Beach, S. R. H., & Whisman, M. A. (2012). Affective disorders. *Journal of Marital and Family Therapy*, 38, 201–19.

Berg, C. A., Wiebe, D. J., & Butner, J. (2011). Affect covariation in marital couples dealing with stressors surrounding prostate cancer. *Gerontology*, 57, 167–72.

Bradford, K., Vaughn, L. B., & Barber, B. K. (2008). When there is conflict: Interparental conflict, parent–child conflict, and youth problem behaviors. *Journal of Family Issues*, 29(6), 780–805.

Buck, A. A., & Neff, L. A. (2012). Stress spillover in early marriage: The role of self-regulatory depletion. *Journal of Family Psychology*, 26(5), 698–708.

Butler, E. A., & Randall, A. K. (2013). Emotional coregulation in close relationships. *Emotion Review*, 5(2), 202–10.

Butner, J., Diamond, L. M., & Hicks, A. M. (2007). Attachment style and two forms of affect coregulation between romantic partners. *Personal Relationships*, 14, 431–55.

Campos, B., Graesch, A. P., Repetti, R., Bradbury T., & Ochs, E. (2009). Opportunity for interaction? A naturalistic observation study of dual-earner families after work and school. *Journal of Family Psychology*, 23(6), 798–807.

Campos, B., Wang, S. W., Plaksina, T., et al. (2013). Positive and negative emotion in the daily life of dual-earner couples with children. *Journal of Family Psychology*, 27(1), 76.

Christensen, A., & Heavey, C. L. (1990). Gender and social structure in the demand/withdraw pattern of marital conflict. *Journal of Personality and Social Psychology*, 59(1), 73.

Chung, G. H., Flook, L., & Fuligni, A. J. (2009). Daily family conflict and emotional distress among adolescents from Latin American, Asian, and European backgrounds. *Developmental Psychology*, 45(5), 1406.

(2011). Reciprocal associations between family and peer conflict in adolescents' daily lives. *Child Development*, 82(5), 1390–6.

Cole, P. M., Martin, S. E., & Dennis, T. A. (2004). Emotion regulation as a scientific construct: Methodological challenges and directions for child development research. *Child Development*, 75(2), 317–33.

Costigan, C. L., Cox, M. J., & Cauce, A. M. (2003). Work-parenting linkages among dual-earner couples at the transition to parenthood. *Journal of Family Psychology*, 17, 397–408.

Crouter, A. C., Bumpus, M. F., Head, M. R., & McHale, S. M. (2001). Implications of overwork and overload for the quality of men's family relationships. *Journal of Marriage and the Family*, 63, 404–16.

Davidov, M., & Grusec, J. E. (2006). Untangling the links of parental responsiveness to distress and warmth to child outcomes. *Child Development*, 77(1), 44–58.

Davila, J., Bradbury, T. N., Cohan, C. L., & Tochluk, S. (1997). Marital functioning and depressive symptoms: Evidence for a stress generation model. *Journal of Personality and Social Psychology*, 73, 849–61.

Deater-Deckard, K., & Petrill, S. A. (2004). Parent–child dyadic mutuality and child behavior problems: An investigation of gene–environment processes. *Journal of Child Psychology and Psychiatry*, 45(6), 1171–9.

Denham, S.A., Bassett, H. H., & Wyatt, T. (2014). The socialization of emotional competence. In J. Grusec. & P. Hastings (Eds.) *Handbook of Socialization: Theory and Research* (2nd edn.) (pp. 590–613). New York, NY: The Guilford Press.

Downey, G., Purdie, V., & Schaffer-Neitz, R. (1999). Anger transmission from mother to child: A comparison of mothers in chronic pain and well mothers. *Journal of Marriage and the Family*, 61, 62–73.

Eldridge, K. A., Sevier, M., Jones, J., Atkins, D. C., & Christensen, A. (2007). Demand-withdraw communication in severely distressed, moderately distressed, and nondistressed couples: Rigidity and polarity during relationship and personal problem discussions. *Journal of Family Psychology*, 21(2), 218.

Gable, S. L., Gonzaga, G. C., & Strachman, A. (2006). Will you be there for me when things go right? Supportive responses to positive event disclosures. *Journal of Personality and Social Psychology*, 91(5), 904.

Gable, S. L., Reis, H. T., Impett, E. A., & Asher, E. R. (2004). What do you do when things go right? The intrapersonal and interpersonal benefits of sharing positive events. *Journal of Personality and Social Psychology*, 87(2), 228.

Gassman-Pines, A. (2011). Associations of low-income working mothers' daily interactions with supervisors and mother-child interactions. *Journal of Marriage and Family*, 73, 67–76.

Goodman, W. B., Crouter, A. C., Lanza, S. T., & Cox, M. J. (2008). Paternal work characteristics and father-infant interactions in low-income, rural families. *Journal of Marriage and Family*, 70, 640–53.

Gottman, J. M., Katz, L. F., & Hooven, C. (1996). Parental meta-emotion philosophy and the emotional life of families: Theoretical models and preliminary data. *Journal of Family Psychology*, 10(3), 243.

Gross, J. J. (2015). Emotion regulation: conceptual and empirical foundations. In J. Gross (Ed.) *Handbook of Emotion Regulation* (2nd edn.) (pp. 3–22). New York, NY: The Guilford Press.

Halberstadt, A. G., & Eaton, K. L. (2002). A meta-analysis of family expressiveness and children's emotion expressiveness and understanding. *Marriage & Family Review*, 34(1–2), 35–62.

Harrist, A. W., & Waugh, R. M. (2002). Dyadic synchrony: Its structure and function in children's development. *Developmental Review*, 22(4), 555–92.

Havighurst, S. S., Wilson, K. R., Harley, A. E., Prior, M. R., & Kehoe, C. (2010). Tuning in to kids: Improving emotion socialization practices from a community trial. *Journal of Child Psychology and Psychiatry*, 51(12), 1342–50.

Hicks, A. M., & Diamond, L. M. (2008). How was your day? Couples' affect when telling and hearing daily events. *Personal Relationships*, 15(2), 205–28.

Holley, S. R., Haase, C. M., & Levenson, R. W. (2013). Age-related changes in demand-withdraw communication behaviors. *Journal of Marriage and Family*, 75(4), 822–36.

Holley, S. R., Sturm, V. E., & Levenson, R. W. (2010). Exploring the basis for gender differences in the demand-withdraw pattern. *Journal of Homosexuality*, 57(5), 666–84.

Katz, L. F., Shortt, J. W., Allen, N. B., et al. (2014). Parental emotion socialization in clinically depressed adolescents: Enhancing and dampening positive affect. *Journal of Abnormal Child Psychology*, 42(2), 205–15.

Kiecolt-Glaser, J. K., McGuire, L., Robles, T. F., & Glaser, R. (2002). Emotions, morbidity, and mortality: New perspectives from psychoneuroimmunology. *Annual Review of Psychology*, 53, 83–107.

Kiecolt-Glaser, J. K., & Newton, T. L. (2001). Marriage and health: his and hers. *Psychological Bulletin*, 127(4), 472–503.

Kitzmann, K. M. (2000). Effects of marital conflict on subsequent triadic family interactions and parenting. *Developmental Psychology*, 36(1), 3.

Klausli, J. F., & Tresch Owen, M. (2011). Exploring actor and partner effects in associations between marriage and parenting for mothers and fathers. *Parenting*, 11(4), 264–79.

Klimes-Dougan, B., Brand, A. E., Zahn-Waxler, C., et al. (2007). Parental emotion socialization in adolescence: Differences in sex, age, and problem status. *Social Development*, 16(2), 326–42.

Krishnakumar, A., & Buehler, C. (2000). Interparental conflict and parenting behaviors: a meta-analytic review. *Family Relations*, 49(1), 25–44.

Langston, C. A. (1994). Capitalizing on and coping with daily-life events: Expressive responses to positive events. *Journal of Personality and Social Psychology*, 67(6), 1112.

Larson, R. W., & Almeida, D. M. (1999). Emotional transmission in the daily lives of families: A new paradigm for studying family process. *Journal of Marriage and the Family*, 61, 5–20.

Larson, R. W., & Gillman, S. (1999). Transmission of emotions in the daily interactions of single-mother families. *Journal of Marriage and the Family*, 61, 21–37.

Larson, R. W., & Richards, M. H. (1994). Family emotions: Do young adolescents and their parents experience the same states? *Journal of Research on Adolescence*, 4(4), 567–83.

Lehman, B. J., & Repetti, R. L. (2007). Bad days don't end when the school bell rings: the lingering effects of negative school events on children's mood, self-esteem, and perceptions of parent-child interaction. *Social Development*, 16(3), 596–618.

Lunkenheimer, E. S., Olson, S. L., Hollenstein, T., Sameroff, A. J., & Winter, C. (2011). Dyadic flexibility and positive affect in parent–child coregulation and the development of child behavior problems. *Development and Psychopathology*, 23(2), 577–591.

Margolin, G., Christensen, A., & John, R. S. (1996). The continuance and spillover of everyday tensions in distressed and nondistressed families. *Journal of Family Psychology*, 10(3), 304.

Matjasko, J. L., & Feldman, A. F. (2005). Emotional transmission between parents and adolescents: The importance of work characteristics and relationship quality. In B. Schneider & L. J. Waite (Eds.), *Being Together, Working*

*Apart: Dual-Career Families and the Work-Life Balance* (pp. 138–58). New York, NY: Cambridge University Press.

Morris, A. S., Silk, J. S., Steinberg, L., Myers, S. S., & Robinson, L. R. (2007). The role of the family context in the development of emotion regulation. *Social Development*, 16(2), 361–88.

Parker, D. M. (2016). *In Sync: Daily Mood and Diurnal Cortisol Synchronization between Pre-adolescents and Their Mothers and Fathers* (Unpublished doctoral dissertation). University of California Los Angeles, California.

Patterson, G. R. (2016). Coercion theory: The study of change. In T. J. Dishion & J. Snyder (Eds.), *The Oxford Handbook of Coercive Relationship Dynamics* (pp. 7–22). New York, NY: Oxford University Press.

Pearl, E., (2009). Parent management training for reducing oppositional and aggressive behavior in preschoolers. *Aggression and Violence*, 14(5), 295–305.

Pettit, G. S., & Arsiwalla, D. D. (2008). Commentary on special section on "Bidirectional parent–child relationships": The continuing evolution of dynamic, transactional models of parenting and youth behavior problems. *Journal of Abnormal Child Psychology*, 36(5), 711–18.

Proulx, C. M., Helms, H. M., & Buehler, C. (2007). Marital quality and personal well-being: A Meta-analysis. *Journal of Marriage and Family*, 69(3), 576–93.

Randall, A. K. & Schoebi, D. (2015). Lean on me: Susceptibility to partner affect attenuates psychological distress over a 12-month period. *Emotion*, 15, 201–10.

Repetti, R. L. (1989). Effects of daily workload on subsequent behavior during marital interaction: The roles of social withdrawal and spouse support. *Journal of Personality and Social Psychology*, 57(4), 651–9.

(1994). Short-term and long-term processes linking job stressors to father-child interaction. *Social Development*, 3(1), 1–15.

(1996). The effects of perceived daily social and academic failure experiences on school-age children's subsequent interactions with parents. *Child Development*, 67(4), 1467–82.

Repetti, R. L., Reynolds, B. M., & Sears, M. S. (2015). Families under the microscope: Repeated sampling of perceptions, experiences, biology and behavior. *Journal of Marriage and Family*, 77, 126–46.

Repetti, R., Robles, T., & Reynolds, B. (2011). Allostatic processes in the family. *Development and Psychopathology*, 23, 921–38.

Repetti, R.L. & Saxbe, D.E. (in press, 2019). The influence of chronic family stressors on adult health. In B. Fiese (Ed.), *APA Handbook of Contemporary Family Psychology: Volume 2. Applications and Broad Impact of Family Psychology*.

Repetti, R. L., Taylor, S. E., & Seeman, T. (2002). Risky families: family social environments and the mental and physical health of offspring. *Psychological Bulletin*, 128, 330–66.

Repetti, R. L., Wang, S., & Saxbe, D. (2009). Bringing it all back home: How outside stressors shape families' everyday lives. *Current Directions in Psychological Science*, 18(2), 106–11.

Repetti, R. L., & Wood, J. (1997). The effects of daily stress at work on mothers' interactions with preschoolers. *Journal of Family Psychology*, 11, 90–108.

Robles, T. F., Slatcher, R. B., Trombello, J. M., & McGinn, M. M. (2013). Marital quality and health: A meta-analytic review. *Psychological Bulletin*, 140, 140–87.

Sallquist, J., Eisenberg, N., Spinrad, T. L., et al. (2010). Mothers' and children's positive emotion: Relations and trajectories across four years. *Social Development*, 19(4), 799–821.

Saxbe, D. E., Margolin, G., Spies Shapiro, L., et al. (2014). Relative influences: Patterns of HPS axis concordance during triadic family interaction. *Health Psychology*, 33(3), 273–81.

Saxbe, D., & Repetti, R. L. (2010). For better or worse? Coregulation of couples' cortisol levels and mood states. *Journal of Personality and Social Psychology*, 98(1), 92.

Schermerhorn, A. C., Cummings, E. M., DeCarlo, C. A., & Davies, P. T. (2007). Children's influence in the marital relationship. *Journal of Family Psychology*, 21(2), 259–69.

Schoebi, D. (2008). The coregulation of daily affect in marital relationships. *Journal of Family Psychology*, 22(4), 595.

Schulz, M. S., Cowan, P. A., Cowan, C. P., & Brennan, R. T. (2004). Coming home upset: Gender, marital satisfaction and the daily spillover of workday experience into couple interactions. *Journal of Family Psychology*, 18, 250–63.

Sears, M. S., Repetti, R. L., Reynolds, B. M., Robles, T. F., & Krull, J. L. (2016a). Spillover in the home: The effects of family conflict on parents' behavior. *Journal of Marriage and Family*, 78(1), 127–41.

Sears, M. S., Repetti, R. L., Robles, T. F., & Reynolds, B. M. (2016b). I just want to be left alone: Daily overload and marital behavior. *Journal of Family Psychology*, 30, 569–79.

Song, Z., Foo, M. D., & Uy, M. A. (2008). Mood spillover and crossover among dual-earner couples: A cell phone event sampling study. *Journal of Applied Psychology*, 93, 443–52.

Sperling, J. & Repetti, R. L. (2018). Understanding emotion socialization through naturalistic observations of parent-child interactions. *Family Relations*, 67, 325–38.

Story, L. B. & Repetti, R. L. (2006). Daily occupational stressors and marital behavior. *Journal of Family Psychology*, 20(4), 690–700.

Thompson, A., & Bolger, N. (1999). Emotional transmission in couples under stress. *Journal of Marriage and the Family*, 61, 38–48.

Timmons, A. C., & Margolin, G. (2015). Family conflict, mood, and adolescents' daily school problems: Moderating roles of internalizing and externalizing symptoms. *Child Development*, 86, 241–58.

Wang, S., & Repetti, R. L. (2014). Psychological well-being and job stress predict marital support interactions: A naturalistic observational study of dual-earner couples in their homes. *Journal of Personality and Social Psychology*, 107, 864–78.

Wang, S., Repetti, R. L., & Campos, B. (2011). Job stress and family social behavior: The moderating role of neuroticism. *Journal of Occupational Health Psychology*, 16, 441–56.

Wile, D. (1981). *After the Honeymoon: How Conflict Can Improve Your Relationship.* New York, NY: Wiley.

Yap, M. B. H., Allen, N. B., Leve, C., & Katz, L. F. (2008). Maternal meta-emotion philosophy and socialization of adolescent affect: The moderating role of adolescent temperament. *Journal of Family Psychology*, 22(5), 688–700.

Zaki, J., & Williams, W. C. (2013). Interpersonal emotion regulation. *Emotion*, 13, 803–10.

Zhou, Q., Eisenberg, N., Losoya, S. H., et al. (2002). The relations of parental warmth and positive expressiveness to children's empathy-related responding and social functioning: A longitudinal study. *Child Development*, 73(3), 893–915.

CHAPTER 8

# Interpersonal emotion dynamics within young adult romantic and peer relationships

*Charlie Champion, Thao Ha, and Thomas Dishion[†]*

One of the most powerful drivers of emotion within interpersonal exchanges is conflict and its management. As romantic relationships grow and endure, partners become more interconnected in emotions and behavior (see Chapter 1 for a conceptual overview on Interpersonal Emotion Dynamics (IED)). IED are the study of the emergent dyadic properties of the relationship as it unfolds over time (Schoebi & Randall, 2015). The way in which romantic partners cope with and recover from conflict is predictive of many individual and relationship outcomes (Cramer, 2000; Gottman & Levenson, 1999; Simon et al., 2008). In fact, not being able to resolve conflicts has been found to be an important predictor for divorce and premarital relationship dissolution (Gottman & Levenson, 1999, Shulman et al., 2006).

Coercive responses to conflict involve using aversive interpersonal behaviors to influence the outcome in one's favor, which in turn strengthens or escalates the coercive pattern through negative reinforcement (Patterson, 1982). Within intimate relationships, coercion can be displayed overtly as verbal threats, displays of anger and contempt, and physical fighting (Slep et al., 2016). As a result of coercion, conflict does not get resolved, which results in outcomes such as low self-esteem and/or depression, relationship dissatisfaction, alcohol use, infidelity, and sexual jealousy (Burke et al., 1988; Carr & VanDeusen, 2004; Frieze, 1983; Goetz & Shackelford, 2006). Most importantly, coercion is considered to be the interaction process that allows for intimate partner violence to emerge and continue (Pence & Paymar, 1986).

These coercive processes can be thought of as an example of an important and impactful IED, especially among romantic relationships in adulthood, as they represent emergent dyadic properties of the relationship as it unfolds over time (Schoebi & Randall, 2015). Coercion develops over time and can be seen across relationships, but importantly is

[†]2018

a dyadic phenomenon that incorporates emotional processes and components of each person involved. As partners become closer, they not only bring their unique emotional experiences into the relationship, but their emotions become intertwined. We can think of coercion as a process that develops from each individual's conflict tactics, as well as the emergent dynamic that is unique to the couple. By conceptualizing coercion as an IED, we can better understand how adult romantic relationships' displays of coercion may be, in part, explained by their past experiences with coercive relationships.

Recent evidence has shown that adolescent friendships could provide an important socialization context that predicts future relationship functioning (e.g., Ha et al., 2016). Little research has examined coercion across relationships, and specifically, whether coercion in adulthood might be learned in adolescence. Unfortunately, observational research on these coercive dynamics is currently lacking. Self-reports are subjective to reporter bias, but more importantly, are not able to capture moment-to-moment changes during conflict discussions, which have been argued to be more sensitive to capturing important interaction dynamics (Weisz & Kazdin, 2010). Therefore, this chapter provides a conceptual overview of coercion as an IED, while highlighting the current methodologies for understanding coercion, and suggests a dynamic system in which to more clearly conceptualize the development of coercion across relationships.

## The importance of coercion in relationships

The use of coercion in close relationships can develop early in life between parents and children. Patterson (1982) initially defined coercion based on reinforcement principles. Parent–child coercion is expressed when either a parent gives in to stop the child from escalating an aversive situation or when a parent reciprocates and escalates the aversive situation. A parent may reciprocate and escalate by yelling at the child to match their aversive behavior, or storming out of the room and slamming the door. In either case, both the parent's and child's behavior is reinforced, creating a powerful socialization context as the child learns how to manage conflicts. This learned pattern of becoming aversive in the face of conflict potentially disrupts the formation of healthy relationships in childhood, or of relationships in which children can successfully manage conflict with parents and peers. Once these coercive patterns are learned, they may extend into adulthood, disrupting the ability to recover from conflict. As early as elementary school (ages 5–9 years old), young children on the playground have been observed engaging in a process of "deviancy training," which involves mutual reinforcement for antisocial behavior (Snyder et al., 2007). Such playground dynamics are not trivial, as one can predict growth in both overt (e.g., physical aggression) and covert (e.g., lying) forms of problematic relationship dynamics in the ensuing years.

During early adolescence (twelve to thirteen years old), individuals experience a shift from primarily parental relationships to more egalitarian relationships with peers (Fuligni & Eccles, 1993). The adolescent transition is a time in which acceptance among peers becomes especially important and youth become more motivated by actions or attitudes that promote rewarding experiences (e.g., Blakemore & Choudhury, 2006). As social learning theory states, individuals are most likely to adopt the behaviors of others who are salient to them (Bandura, 1986). When friends select each other based on antisocial ideas or behaviors, "deviancy training" may occur, in which these ideas and behaviors become reinforced and act as a "glue" that keeps friendships together. During adolescence, deviancy training is displayed through mutual reinforcement of antisocial behaviors, ideas or norms, through showing support of deviancy. Deviancy training can result in disinhibiting of a variety of behaviors, including drug use, rule breaking, and forms of aggression such as bullying and violence (Dishion et al., 2004). In many ways, the coercive process is contagious, such that when a friend expresses a deviant norm and the other escalates, both inadvertently reinforce one another for deviant behavior (see Dishion & Tipsord, 2011). Research on the coercive process has concluded that deviancy training in adolescence is predictive of antisocial behaviors not only during adolescence, but extending into adulthood as well, such that friends who engaged in deviant talk were more likely to engage in antisocial behaviors as adults, controlling for their own levels of antisocial behavior (Dishion et al., 2004). To date, there is little research on how this kind of deviancy training can actually impact the interpersonal emotion dynamics of future relationships. For example, does the reinforcement of coercive and manipulative behavior in romantic relationships in general actually increase the likelihood of these patterns occurring in romantic relationships in the future?

## Coercion across relationships

Developmental researchers have long been interested in how friendship dynamics might impact the long-term quality of romantic, intimate relationships in late adolescence and early adulthood. For example, Capaldi et al. (2001) examined how male adolescent friendships can promote aggression toward females six years later. Adolescent male friend pairs (age seventeen to eighteen) participated in a 25-minute videotaped interaction that included discussing things they liked and disliked about women in their lives. These males also participated in a 40-minute videotaped interaction task with their romantic partner at age nineteen to twenty-four and were assessed on a variety of indicators measuring level of aggression toward their partner. The findings revealed male friendship support for hostile statements about women during late adolescence was predictive of aggression toward romantic partners in early adulthood, controlling for their general tendency to be antisocial. Stocker and Richmond (2007) also investigated the association between hostility in adolescent friendships and hostility in future romantic relationships. Self-reports of hostility in friendships were collected at age fourteen to sixteen, and then self-reports of hostility in romantic relationships were collected at age seventeen to nineteen. The results indicated that more hostility in adolescent friendships was predictive of more hostility in young adult romantic relationships. In other words, IEDs reinforced in adolescence may be more likely to be repeated or more readily replicated in future relationships.

Recently, Ha et al. (2016) extended these findings to the study of sexual assault. Sexual assault can be defined by practices such as offering alcohol or drugs to a potential partner to "relax" with the intention of encouraging sex, or to go further after someone said no. More intense forms of sexual assault include forced sexual intercourse, resulting in arrests or legal involvement. Ha and colleagues examined how observations of adolescent friendship coercive discussions of romantic relationships actually predicted future sexual assault incidents as young adults. At age sixteen to seventeen, adolescents participated in a 45-minute videotaped discussion with a same-sex friend. Their discussions were coded for displays of coercive relationship talk, which was based on a variety of factors such as the extent to which the dyad made negative, hostile references toward others, and exhibited deviancy training, which involves mutual reinforcement of negative talk. Results revealed that higher levels of observed coercive relationship talk with a same-sex friend was predictive of reported sexual assault in adulthood. Together, these findings suggest that adolescent friendships potentially socialize future relationship coercion, or in other words, are central to the development of interpersonal emotion dynamics.

## Coercion as a dynamic system

While it is clear that coercion is potentially harmful to the well-being of interpersonal relationships, little research has investigated the stability of coercion across contexts. A dynamic systems (DS) framework can be useful to apply to the study of the variety of forms that coercion can take in various relationships (e.g., family, friends, intimate) and offers an explanation for how interpersonal emotion dynamics may arise and be maintained across relationships. Specifically, DS states that the display of "attractors," or dynamic patterns that dyads spend most time in, can be thought of as reflecting both the learning history of the individuals as well as the "pull" of the relationship, or in other words, an "attractor" (see Chapter 4). In this sense, coercion in adult romantic relationships is a potential emergent property of the relationship, which partially reflects the history of each partner, as well as factors such as the context and initial conditions of the relationship (Granic & Patterson, 2006; Thelen & Smith, 1996). Thus, individuals can get caught in a coercive cycle, and the conflict can very much be experienced as an "attractor." Alternatively, coercion in close relationships could function as a "repeller." From a DS framework, coercion and conflict in close relationships is avoided. Consistent with this view is the finding that in healthy families, or families who peacefully manage and recover from conflict, parents and adolescents were able to discuss a conflict and stay in the neutral-positive area of a state space grid throughout the discussion; a pattern that predicted positive adjustment outcomes for adolescents two years later (Dishion et al., 2012). From this perspective comes the prediction that stability in negative relationships across contexts results from the inability to select and maintain positive relationship dynamics, engaging in positive exchanges and resolving conflict without coercion automatically.

There is another level of complexity to studying and understanding relationship dynamics across systems. For example, adolescent friendships engage in little conflict (Dishion et al., 1995). When friends fight, they tend to move on and find other friends. However, friends can come together and join into a coalition, and encourage coercion toward others. Initially, this dynamic of friends connecting by engaging in deviant talk and deviancy training (Dishion et al., 1996) was found to be highest when both friends were antisocial, and it predicted escalations in problem behavior over time (e.g., Granic & Dishion, 2003). The findings that a history of antisocial behavior predicted high levels of deviancy training, which in turn predicted escalations in later aggression (e.g., Van Ryzin & Dishion, 2013) suggest that the process of coercion can look different from relationship to relationship.

In some ways, committed adult romantic relationships can be similar to family dynamics when examining constructs such as interdependence. One salient issue among cohabitating couples in particular, is that the behaviors and emotions of one person can dramatically affect the life of the partner, such as persons directly impacting their partner's well-being,

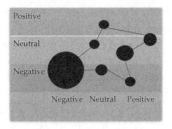

Figure 8.1.  Couple high on coercion

*Note:* Size of the plot point represents duration. Axes represent male and female.

i.e., interdependency among partners (Kelley & Thibaut, 1979). Thus, conflict does emerge in romantic relationships and, it appears, coercive dynamics emerge as important predictors for the happiness and well-being of both partners. It is not surprising that flexibility within committed relationships, with respect to communication, is thought to be more important in predicting outcomes, such as psychopathology, than level of conflict or hostility within an interaction (Bui-Wrzosinska, 2013; Gottman & Notarius, 2000).

A graphic representation of moment-to-moment interaction processes is called a state space grid (see Hollenstein, 2013). State space grids represent how interactions between two people unfold in real time. This state space grid (Figure 8.1) describes a couple that moves across different states, such as negativity, positivity, and neutrality, throughout the interaction. Specifically, Figure 8.1 displays a hypothetical state space grid representing the interaction of a highly coercive couple. This couple spends the longest durations in negative talk displayed by both partners. While this couple also spends time in more neutral or positive states, the clear attractor in this example is the dyadic coercive state in which both partners are reinforcing their negative behaviors and affect. In contrast, couples with healthy conflict resolution styles would move about the grid throughout the interaction, without spending time in the coercive zone. Slep et al. (2016) describe the coercive process in couples to be such that those who respond to conflict coercively, through escalation, are likely to continue to display coercion in conflict discussions, highlighting the negative reinforcement cycle described by DS. Further, research has found that couples who get stuck in coercive interaction patterns are not able to flexibly revert to positive emotions in order to recover from a conflict conversation task, and instead stay "stuck" in a negative state (Gottman & Levenson, 1999).

## Using DS to conceptualize adolescent IED

To date, most longitudinal research linking observed friendships with couple aggression in adulthood has focused primarily on males (e.g., Capaldi et al., 2001). It is important to note, however, that studies linking hostility or aggression among adolescent friendships and adult romantic partners may each be capturing different aspects of this coercive IED. For example, Capaldi et al. (2001) examined talk that was specifically hostile toward females. Other studies have included aggression toward others as well as one's partner, and hostility's definition can range from relational to physical.

Importantly, in the only previous observation study with both female and male friendships, coercive relationship talk was prognostic of future sexual assault for both males and females (Ha et al., 2016). In contrast, Capaldi and Owen (2001) only examined males when linking observations of coercion in adult romantic partners. Thus, there is less research on the developmental trajectories leading to coercive IED among females. The current findings, however, are suggestive of a need to more carefully study female relationship formation, in light of longitudinal research conducted by Odgers et al. (2008). Odgers et al. (2008) unveiled two developmental pathways of antisocial behavior in males and females from childhood through adulthood. The life-course persistent pathway (LCP) was characterized by social and familial deficits that develop in childhood and persist into adulthood, while the adolescent limited pathway (AL) was characterized as normative antisocial type behavior that develops in adolescence and shortly dissipates, without significant antisocial behavior in adulthood. Results revealed that both developmental pathways emerged for females. However, interestingly, females experienced poorer outcomes at age thirty-two compared to males, as evidenced by increased antisocial behavior, poor health, family difficulties, and economic problems. These findings support the hypothesis of similarity in the socialization of antisocial behavior, or coercive IEDs, for males and females, but that the impact of antisocial behavior in childhood may have more serious consequences for adult adjustment for females.

Most recently, the link between deviancy training in adolescence and displays of coercion in romantic relationships was investigated to further understand the development of coercion as a form of IED across relationships. Furthermore, because less is known about whether these links are relevant for females, gender was examined as a moderator of the socializing of friendships on romantic relationships, using the same data described in Ha et al. (2016). This study was part of a larger project called Project Alliance, in which the Family Check-Up (FCU; Dishion & Kavanagh, 2003), a family-centered intervention, was implemented starting in middle school with the goal of reducing problem behavior through entire family engagement, motivational interviewing, and targeted feedback to improve parenting practices.

Data from when the youth were on average seventeen years of age at the first assessment and twenty-eight years of age at the second assessment were examined. At age seventeen, participants were asked to participate in a videotaped interaction with a same-sex friend and these interactions were coded for deviancy training, which was defined as "rule break," or by verbal and nonverbal behaviors that were not relevant to the task or violated community and societal standards. The percentage of time the individual spent engaging in rule break was averaged across both the participant and the peer, with a higher percentage indicating more deviant influence within the pair.

At age twenty-eight, participants again completed a videotaped interaction, but this time with their romantic partner. These videotaped interactions were coded for coercion, using a micro coding system (Peterson et al., 2008), in accordance with the DS framework, and included verbal, physical, and affect codes ranging from positive to negative, as well as behavior change codes, such as "directive." The percentage of time the individual spent displaying: anger/disgust toward their partner, responding negatively toward their partner, verbally giving their partner directives in a negative way and displaying stonewalling behaviors toward their partner were averaged across tasks, with a higher percentage indicating more coercive displays (e.g., Dishion et al., 2012).

Interestingly, and in some contrast to previous research (Capaldi et al., 2001), bivariate correlations among indicators of deviancy training and coercive relationship dynamics were significant for females but not males. Results of this study revealed that, surprisingly, the interaction of deviancy training in adolescence by gender significantly predicted coercion in adulthood over and above the predictors individually. In other words, gender significantly moderated the positive association between adolescent deviancy training and adult coercion such that, only for females, higher levels of deviancy training with peers at age seventeen was predictive of higher levels of coercion at age twenty-eight.

This finding supports previous literature that peers are a unique risk factor in the development of coercion, but highlights that this may be especially true for females. The findings reported by Odgers et al. (2008) may be most relevant, in that the life course persistent antisocial females in that longitudinal study had the most serious negative life outcomes. One conceivable hypothesis is that males drop out of being coercive when they enter into a relationship with a non-antisocial female, explaining why their trajectory is not always stable. It may be possible that females with high levels of antisocial behavior in adolescence are less likely to select prosocial males as partners ten years later, however, there is little research on the relationship outcomes except for the current longitudinal study. There is some support for this hypothesis, as previous research has shown that males' level of violence changed across romantic relationships as a function of their partner's level of aggression (Shortt et al., 2012), but this is a gap in the literature for future studies to explore.

Taken together, this review, along with most recent findings, posits that adolescent friendships play a role in the developmental of interpersonal emotion dynamics. It appears that adolescents may go through an important socialization process with their friends that either creates or enhances their norms and behaviors about interpersonal dynamics, and specifically, the ways in which they respond to and manage conflict in close relationships. For many adolescents, friendships may be the first exposure to talking about or forming ideas about romantic and sexual relationships. Because of the importance of friendship during adolescence, it posits that these relationships are highly influential. In other words, the interpersonal dynamics learned throughout the lifespan, but particularly solidified in adolescence, may display themselves in adult romantic relationships. From a DS perspective, this posits that adolescent friendships may work to strengthen or reinforce coercive attractors and are an important part of the coercive trajectory across contexts.

While these findings are striking, it does not necessarily imply that youth "learn" to be coercive within intimate relationships later in life. An alternative perspective is that "antisocial traits" reveal themselves in relationships with friends and later in romantic relationships if unabated. Further, it is currently unclear whether socialization or selection effects are most at play in the development of problematic relationship dynamics. While socialization during adolescence appears to play a role, the coercive cycle, established in early childhood, may cause adolescents to select into coercive peer groups in which little socialization takes place. More research teasing apart the direct influence of peer relationships in adolescence is necessary to better understand the amount they contribute to the development of coercion in later relationships. This would be particularly important to tease apart for the purposes of prevention efforts targeting peer relationships in adolescence.

## Future research

First, it will be important for future research to focus efforts on better understanding how coercion develops as an IED by continuing to examine coercive patterns throughout relationships (i.e., childhood through adulthood). Importantly, future research will utilize observational studies in order to assess coercion through moment-to-moment interactions, or within the framework of dynamic systems theory. Longitudinal observational studies will continue to inform whether reinforcement of coercive relationship ideals specifically increases this IED occurring in real life future relationships.

Coercive patterns are an important target of prevention work in couples therapy. However, little prevention effort currently exists that targets coercive dynamics (e.g., Cordova et al., 2001). Prevention is an especially important area, given that coercive dynamics become more solidified over time. This review begins to shed light on ways in which prevention efforts might be utilized in premarital relationships (see Baucom et al., 1998; Slep, et al., 2016). In addition, there are hundreds of randomized studies showing that parent–child coercive interaction dynamics can be reduced using interventions that promote parents' use of positive behavior support and behavior management practices (see Forgatch & Kjøbli, 2016; Weisz & Kazdin, 2010). Such interventions are typically delivered when couples and families are experiencing distress. A more preventive approach is relationship education; however, to date, that approach (Holt et al., 2016) has yet to yield enduring effects on future relationship dynamics. Future research would determine at what age and in which context can interventions target beliefs and skills that can improve both who a partner selects and how conflict can be effectively managed and problems solved. The evidence reviewed in this chapter suggests that adolescent friendships may be the age and context at which to intervene.

## References

Bandura, A. (1986). *Social Foundations of Thought and Action: A Social Cognitive Theory*. Englewood Cliffs, NJ: Prentice Hall.

Baucom, D. H., Shoham, V., Mueser, K. T., Daiuto, A. D., & Stickle, T. R. (1998). Empirically supported couple and family interventions for marital distress and adult mental health problems. *Journal of Consulting and Clinical Psychology*, 66(1), 53–88.

Blakemore, S. J., & Choudhury, S. (2006). Development of the adolescent brain: implications for executive function and social cognition. *Journal of Child Psychology and Psychiatry*, 47, 296–312.

Bui-Wrzosinska, L. (2013). Conflict as an attractor: a dynamical systems perspective on the dynamics of conflict. In A. Nowak, K. Winkowska-Nowak & D. Bree (Eds.), *Complex Human Dynamics* (pp. 227–42). Berlin Heidelberg: Springer.

Burke, P. J., Stets, J. E., & Pirog-Good, M. A. (1988). Gender identity, self-esteem, and physical and sexual abuse in dating relationships. *Social Psychology Quarterly*, 51, 272–85.

Capaldi, D. M., Dishion, T. J., Stoolmiller, M., & Yoeger, K. (2001). Aggression toward female partners by at-risk young men: the contribution of male adolescent friendships. *Developmental Psychology*, 37, 61–73.

Capaldi, D. M., & Owen, L. D. (2001). Physical aggression in a community sample of at-risk young couples: gender comparisons for high frequency, injury, and fear. *Journal of Family Psychology*, 15(3), 425.

Carr, J. L., & VanDeusen, K. M. (2004). Risk factors for male sexual aggression on college campuses. *Journal of Family Violence*, 19(5), 279–89.

Cordova, J. V., Warren, L. Z., & Gee, C. B. (2001). Motivational interviewing as an intervention for at-risk couples. *Journal of Marital and Family Therapy*, 27(3), 315–26.

Cramer, D. (2000). Relationship satisfaction and conflict style in romantic relationships. *The Journal of Psychology*, 134(3), 337–41.

Dishion, T. J., Andrews, D. W., & Crosby, L. (1995). Antisocial boys and their friends in early adolescence: relationship characteristics, quality, and interactional process. *Child development*, 66(1), 139–151.

Dishion, T. J., Forgatch, M., Van Ryzin, M., & Winter, C. (2012). The nonlinear dynamics of family problem solving in adolescence: the predictive validity of a peaceful resolution attractor. *Nonlinear Dynamics, Psychology, and Life Sciences*, 16(3), 331–52.

Dishion, T. J., & Kavanagh, K. (2003). *Intervening in Adolescent Problem Behavior: A Family-Centered Approach*. New York, NY: Guilford Press.

Dishion, T. J., Nelson, S. E., Winter, C. E., & Bullock, B. M. (2004). Adolescent friendship as a dynamic system: entropy and deviance in the etiology and course of male antisocial behavior. *Journal of Abnormal Psychology*, 32, 651–63.

Dishion, T. J., Spracklen, K. M., Andrews, D. W., & Patterson, G. R. (1996). Deviancy training in male adolescent friendships. *Behavior Therapy*, 27(3), 373–90.

Dishion, T. J., & Tipsord, J. M. (2011). Peer contagion in child and adolescent social and emotional development. *Annual Review of Psychology*, 62, 189–214.

Forgatch, M. S., & Kjøbli, J. (2016). Parent management training – Oregon model: adapting intervention with rigorous research. *Family Process*, 55(3), 500–13.

Frieze, I. H. (1983). Investigating the causes and consequences of marital rape. *Signs*, 8(3), 532–53.

Fuligni, A. J., & Eccles, J. S. (1993). Perceived parent-child relationships and early adolescents' orientation toward peers. *Developmental Psychology*, 29(4), 622–32.

Goetz, A. T., & Shackelford, T. K. (2006). Sexual coercion and forced in-pair copulation as sperm competition tactics in humans. *Human Nature*, 17(3), 265–82.

Gottman, J. M., & Levenson, R. W. (1999). Rebound from marital conflict and divorce prediction. *Family Process*, 38, 287–92.

Gottman, J. M., & Notarius, C. I. (2000). Decade review: observing marital interaction. *Journal of Marriage and Family*, 62(4), 927–47.

Granic, I., & Dishion, T. J. (2003). Deviant talk in adolescent friendships: a step toward measuring a pathogenic attractor process. *Social Development*, 12(3), 314–34.

Granic, I., & Patterson, G. R. (2006). Toward a comprehensive model of anti-social development: a dynamic systems approach. *Psychological Review*, 113(1), 101–31.

Ha, T., Kim, H. Christopher, C., Caruthers, A., & Dishion, T. J. (2016). Predicting sexual coercion in early adulthood: the transaction between maltreatment, gang affiliation, and adolescent socialization of coercive relationship norms. *Development and Psychopathology*, 28, 707–20.

Hollenstein, T. (2013). *State Space Grids* (pp. 11–33). Springer US.

Holt, L. J., Mattanah, J. F., Schmidt, C. K., et al. (2016). Effects of relationship education on emerging adults' relationship beliefs and behaviors. *Personal Relationships*, 23(4), 723–41.

Kelly, H. & Thibaut, J. (1979). Interpersonal relations-a theory of interdependence. *Applied Ergonomics*, 249.

Odgers, C. L., Moffitt, T. E., Broadbent, J. M., et al. (2008). Female and male anti-social trajectories: from childhood origins to adult outcomes. *Development and Psychopathology*, 20(02), 673–716.

Patterson, G. R. (1982). *Coercive Family Process* (Vol. 3). Eugene, OR: Castalia Publishing Company.

Pence, E., & Paymar, M. (1986). *Power and Control: Tactics of Men Who Batter.* Duluth, MN: Minnesota Program Development.

Peterson, J., Winter, C., Jabson, J., & Dishion, T. J. (2008). *Relationship Affect Coding System.* Unpublished coding manual, University of Oregon, Child and Family Center, Eugene.

Schoebi, D., & Randall, A. K. (2015). Emotional dynamics in intimate relationships. *Emotion Review*, 7(4), 342–8.

Shortt, J. W., Capaldi, D. M., Kim, H. K., et al. (2012). Stability of intimate partner violence by men across 12 years in young adulthood: effects of relationship transitions. *Prevention Science*, 13, 360–9.

Shulman, S., Tuval-Mashiach, R., Levran, E., & Anbar, S. (2006). Conflict resolution patterns and longevity of adolescent romantic couples: a 2-year follow-up study. *Journal of Adolescence*, 29(4), 575–88.

Simon, Valerie A., Kobielski, Sarah J., & Martin, S. (2008). Conflict beliefs, goals, and behavior in romantic relationships during late adolescence. *Journal of Youth Adolescence*, 37, 324–35.

Slep, A. M. S., Heyman, R. E., & Lorber, M. F. (2016). Coercive process and intimate partner violence in committed relationships. In T. J. Dishion & J. J. Snyder (Eds.), *The Oxford Handbook of Coercive Relationship Dynamics.* Oxford: Oxford University Press.

Snyder, J., Schrepferman, L., Brooker, M., & Stoolmiller, M. (2007). The roles of anger, conflict with parents and peers, and social reinforcement in the early development of physical aggression. In T. A. Cavell & K. T. Malcolm (Eds.), *Anger, Aggression and Interventions for Interpersonal Violence* (pp. 187–214). Mahwah, NJ: Erlbaum.

Stocker, C. M., & Richmond, M. K. (2007). Longitudinal associations between hostility in adolescents' family relationships and friendships and hostility in their romantic relationships. *Journal of Family Psychology*, 21, 490–7.

Thelen, E., & Smith, L. B. (1996). *A Dynamic Systems Approach to the Development of Cognition and Action*. Cambridge, MA: MIT Press.

Van Ryzin, M. J., & Dishion, T. J. (2013). From antisocial behavior to violence: a model for the amplifying role of coercive joining in adolescent friendships. *Journal of Child Psychology and Psychiatry*, 56, 661–9.

Weisz, J. R., & Kazdin, A. E. (Eds.). (2010). *Evidence-based Psychotherapies for Children and Adolescents*. New York, NY: Guilford Press.

# CHAPTER 9

# Interpersonal emotion dynamics within intimate relationships

*Sharon Shenhav, Arpine Hovasapian, and Belinda Campos*

Emotions are central to relationships (e.g., English et al., 2013; Keltner & Haidt, 2001; Knobloch & Metts, 2013; Shiota et al., 2004). In the course of their interactions, relationship partners shape, and in turn are shaped by, each other's emotions (Butner et al., 2007; Saxbe & Repetti, 2010; Schoebi, 2008). These shaping processes, termed *interpersonal emotion dynamics*, reflect partners' interconnection and have implications for their relationship outcomes (Schoebi & Randall, 2015; see also Chapter 1 for a review of relevant theories and models). The goal of this chapter is to review the emotion dynamics that are characteristic of intimate relationships, with a focus on romantic relationships (for family relationships and friendships, see Chapters 7 and 8). Interpersonal emotion dynamics in psychological processes that form, maintain, and dissolve romantic relationships are reviewed and, whenever possible, we also weave in current knowledge of variation in these dynamics that stem from relationship partners' broader social contexts. Our chapter then concludes with a wish list for future directions on this topic that can broaden and deepen the field's understanding of emotion dynamics in intimate relationships.

## What is an intimate relationship?

Intimate relationships are defined by the special, accumulated knowledge, deep interdependence, shared commitment, and feelings of caring, trust, and responsiveness (Miller, 2015) that people can have for each other. According to Prager and Roberts (2004), people in intimate relationships have *intimate interactions* that involve self-disclosure, shared understanding, and sustained, positive involvement that communicates the basic positive regard that relationship partners have for each other. These interactions typically involve emotions, which we define as brief, automatic reactions to goal relevant stimuli (Keltner & Lerner, 2010). The signaling features of emotions – facial expressions, body movements, touch, and vocal tones – carry information from one person to another in the course of these interactions (e.g., Keltner & Lerner, 2010). These features are spontaneous and brief, allowing partners to exchange information quickly (e.g., Shiota et al., 2004) and rely on these signals when forms of nonverbal communication are preferred (e.g., flirting) or when one is reluctant to verbally express feelings (e.g., anger, sadness, or sexual desire) (Eibl-Eibesfeldt, 1989; Prager & Roberts, 2004). Intimate relationships are chiefly characterized by interactions that reveal parts of the self to a partner that are otherwise kept private, but not all intimate interactions carry deep meaning. For example, partners may learn each other's childhood food preferences and current pet peeves but also come to understand a partner's relationship expectations for love and support during life's difficult periods. All reveal important parts of the self, but only the latter is deeply meaningful for the relationship. Intimate interaction can also be simple moments of shared amusement or responding to another's sadness.

Intimacy is a primary feature of romantic relationships and this quality has become more tightly entwined into couple relationship ideals in the last fifty years (Finkel et al., 2015). Intimacy is both created by emotion interaction and reflected in its course. Emotion, particularly positive emotion, is critical to forming and maintaining desired levels of intimacy that are rewarding to partners in these relationships (Huston et al., 2001; Shiota et al., 2004). The emotions expressed in the course of relationship interactions can signal intentions to affiliate or avoid (Campos et al., 2015), communicate the rewards, sorrows, or injuries obtained in the course of an interaction (Schoebi, 2008), solidify the commitments that bind a relationship (Gonzaga et al., 2001), or set in motion processes that portend the end of a relationship (Levenson & Gottman, 1983). For example, a partner's happiness during time spent together is rewarding and an angry response to inconsideration lets a partner know that there is relationship repair work to be done. As these examples show, emotions facilitate adaptive responding, including in the context of forming, maintaining, and, if needed, dissolving intimate relationships (e.g., Keltner & Gross, 1999; Lazarus, 1991; Levenson, 1999).

## Intimate relationship formation

In this section, we review research regarding relationship formation in romantic and non-romantic contexts. The latter provides important information that is applicable to the initiation and maintenance of romantic relationships (e.g., liking, closeness, enjoyment, similarity; Luo & Zhang, 2009; Tidwell et al., 2013; Vittengl & Holt, 2000). Indeed, emotion dynamics in non-romantic contexts can be key precursors to romantic relationship formation.

Emotional experiences and expressions are salient cues that we use to form impressions of others. If we are lucky, these initial social interactions with others will be accompanied by positive emotions. Positive emotion signals carry important information regarding with whom it might be promising to pursue a relationship (Berrios et al., 2015; Campos et al., 2015). Is the person smiling genuinely at us? Do we feel happy interacting with the person? Do we feel drawn to this person? These emotions may set in motion certain psychological processes (e.g., attraction, closeness) through which we can begin to accumulate knowledge of others and thereby establish intimacy with a relationship partner. Particularly when there is an opportunity to form a new relationship, research supports the notion that we are both aware of and responsive to others' positive emotions, a process termed "positive emotion attunement" (Campos et al., 2015). In fact, beyond reports of our own positive emotions and our own displays of positive emotions, the positive emotional displays of others (e.g., Duchenne smiles which indicate a genuine smile) have been shown to elicit feelings of closeness (Campos et al., 2015).

In romantic contexts, positive emotionality has been tied to romantic attraction. Using a speed dating paradigm, which allows for examination of interpersonal emotion dynamics present in settings designed for romantic relationship formation, researchers found that those who elicited positive affect in others were also more likely to be romantically desired by others (Berrios et al., 2015). In other words, when an individual reported feeling positive (e.g., enthusiastic, happy) after an interaction with an opposite-sex partner, they were also more likely to report having romantic interest in that person (i.e., saying yes to wanting to see them again).

There is also evidence that our attraction to potential romantic partners varies as a function of their emotional displays. For example, particular emotional displays (happiness in women, pride in men) have been associated with increased sexual attraction (Tracy & Beall, 2011). With the increase in the use of technology for initiating romantic relationships, these processes need not occur in moment-to-moment interactions. Emotions that are elicited by viewing a photograph (e.g., feelings of attraction) (Tracy & Beall, 2011) can be an important precursor to relationship initiation. For example, sending a message and starting a conversation can set the stage for establishing a desired relationship. This courtship behavior may then become the foundation for other relationship building processes (e.g., self-disclosure, responsiveness) that encourage intimacy (Reis & Shaver, 1988).

Self-disclosure, the process by which individuals reveal personal information about themselves, provides opportunities for interaction partners to share and respond to one another. As Reis and Shaver (1988) propose in their interpersonal process model of intimacy, one person's disclosure and a partner's subsequent response are essential in promoting intimacy. Research applying this model has found that participants' daily life emotional self-disclosure (i.e., expressing one's emotions) is more predictive of intimacy than factual self-disclosure (Laurenceau et al., 1998). Further, self-disclosure often involves reciprocity norms; if one member of a dyad discloses something, the other responds in kind. Experimental paradigms examining solicited and unsolicited self-disclosure in previously unacquainted dyads find that self-disclosure leads to greater levels of liking, closeness, and perceptions of similarity (Reis et al., 2011; Sprecher et al., 2013a,b; Vittengl & Holt, 2000). Moreover, greater liking is associated with an increase in positive affect in the interaction partner (Vittengl & Holt, 2000). Positive emotions are also amplified when self-disclosure occurs reciprocally as compared to only one partner disclosing or turn-taking disclosures in two separate interactions (Sprecher et al., 2013b). However, self-disclosure may also disappoint. If a partner's self-disclosure reduces perceptions of similarity, liking decreases (Norton et al., 2007).

According to Sprecher et al. (2013b), self-disclosure should be considered in its dyadic context and the extent to which there are opportunities to respond to self-disclosures in positive ways. Responsiveness, the way a receiver reacts, plays a key role in the social or romantic attraction that may or may not follow self-disclosure. For example, is the listener supportive and understanding, or bored and uninterested? Reis et al. (2004) assert that "perceived responsiveness to the self is a basic concept in the study of closeness and intimacy" (Reis et al., 2004, p. 221). In fact, perceptions of partner responsiveness emerge as a mediator between self and partner disclosure and intimacy (Laurenceau et al., 1998), as well as sexual desire (Birnbaum & Reis, 2012). Perceiving a partner as responsive has also been found to elicit positive emotions (e.g., feeling happy and enthusiastic) that led to romantic interest in a speed-dating study (Berrios et al., 2015). However, the effectiveness of responsiveness hinges on the extent to which an interaction partner's responsiveness is perceived to be appropriate and genuine; if not, responsiveness may not lead to increases in romantic attraction (Birnbaum & Reis, 2012). Although there are exceptions, the interpersonal emotion dynamics involved in self-disclosure and responsiveness often evoke feelings of being supported, understood, accepted, and cared for (e.g., Reis et al., 2004, 2011). These feelings tend to increase social attraction (Reis et al., 2011), sexual desire (Birnbaum & Reis, 2012) and intimacy (e.g., Berrios et al., 2015; Laurenceau et al., 1998) across romantic and non-romantic contexts.

The emotions and processes reviewed thus far play an important role in romantic relationship initiation and formation. These relationship-building processes tend to occur naturally and if successful, individuals move past these initial encounters and progress toward interpersonal emotion dynamics that are central to the maintenance of romantic relationships.

## Intimate relationship maintenance

In ongoing relationships, the emotional lives of partners become intertwined through specific patterns of emotion coordination (Randall et al., 2013). Emotion coordination processes are particularly relevant to the maintenance of romantic relationships, although they play a role in initiation and dissolution as well. Coordination is associated with healthy relationship processes, such as understanding and sensitivity, but also undesirable processes, such as when negative affect is reciprocated during conflict (Levenson & Gottman, 1983; Schoebi, 2008). Two subtypes of emotion coordination are transmission (one partner's emotions predicting the other's emotions later in time) and synchronization (the rising and falling of partners' emotions in unison) (Randall & Butler, 2013; see also Chapter 2 for graphical representations and additional information on these between-individual emotion dynamics).

### Transmission

Transmission is the process by which mood, affect, or behavior transfers from one person to the other at a later time point (Larson & Almeida, 1999). Transmission is common in intimate relationships. For example, one study observed the daily emotional states of marital couples while one partner was preparing for a stressful event – the New York Bar Examination (Thompson & Bolger, 1999). The exam taker's depressed mood was related to their partner feeling less positive and more negative in their own daily mood. This association declined as the test date approached, indicating that partners made allowances for their stressed out loved ones and, in so doing, were able to be supportive when it was most needed. Through these processes, the emotional lives of partners may become synchronized – rising and falling in unison.

*Synchronization*

As an example of emotion synchronization, researchers have found that day-to-day fluctuations in physiological and affective states link over time (Saxbe & Repetti, 2010). This has been found in cortisol levels and self-reported mood states (Papp et al., 2013). Synchrony occurs because partners often engage in activities together, but it also occurs when individuals experience positive or negative emotions separately and later share their emotions with their partners. One may become elated when hearing good news from one's partner or sad when empathetically reacting to their partner's rough day (Gable & Reis, 2010).

*Convergence and divergence of emotions*

Synchronization and transmission may lead to emotional reactions that converge toward or diverge away from equilibrium (a state of emotional and physiological stability). Randall et al. (2013) note that neither pattern of emotion coordination is inherently good or bad. A convergent pattern can promote mutual positive affect or mutual hostility. A divergent pattern can promote a balanced emotional state across partners during times of stress or can lead to incompatible emotional states.

Examples of convergent and divergent emotion coordination patterns can be seen in conflict situations. During conflict, negative emotions can become "contagious" and have deleterious effects on the relationships, especially if it goes unresolved (Levenson & Gottman, 1985). Conflict often becomes difficult to resolve because partners become trapped in spiraling patterns of negative emotions in their responses and counter-responses to each other. In Saxbe and Repetti's (2010) daily diary study, less satisfied couples showed greater synchrony of negative mood and cortisol, likely because of the added effect of their negative patterns of emotional reactivity.

Conversely, partners often learn to respond to each other in ways that stabilize negative emotions when conflicts occur. For example, Krokoff (1991) found that couples who were able to resolve relational disagreements using humor lessened the averseness of their conflict by allowing for an avenue to express negative affect. Thus, instead of reacting in a similar negative emotional tone to one's partner, reacting differently (i.e., with a positive tone) brought emotions back to equilibrium.

Convergence of emotions in intimate relationships can happen because partners: (a) react to the outside world together and/or (b) react to each other (Butler, 2015). When reacting to the outside world, intimate partners come to converge in their emotional reactions by developing similar appraisal patterns to stimuli in their environment. In a study that tested emotional responses to an experimental stressor over two time-points, couples came to develop similar patterns of emotional response after a six-month period, even when they were not in the presence of their partner (Anderson et al., 2003). This finding suggests that discussing emotional events and appraisals of events could help couples become more emotionally coordinated.

What are the specific ways in which relationship partners come to converge in their emotional reactions to external stimuli? First, in each other's presence, one person's expressive reaction can influence the other person's focus of attention and provide information about the environment. For example, infants will not crawl over a plexi-glass cliff if they see an expression of fear in their mother (Sorce et al., 1985). Similarly, in adult romantic relationships, an expression of worry can signal to one's partner that there is a threat nearby (Parkinson & Simons, 2012). Second, when people tell each other about past emotional events, the sharing process involves interpreting, clarifying, reevaluating, and questioning details of the experience between the speaker and the listener. This analysis of the event leads people to adopt similar appraisals in future events (Pasupathi, 2001). Though developing shared appraisals is ubiquitous across all types of dyadic relationships, it is particularly prevalent in the intimate relationship context, where people share their emotions frequently (Gable & Reis, 2010). For example, when couples share news about their day with each other, their responses might reinforce certain interpretations and appraisals of the shared events. Reis et al. (2010) found that sharing positive emotional experiences often builds relationship ties because romantic partners respond to each other's good news in ways that increase appraisals of importance for the event.

Emotions may also converge because partners develop joint coping strategies to deal with outside threats. Certain environmental challenges (e.g., societal disapproval of relationship) may cause romantic partners to converge more closely with one another. For example, young intercultural couples often experience parental disapproval and parental conflict, particularly if they are first- or second-generation immigrants (Shenhav et al., 2017). To protect against negative outside influences, interracial partners often engage in insulation (avoiding problematic situations) and negotiation (deciding together to how respond to situations; Foeman & Nance, 2002). By developing joint coping strategies to deal with threats to the relationship, partners' emotional reactions to external influences converge.

## Factors influencing emotion coordination

It is important to note that there is much variation in the amount of emotion coordination couples experience. Factors that influence the degree of coordination between couples occur on the individual, dyadic, and broader social contextual levels. For example, Butner et al. (2007) found that people high in attachment avoidance are less impacted by changes in their partners' affect. On a dyadic level, relationship quality affects emotion coordination; couples with low marital satisfaction tend to be less effective in modulating each other's arousal during conflict (Levenson & Gottman, 1983). Additionally, physiological synchrony (cortisol associations) is related to physical proximity (spending more time together) as well as communication behaviors (expressions of support; Papp et al., 2013; Repetti et al., 2011). On a cultural level, couples who endorse more collectivistic values are more emotionally interdependent than those who endorse individualistic values (Schoebi et al., 2010).

Additionally, a daily diary study found that couples in arranged marriages have been found to be less synchronized than those in love marriages (Randall et al., 2011). Addressing these kinds of cultural differences in emotion dynamics during the maintenance phase of a relationship is a promising area of future research. For example, emotion coordination processes may unfold differently in partners who come from different cultural backgrounds – each with its own set of norms regarding emotional expression, communication, and expectations of the degree to which commitments are voluntary or indissoluble.

## Interpersonal emotion regulation

Interpersonal emotion regulation refers to the automatic or deliberate attempt to regulate another's emotional state (Zaki & Williams, 2013). One form of emotion regulation that has been studied in intimate relationships is the coregulation of emotions – or the bidirectional oscillating pattern of affective arousal and dampening that dynamically maintains an equilibrium state (Butler & Randall, 2013). In intimate relationships, this coregulation can contribute to emotional and physiological stability in the relationship. In a daily diary study, Butner et al. (2007) found that romantic partners' levels of positive and negative affect covaried above and beyond the influence of their shared daily interactions. This effect was stronger on days that couples spent more time together. More deliberate efforts toward interpersonal emotion regulation occur in many forms. Niven et al. (2009) list hundreds of specific interpersonal emotion regulation strategies. One distinction among strategies is that some focus on improving affect (e.g., reframing a negative event in a positive light), while others worsen affect (e.g., complaining about a target's behavior). Another focus is on cognitive mechanisms (changing a target's thoughts) or behavioral strategies (using behavior to change emotions, with no direct attempt to change thoughts).

Emotion regulation strategies are often used during distressing times to deliberately change emotions, but people also regulate each other's emotions through everyday interactions (Gable et al., 2004). When partners experience everyday emotional events, they often talk openly with each other about the circumstances of the event as well as their feelings and responses. People share over 80% of emotional experiences with others (Rimé et al., 1998). Sharing emotions is one way in which they can become coordinated across partners. For negative events, sharing often dissolves the emotional impact, although this is not always the case (Rimé, 2009). For positive events, sharing with loved ones allows people to savor and capitalize on the good things that happen to them. Sharing positive emotions with relationship partners is associated with increased positive affect and relationship quality, particularly when partners respond in enthusiastic ways (Gable et al., 2004). That is, sharing positive events allows people to up-regulate, or capitalize on, positive life events.

## Intimate relationship dissolution

Despite the myriad ways in which couples are emotionally entwined, partners often find themselves diverging away from each other. At times, our own and our partner's emotional reactions and behaviors can lead to discontentment and, if not resolved, the potential dissolution of the relationship. The following section reviews processes and vulnerabilities in romantic couples experiencing relationship conflict and facing relationship dissolution.

Although all couples experience periods of uncertainty, as well feelings of dissatisfaction and enduring of conflicts, the ways in which couples behave and affectively respond to one another in these situations varies. Uncertainty may be a particularly difficult emotion to experience within a relationship. For example, relational uncertainty has been associated with feelings of anger and sadness (Knobloch & Theiss, 2010). Further, a partner's report that the relationship is in turmoil is a more direct predictor of an individual's relational uncertainty than one's own reports of relationship turmoil (Knobloch & Theiss, 2010). This finding highlights the dynamic nature of emotional experiences within couples, such that one relationship partner can influence the emotional experiences of the other. Moreover in conflict interactions, relationally uncertain couples (i.e., those who were contemplating dissolution) exhibited higher levels of emotional congruency of negative emotions (i.e., both members of the couple reported similarity in negative emotion experienced) than couples who were not relationally uncertain. Such negative emotionality was suggested to hinder positive behavior, such as exhibiting responsiveness to one's partner during a conflict discussion (Ebesu Hubbard, 2001).

Particular patterns of negativity in spousal interactions have been identified as predictive of divorce. These interactions generally follow a pattern of conflict among heterosexual couples that begin with a harsh start (e.g., criticism typically initiated by the wife) that is met with a rejection to be influenced (typically by the husband), followed by a reciprocation of low-intensity negativity by the wife, and the absence of negativity reduction by the husband (Gottman et al., 1998). This pattern illustrates that dynamic processes during conflict interactions can make relationship dissolution likely, however there are also avenues through which either partner could adjust their affective behavior, which may in turn influence the subsequent emotionality adopted by the other partner. Current evidence suggests that the emotion experience of contempt is particularly damaging to intimate relationships. In a love paradigm task, higher levels of contempt (as coded by observers) predicted husbands' serious consideration or active steps toward divorce over a year later. For wives, higher levels of contempt and lower levels of affection during conflict interactions were predictive of divorce (Graber et al., 2011). Notably, however, gender-specific patterns of affective behavior that are predictive of relationship dissolution may be contingent on contextual factors (e.g., socioeconomic status, age of relationship partners, presence of children), and may not always replicate across all participant samples (e.g., Kim et al., 2007).

Couples' behavioral and emotional patterns during nonconflict interactions that are expected to be positive (e.g., how one reacts to their partner's announcement of a job promotion) also provide insight into interpersonal dynamics that contribute to relationship dissolution. Opportunities for partners to offer support and convey understanding, validation, and caring can go wrong and violate expectations in ways that are particularly hurtful to couples' current and future relationship health (Gable et al., 2006). In Gable et al. (2006) study, men and women whose relationships dissolved (as reported at Time 2) rated their partners as reacting in ways that exhibited less understanding, validation, and care in positive event discussions (rated at Time 1) as compared to those men and women whose relationships did not dissolve; no differences were found for responsiveness in negative event discussions (Gable et al., 2006). Interpersonal exchanges among romantic partners carry a certain level of expectation and, thus, a lack of partner positivity violates the expectation of partner responsiveness to the other's sharing of positive experiences and emotion (Gable et al., 2004).

Perceptions of and responses to partners may be based upon objective assessments of a partner's verbal (e.g., an empathic comment) and non-verbal (e.g., Duchenne smile, a hug) communication but are also influenced by subjective factors (Reis & Shaver, 1988). Attachment styles are one such factor that may shape emotion dynamics in ways that increase a couple's vulnerability to dissatisfaction and dissolution. For example, individuals low in attachment anxiety (and thus, higher in secure attachment) report lower levels of distress when partners behave more positively (e.g., apologizing) during conflict. For their anxious counterparts however, distress is not contingent on partner behavior. These participants feel distressed and believe that the conflict will lead to negative repercussions for their relationship future even when partners behave positively (Campbell et al., 2005). This negativity bias extended to the partners of anxiously attached individuals as well; they also believed that conflicts would negatively affect the future of their relationship (Campbell et al., 2005). These negative relationship beliefs may then influence actual behavior adopted in conflict interactions and create cyclical effects. For example, expectations of partner rejection led women who are rejection-sensitive to exhibit greater negativity during conflict discussions, which may subsequently cause the partner to be rejecting (Downey et al., 1998).

There is also evidence that once relationship partners are unhappy, they are likely to engage in relationship-distressing attributions (Sumer & Cozzarelli, 2004). For example, individuals may attribute negative intentions to their partners' behaviors in such a way that focuses attention on negative aspects of partner behavior and glosses over positive aspects (Collins et al., 2006; Sumer & Cozzarelli, 2004). Individuals' relationship distressing attributions have implications for couple outcomes as they encourage a cycle of relationship dissatisfaction (Jacobson et al., 1985), increase likelihood of engaging in behaviors that result in relationship conflict (Collins et al., 2006; Hall & Fincham, 2006) and impede positive relationship processes such as forgiveness (Hall & Fincham, 2006). Altogether, these processes serve to move partners away from a stable, sustaining equilibrium.

Although not all relationships last, people's emotional lives can remain entwined with the emotions of their partner for a period of time. Individuals who had recently experienced a break-up reported emotions such as love, sadness, anger, and relief, as well as greater variability in daily emotion than individuals in intact relationships (Sbarra & Emery, 2005). However, emotional recovery does occur. For example, after one month, no differences in sadness were reported among those who experienced a break-up as compared to those whose relationships stayed intact (Sbarra & Emery, 2005). In this regard, research comparing those who adjust well to those who adjust poorly to a break-up is particularly noteworthy. Those classified as good adjusters reported co-occurring emotions of love and sadness, whereas poor adjusters were less likely to report sadness or anger when they reported love/longing for their ex-partner (Sbarra & Ferrer, 2006). The authors utilize Emery's (1994) model of post-relationship affective processing to explain this finding, noting that this pattern of emotion co-occurrence may be an indicator of emotional resolution to the break-up (Sbarra & Ferrer, 2006).

## Conclusions and a wish list for future directions

Research on intimate relationships has always implicitly focused on interpersonal emotion dynamics but the explicit focus on these processes is now growing (e.g., Butler, 2011; Butner et al., 2007; Randall et al., 2013; Schoebi, 2008; Schoebi & Randall, 2015). From studies directly addressing this important topic, we are learning how emotion exchanges shape willingness to enter relationships, promote commitment, and can engender relationship-enhancing or relationship-harming processes (Campos et al., 2015; Gable et al., 2004; Gonzaga et al., 2001; Levenson & Gottman, 1983). We are also learning about the moment-by-moment processes through which couples come to be emotionally linked and the ways they deviate and return to their relationship's emotional equilibrium (Butler, 2015). At all times, this rich and interesting area of investigation is pushing forward advances in processes, methods, and data analyses that stand to reveal new insights about the interpersonal emotion dynamics that characterize this important relationship type.

As this area of study grows, we have a wish list for the future. Our wishes are relevant to all relationship stages and have been mentioned throughout this chapter. First, we hope researchers will systematically address the diversity of human experience. More research on these processes across cultures, genders, sexual orientations, social classes, and ages is needed. Second, we hope for more studies of short-term, even fleeting emotion dynamics that may be more typical of daily intimacy than deeply involved emotion-laden interactions (Campos et al., 2009; Wang & Repetti, 2014). Third, we hope researchers address interpersonal emotion dynamics as relationships change over time. For example, how do these processes change as individuals move from friendship to romantic partnerships or from romantic partners to family (as happens via marriage)? Do changes occur in a linear or nonlinear fashion? Additionally, we hope that research on interpersonal emotion dynamics within romantic relationships extend to include the influence of each partner's individual and shared social networks (e.g., family members and close friends). For example, might support from a couple's social network be protective against negative consequences of particular emotional dynamics within the couple? Last, but not least, we hope future work will use the newest analytic approaches and methods described throughout this book (see Chapters 3 and 4) to bring greater precision to our understanding of the moment-by-moment ways that emotion dynamics unfold in intimate relationships. Our wish list is a tall order. But the chapters in this volume show that the field is up for the challenge.

## References

Anderson, C., Keltner, D., & John, O. P. (2003). Emotional convergence between people over time. *Journal of Personality and Social Psychology*, 84, 1054–68.

Berrios, R., Totterdell, P., & Niven, K. (2015). Why do you make us feel good? Correlates and interpersonal consequences of affective presence in speed-dating. *European Journal of Personality*, 29, 72–82.

Birnbaum, G. E., & Reis, H. T. (2012). When does responsiveness pique sexual interest? Attachment and sexual desire in initial acquaintanceships. *Personality and Social Psychology Bulletin*, 38, 946–58.

Butler, E. A. (2011). Temporal interpersonal emotion systems: The "TIES" that form relationships. *Personality and Social Psychology Review*, 15, 367–93.

(2015). Interpersonal affect dynamics: It takes two (and time) to tango. *Emotion Review*, 7, 336–41.

Butler, E. A., & Randall, A. K. (2013). Emotional coregulation in close relationships. *Emotion Review*, 5(2), 202–10.

Butner, J., Diamond, L. M., & Hicks, A. M. (2007). Attachment style and two forms of affect coregulation between romantic partners. *Personal Relationships*, 14, 431–55.

Campbell, L., Simpson, J. A., Boldry, J., & Kashy, D. A. (2005). Perceptions of conflict and support in romantic relationships: The role of attachment anxiety. *Journal of Personality and Social Psychology*, 88, 510–31.

Campos, B., Graesch, A. P., Repetti, R., Bradbury, T., & Ochs, E. (2009). Opportunity for interaction? A naturalistic observation study of dual-earner families after work and school. *Journal of Family Psychology*, 23, 798–807.

Campos, B., Schoebi, D., Gonzaga, G. C., Gable, S. L., & Keltner, D. (2015). Attuned to the positive? Awareness and responsiveness to others' positive emotion experience and display. *Motivation and Emotion*, 39, 780–94.

Collins, N. L., Ford, M. B., Guichard, A. C., & Allard, L. M. (2006). Working models of attachment and attribution processes in intimate relationships. *Personality and Social Psychology Bulletin*, 32, 201–19.

Downey, G., Freitas, A. L., Michaelis, B., & Khouri, H. (1998). The self-fulfilling prophecy in close relationships: Rejection sensitivity and rejection by romantic partners. *Journal of Personality and Social Psychology, 75*, 545–60.

Ebesu Hubbard, A. (2001). Conflict between relationally uncertain romantic partners: The influence of relational responsiveness and empathy. *Communication Monographs, 68*, 400–14.

Eibl-Eibesfeldt, I. (1989). *Human Ethology.* New York, NY: Aldine de Gruyter.

Emery, R. E. (1994). *Renegotiating Family Relationships: Divorce, Child Custody, and Mediation.* New York, NY: Guilford Press.

English, T., John, O. P., & Gross, J. J. (2013). Emotion regulation in close relationships. In J. A. Simpson & L. Campbell (Eds.), *The Oxford Handbook of Close Relationships* (pp. 500–13). Oxford, UK: Oxford University Press.

Finkel, E. J., Cheung, E. O., Emery, L. F., Carswell, K. L., & Larson, G. M. (2015). The suffocation model: Why marriage in America is becoming an all-or-nothing institution. *Current Directions in Psychological Science, 24*, 238–44.

Foeman, A., & Nance, T. (2002). Building new cultures, reframing old images: Success strategies of interracial couples. *Howard Journal of Communications, 13*, 237–49.

Gable, S. L., Gonzaga, G. C., & Strachman, A. (2006). Will you be there for me when things go right? Supportive responses to positive event disclosures. *Journal of Personality and Social Psychology, 91*, 904–17.

Gable, S. L., & Reis, H. T. (2010). Good news! Capitalizing on positive events in an interpersonal context. *Advances in Experimental Social Psychology, 42*, 195–257.

Gable, S. L., Reis, H. T., Impett, E. A., & Asher, E. R. (2004). What do you do when things go right? The intrapersonal and interpersonal benefits of sharing positive events. *Journal of Personality and Social Psychology, 87*, 228–45.

Gonzaga, G. C., Keltner, D., Londahl, E. A., & Smith, M. D. (2001). Love and the commitment problem in romantic relations and friendship. *Journal of Personality and Social Psychology, 81*, 247–62.

Gottman, J. M., Coan, J., Carrere, S., & Swanson, C. (1998). Predicting marital happiness and stability from newlywed interactions. *Journal of Marriage and the Family, 60*, 5–22.

Graber, E. C., Laurenceau, J. P., Miga, E., Chango, J., & Coan, J. (2011). Conflict and love: Predicting newlywed marital outcomes from two interaction contexts. *Journal of Family Psychology, 25*(4), 541–50.

Hall, J. H., & Fincham, F. D. (2006). Relationship dissolution following infidelity: The roles of attributions and forgiveness. *Journal of Social and Clinical Psychology, 25*, 508–22.

Huston, T. L., Caughlin, J. P., Houts, R. M., Smith, S. E., & George, L. J. (2001). The connubial crucible: Newlywed years as predictors of marital delight, distress, and divorce. *Journal of Personality and Social Psychology, 80*, 237–52.

Jacobson, N. S., McDonald, D. W., Follette, W. C., & Berley, R. A. (1985). Attributional processes in distressed and nondistressed married couples. *Cognitive Therapy and Research, 9*(1), 35–50.

Keltner, D., & Gross, J. J. (1999). Functional accounts of emotions. *Cognition and Emotion*, 13, 467–80.

Keltner, D., & Haidt, J. (2001). Social functions of emotions. In T. J. Mayne & G. A. Bonanno (Eds.), *Emotions: Current Issues and Future Directions* (pp. 192–213). New York, NY: The Guilford Press.

Keltner, D., & Lerner, J. S. (2010). Emotion. In D. T. Gilbert, S. T. Fiske, & G. Lindsay (Eds.), *The Handbook of Social Psychology* (5th edn., pp. 312–47). New York, NY: McGraw Hill.

Kim, H. K., Capaldi, D. M., & Crosby, L. (2007). Generalizability of Gottman and colleagues' affective process models of couples' relationship outcomes. *Journal of Marriage and Family*, 69, 55–72.

Knobloch, L. K., & Metts, S. (2013). Emotion in relationships. In J. A. Simpson & L. Campbell (Eds.), *The Oxford Handbook of Close Relationships* (pp. 514–34). New York, NY: Oxford University Press.

Knobloch, L. K., & Theiss, J. A. (2010). An actor – partner interdependence model of relational turbulence: Cognitions and emotions. *Journal of Social and Personal Relationships*, 27, 595–619.

Krokoff, L. J. (1991). Job distress is no laughing matter in marriage, or is it? *Journal of Social and Personal Relationships*, 8, 5–25.

Larson, R., & Almeida, D. (1999). Emotional transmission in the daily lives of families: A new paradigm for studying family process. *Journal of Marriage and Family*, 61, 5–20.

Laurenceau, J. P., Barrett, L. F., & Pietromonaco, P. R. (1998). Intimacy as an interpersonal process: The importance of self-disclosure, partner disclosure, and perceived partner responsiveness in interpersonal exchanges. *Journal of Personality and Social Psychology*, 74, 1238–51.

Lazarus, R. S. (1991). *Emotion and Adaptation*. New York, NY: Oxford University Press.

Levenson, R. W. (1999). The intrapersonal functions of emotion. *Cognition & Emotion*, 13, 481–504.

Levenson, R. W., & Gottman, J. M. (1983). Marital interaction: Physiological linkage and affective exchange. *Journal of Personality & Social Psychology*, 45, 587–97.

(1985). Physiological and affective predictors of change in relationship satisfaction. *Journal of Personality and Social Psychology*, 49(1), 85–94.

Luo, S., & Zhang, G. (2009). What leads to romantic attraction: Similarity, reciprocity, security, or beauty? Evidence from a speed-dating study. *Journal of Personality*, 77, 933–64.

Miller, R. S. (2015). *Intimate Relationships* (7th edn.). New York, NY: McGraw Hill.

Niven, K., Totterdell, P., & Holman, D. (2009). A classification of controlled interpersonal affect regulation strategies. *Emotion*, 9(4), 498–509.

Norton, M. I., Frost, J. H., & Ariely, D. (2007). Less is more: The lure of ambiguity, or why familiarity breeds contempt. *Journal of Personality and Social Psychology*, 92, 97–105.

Papp, L. M., Pendry, P., Simon, C. D., & Adam, E. K. (2013). Spouses' cortisol associations and moderators: Testing physiological synchrony and connectedness in everyday life. *Family Process*, 52, 284–98.

Parkinson, B., & Simons, G. (2012). Worry spreads: Interpersonal transfer of problem-related anxiety. *Cognition and Emotion*, 26, 462–79.

Pasupathi, M. (2001). The social construction of the personal past and its implications for adult development. *Psychological Bulletin*, 127, 651–72.

Prager, K. J., & Roberts, L. J. (2004). Deep intimate connection: self and intimacy in couple relationships. In D. J. Mashek & A. Aron (Eds.), *Handbook of Closeness and Intimacy* (pp. 43–60). Mahwah, NJ: Lawrence Erlbaum Associates.

Randall, A. K., & Butler, E. A. (2013). Attachment and emotion transmission within romantic relationships: Merging intrapersonal and interpersonal perspectives. *Journal of Relationships Research*, 4(e10), 1–10.

Randall, A. K., Corkery, S. A., Duggi, D., Kamble, S. V., & Butler, E. A. (2011). "We're having a good (or bad) day": Differences in emotional synchrony in married couples in the United States and India. *Family Science*, 2(3), 203–11.

Randall, A. K., Post, J. H., Reed, R. G., & Butler, E. A. (2013). Cooperating with your romantic partner: Associations with interpersonal emotion coordination. *Journal of Social and Personal Relationships*, 30(8), 1072–95.

Reis, H. T., Clark, M. S., & Holmes, J. G. (2004). Perceived partner responsiveness as an organizing construct in the study of intimacy and closeness. In D. J. Mashek & A. Aron (Eds.), *Handbook of Closeness and Intimacy* (pp. 201–25). Mahwah, NJ: Lawrence Erlbaum Associates.

Reis, H. T., Maniaci, M. R., Caprariello, P. A., Eastwick, P. W., & Finkel, E. J. (2011). Familiarity does indeed promote attraction in live interaction. *Journal of Personality and Social Psychology*, 101, 557–70.

Reis, H. T., & Shaver, P. (1988). Intimacy as an interpersonal process. In S. Duck (Ed.), *Handbook of Personal Relationships* (pp. 367–89). Chichester, England: Wiley.

Reis, H. T., Smith, S. M., Carmichael, C. L., et al. (2010). Are you happy for me? How sharing positive events with others provides personal and interpersonal benefits. *Journal of Personality and Social Psychology*, 99, 311–29.

Repetti, R. L., Wang, S. W., & Saxbe, D. E. (2011). Adult health in the context of everyday family life. *Annals of Behavioral Medicine*, 42, 285–93.

Rimé, B. (2009). Emotion elicits the social sharing of emotion: Theory and empirical review. *Emotion Review*, 1, 60–85.

Rimé, B., Finkenauer, C., Luminet, O., Zech, E., & Philippot, P. (1998). Social sharing of emotion: New evidence and new questions. *European Review of Social Psychology*, 9, 145–89.

Saxbe, D., & Repetti, R. L. (2010). For better or worse? Coregulation of couples' cortisol levels and mood states. *Journal of Personality and Social Psychology*, 98, 92–103.

Sbarra, D. A., & Emery, R. E. (2005). The emotional sequelae of nonmarital relationship dissolution: Analysis of change and intraindividual variability over time. *Personal Relationships*, 12(2), 213–32.

Sbarra, D. A., & Ferrer, E. (2006). The structure and process of emotional experience following nonmarital relationship dissolution: Dynamic factor analyses of love, anger, and sadness. *Emotion*, 6(2), 224–38.

Schoebi, D. (2008). The coregulation of daily affect in marital relationships. *Journal of Family Psychology*, 22, 595–604.

Schoebi, D., & Randall, A. K. (2015). Emotional dynamics in intimate relationships. *Emotion Review*, 7(4), 342–8.

Schoebi, D., Wang, Z., Ababkov, V., & Perrez, M. (2010). Affective interdependence in married couples' daily lives: Are there cultural differences in partner effects of anger? *Family Science*, 1, 83–92.

Shenhav, S., Campos, B., & Goldberg, W. (2017). Dating out is intercultural: Experience and perceived parent disapproval by ethnicity and immigrant generation. *Journal of Social and Personal Relationships*, 34(3), 397–422.

Shiota, M. N., Campos, B., Keltner, D., & Hertenstein, M. J. (2004). Positive emotion and the regulation of interpersonal relationships. In P. Philippot & R. S. Feldman (Eds.), *The Regulation of Emotion* (pp. 127–55). Mahwah, NJ: Lawrence Erlbaum Associates.

Sorce, J. F., Emde, R. N., Campos, J. J., & Klinnert, M. D. (1985). Maternal emotion signaling: Its effect on the visual cliff behavior of 1 year olds. *Developmental Psychology*, 21, 195–200.

Sprecher, S., Treger, S., & Wondra, J. D. (2013a). Effects of self-disclosure role on liking, closeness, and other impressions in get-acquainted interactions. *Journal of Social and Personal Relationships*, 30, 497–514.

Sprecher, S., Treger, S., Wondra, J. D., Hilaire, N., & Wallpe, K. (2013b). Taking turns: Reciprocal self-disclosure promotes liking in initial interactions. *Journal of Experimental Social Psychology*, 49, 860–6.

Sumer, N., & Cozzarelli, C. (2004). The impact of adult attachment on partner and self-attributions and relationship quality. *Personal Relationships*, 11, 355–71.

Thompson, A., & Bolger, N. (1999). Emotional transmission in couples under stress. *Journal of Marriage and the Family*, 61, 38–48.

Tidwell, N. D., Eastwick, P. W., & Finkel, E. J. (2013). Perceived, not actual, similarity predicts initial attraction in a live romantic context: Evidence from the speed-dating paradigm. *Personal Relationships*, 20, 199–215.

Tracy, J. L., & Beall, A. T. (2011). Happy guys finish last: the impact of emotion expressions on sexual attraction. *Emotion*, 11, 1379–87.

Vittengl, J. R., & Holt, C. S. (2000). Getting acquainted: The relationship of self-disclosure and social attraction to positive affect. *Journal of Social and Personal Relationships*, 17, 53–66.

Wang, S. W., & Repetti, R. L. (2014). Psychological well-being and job stress predict marital support interactions: A naturalistic observational study of dual-earner couples in their homes. *Journal of Personality and Social Psychology*, 107, 864–78.

Zaki, J., & Williams, W. C. (2013). Interpersonal emotion regulation. *Emotion*, 13, 803–10.

# CHAPTER 10

# Next steps toward understanding interpersonal emotion dynamics

*Emily A. Butler*

All the things we do, from the mundane details of daily life to global social movements, are interpersonal co-creations of behavior and shared meaning. Emotion is one of the primary aspects of this multilayered interpersonal system that coordinates and directs what we co-create, whether it be a love affair or a war. Emotion communicates intentions, organizes our behavior through patterns of interpersonal reactivity, and can contribute to shared or conflicting motivations. Due to the centrality of interpersonal emotion dynamics (IED) in every aspect of human behavior, developing an accurate, explanatory understanding of them is one of the most pressing scientific challenges facing us. Thus the overarching goals of IED research are to propose, systematically test and refine theory. Those goals in turn require establishing high-quality data collection procedures, strong research methods and sophisticated data analytic tools. The chapters in this book attest to the advances that are being made, but much is left to be done.

## Centrality of coordination

At a general level of abstraction, the overarching questions we face regarding IED are about coordination within dynamic systems. Coordination refers to how processes change together across time (Butner et al., 2014). Coordination is at the heart of understanding the temporal organization of the elements of a complex entity as they work together to produce some higher-level behavior or state. What factors bring about or impair interpersonal emotion coordination? What patterns of coordination are common and what are their pragmatic effects in terms of wellbeing and performance? Are coordination at the physiological, behavioral, and experiential level related to each other? Is interpersonal emotional coordination a cause or a consequence of behavioral coordination? For example, existing evidence suggests that both empathy and conflict are associated with increased interpersonal coordination, but it is unclear whether the same mechanisms are at work (Butler & Randall, 2013; Timmons et al., 2015). In the case of empathy, it may be the capacity to share a range of emotions that produces coordination, while with conflict it may be interpersonal reactivity to negative affect that drives it. In addition, empathy and conflict may both produce coordination, but empathy may contribute to a stable interpersonal emotional pattern (co-regulation), while conflict may lead to negative escalation. These are just a few examples of the many unanswered questions that need to be addressed if we are to truly understand IED in a way that can inform prediction and intervention.

## The need for greater mathematical sophistication

One prerequisite for systematic knowledge accumulation is to have clear definitions and operationalizations of our theoretical constructs. The field of IED has historically been plagued by fuzzy definitions and weak theory, with the result being a lack of clear theoretical predictions. Happily, this is changing, and several of the chapters in this volume contribute to this advance. For example, Chapter 1 provides a much-needed theoretical overview, and Sels and colleagues (Chapter 2) provide a useful distinction between dynamic processes that occur between individuals versus dynamics that involve the interpersonal system as a whole. As another example, Butner and colleagues (Chapter 3) provide concise definitions of emotional reactivity, which entails an interpersonal system undergoing a change in emotional state following a perturbation, versus regulation, which entails a homeostatic return to a previous emotional pattern.

What makes the prior definitions particularly powerful is that they can be directly translated into mathematical models, as demonstrated by both chapters. The advantage of having a mathematical model for a particular aspect of theory is that the key theoretical constructs are represented in an explicit and testable way. The potential of this approach is immediately apparent if we compare our ability to predict human behavior (where mathematical modeling is still relatively rare) compared to predicting the weather (where such modeling has been central since computers made it tractable starting in the 1950s). We find it reasonable to get upset if the weather report predicts sunshine a week in the future, when in fact there is an occasional shower that day, but currently we have no hope of predicting a person's behavior to that degree of specificity. Indeed, doing so should be a central goal for future IED research.

If we could predict IED with as much accuracy as we can predict the weather it would open up a range of technological innovations. For example, a skilled therapist could probably recognize all the IED patterns and feedback loops discussed in this book and suggest interventions where appropriate. But if we could get the human observer out of the loop it would allow innovations such as a "real-time relationship app" that could alert you when you need to change your behavior if you want to avoid a fight with your partner. For example, existing apps such as StayGo (https://staygoapp.com/) provide global advice about whether to stay or leave a current romantic relationship, but do not speak to real-time dynamic behaviors such as how to respond to a comment your partner just made. Such automatic detection of IED demands measuring emotionally relevant variables such as language and physiology in real-time, which is becoming a practical option with current smartphone-based technology. It also demands theory-based mathematical modeling and machine learning techniques, similar to standard approaches in many other fields of science.

One implication of this is that to benefit from the power of dynamic systems science as it is applied in other fields, we need to become more sophisticated in our mathematical training. A growing body of work with relevance to IED is starting to appear (Chow et al., 2007, , 2009; Hamaker & Grasman, 2012; Lodewyckx et al., 2010; Yang & Chow, 2010), but most social science students (and faculty for that matter) do not have the basic training in mathematics to be able to understand that work, yet alone extend it. The result is that there are isolated examples in the literature, but not any systematic accumulation. In summary, one important step for advancing our knowledge about IED is to start retooling our undergraduate and graduate training programs in order to produce a more mathematically informed generation of social scientists. In the interim, those in the field who do have the training can contribute by writing approachable, tutorial style publications, similar to Chapter 3 in this volume, that provide a clear explanation of basic dynamic system concepts and modeling fundamentals.

## The need to revisit within-person processes

The work in this volume is inspired by the fact that most emotional episodes occur in the context of social interaction or relationships, yet the study of emotion was traditionally focused on the individual (see Chapter 1). This new emphasis on interpersonal emotion has generated much important work, including that described in this book. One thing that is becoming clear, however, is that we need to cycle back to understanding emotion within individual people better in order to make progress in understanding interpersonal dynamics. For example, it remains an open question whether, or under what conditions, the various aspects of emotional responding (physiology, expression, experience, etc.) become coordinated (i.e., concordant, synchronized, coherent) over time within individuals (Butler et al., 2014; Hubbard et al., 2004; Moscovitch et al., 2010). Yet any theory about IED needs to be compatible with the answer and may in fact depend upon it. Thus making progress on the question of when and how different aspects of emotion become coordinated over time within individuals is a prerequisite for the optimal development of theories on IED.

Revisiting the question of how the multivariate aspects of emotion behave within a person raises a set of sub-questions, one of which is how to model the multiple aspects of emotion. Do we need separate models for each emotional component in isolation, such as having one model for skin conductance, another for self-report and a third for heart rate? For example, skin conductance often has a clear linear trend which is not present in most heart rate data. Does that matter? Do we need to model the lag times between variables that respond at different rates and, if so, how do we learn what those intrinsic lags are, or worse, whether they vary across conditions? Or do these variables behave differently in the context of an interpersonal system, making isolated sub-models irrelevant? And perhaps most vexingly, what frequencies of oscillation are relevant to understanding emotion dynamics either within or between people? Take for example heart rate. We know that there are multiple frequencies of heart rate variability and that they are driven by different combinations of sympathetic and parasympathetic activation (Beauchaine, 2001). Are any or all of those frequencies relevant to emotion, either individually or interpersonally? How do within-person oscillations relate to between-person coupling? We have a lot of work left to do, both at the within-person level but embedded in social contexts (as compared to the historical focus on within-person processes in nonsocial contexts) and at the between-person level.

## Interpersonal-state models of biology

Interpersonal coordination of physiological processes is perhaps the most relevant aspect of IED when it comes to understanding connections to physical health. To date, most research in this domain has focused on peripheral autonomic responses, or a small set of hormones such as cortisol and oxytocin (see Chapter 6 for a review). Recent work is branching out into other biological systems, however, such as additional hormones and immune functioning (Chapter 5), body temperature and cortical functioning (Babiloni & Astolfi, 2014; Reeck et al., 2016). For example, as reported in Chapter 5, genetic differences in the serotonin system have been associated with empathy and susceptibility to partner emotion, while inflammation has been associated with sensitivity to rejection and social threat. Along similar lines, body temperature regulation has been associated with social safety, integration, and attachment (Ijzerman et al., 2017). At the cortical level, recent theoretical work on the neural bases of interpersonal emotion regulation has suggested a series of processing steps, including emotion generation circuits in a person responding emotionally, followed by regulatory control circuits in the brain of a social partner attempting to regulate the other (Reeck et al., 2016).

Although this new work across biological domains is exciting, so far it has been limited to between-person models (Chapter 2: models of sequential processes occurring between parts of a system, to be distinguished from models characterizing the system as a whole). An important next step toward understanding the specific form of IED that has been termed "co-regulation" will be to investigate this broad range of biological processes from the perspective of interpersonal-state dynamics instead. Biological co-regulation has been defined as a "... complex commingling of physiological states, ... whereby each individual within the relationship serves as the primary physiological regulator for their partner" (Sbarra & Hazan, 2008, p. 20). This definition implies that co-regulation must be understood as an aspect of the interpersonal system as a whole, not as a sequence of individual responses. Although there has been speculation about such interpersonal states, such as dynamic interpersonal feedback loops for oxytocin (Chapter 5) or co-regulation of body temperature (Ijzerman et al., 2017), to date empirical evidence is lacking because studies have not combined real-time measurement of biological variables from interacting partners with modeling procedures that treat the social unit as a whole as a system (e.g., interpersonal state dynamics). Similarly, although the technological break-through of hyperscanning has made it possible to simultaneously record real-time brain functioning from multiple interacting social partners, so far work has focused on nonemotional aspects of social interaction, such as behavioral or speech coordination, or between-person processes such as emotional expression being received and decoded by an observer (Babiloni & Astolfi, 2014). Such new forms of IED data bring with them additional mathematical modeling challenges for representing and testing theories about interpersonal-state dynamics. Again, we have much to do.

## Reciprocal connections with relationship quality

Another complexity is that IED can both reflect relationship quality and, at the same time, actively contribute to it. For example, Chapter 9 provides a review of emotional processes that play an active role in the formation, maintenance, and dissolution of close relationships. But the reverse direction of causality also clearly occurs. Unhappy relationships generate more coordinated negative emotions due to conflicts, while happy relationships provide ample opportunities for coordinated positive emotions. Evidence reviewed in Chapter 7 supports the idea that feedback cycles can form between relationship quality and IED. In other words, relationship quality can give rise to different patterns of IED, which in turn contribute to changes in relationship quality. For example, as people become dissatisfied in a relationship they become more likely to make negative partner attributions, which promotes negative emotional reactivity and escalation in both partners, which increases dissatisfaction, etc. One challenge facing us to figure out where in these chains we can optimally intervene to break negative cycles and promote positive ones. One encouraging fact is that feedback spirals can be broken by influencing any one variable within the system, as evidenced by successful therapeutic interventions such as Cognitive Behavioral Therapy. This suggests we only need to find a malleable point in the system – any variable that is amenable to change – even if it is not the obvious "symptom" or natural target for intervention. Further, it may take only small effects to tip a system, so we do not necessarily have to uncover big effects to produce pragmatically relevant changes.

## Does meaning matter?

Several chapters in this volume consider specific behavioral IED patterns, such as coercion (Chapter 8) or demand-withdraw and capitalization (Chapter 7). Each of these are characterized by a particular interpersonal sequence of behaviors that are mutually reinforcing and can be conceptualized as attractors, or points of high return and stability. One question that arises when considering such behavioral sequences is what level of abstraction is optimal for thinking about IED. Specifically, each of these patterns could be represented with a fairly similar positive feedback model, whereby behavior A elicits behavior B, which elicits more behavior A, etc. Yet the interpersonal consequences of demand-withdraw are quite different than capitalization of positive emotion (see Chapter 7). Is progress more likely to be made by drawing abstract distinctions between different patterns, such as whether they involve positive versus negative emotion, or does the specific interpersonal meaning of the behaviors matter? In other words, do we need to include more content or semantics in our characterization of IED? Perhaps statistical patterns of interdependence are meaningless without a higher level of meaning construction. And if so, where does that meaning come from and at what point does it become so specific that it only applies to one social interaction out of a million? These questions lead to further questions about cultural specificity of meaning and whether IED processes generalize across cultural contexts. To date there is almost no research on IED cross-culturally, although extensive evidence shows that most aspects of emotional responding and social relationships vary across cultures (Boiger & Mesquita, 2012; Mesquita & Boiger, 2014), making this an important direction for future research.

## Methodological next steps

In addition to a lack of cross-cultural work, the rarity of experimental designs is another methodological limitation for the field (see Chapter 4 for an overview of methods for studying IED). One interesting possibility is to use acetaminophen to manipulate emotional reactivity. For example, evidence suggests that acetaminophen acts as an emotional blunter (Chapter 5). This could allow a systematic investigation of the conditions under which reduced emotional reactivity enhances co-regulation of emotion versus impedes it. One testable hypothesis is that blunted reactivity would enhance co-regulation and prevent negative escalation in the context of conflict, but impede co-regulation and interpersonal connection in the context of providing social support or sharing positive emotions with a partner.

Another challenge for systematic knowledge accumulation is the difficulty of collecting data appropriate for IED from large samples or over extended periods of time. By definition, studying dynamics requires repeated measurements over time, which dramatically increases the difficulty of data collection and participant burden. As a result, essentially all of what we know comes from relatively small samples and limited time frames. The internet is starting to change this in some regards, in that work is beginning to emerge where IED are investigated across large online social networks, resulting in very large sample sizes (Coviello et al., 2014). But to date, this work has been limited to processes that unfold unidirectionally across large networks, such as contagion. A next step would be to find ways to use the fact that almost everyone in the industrialized world interacts socially over the internet to track bidirectional emotional processes over time within specific close relationships, but from a large number of such relationships.

Finding a way to collect temporally dense data from large samples may help to tackle another challenge, which is the difficulty of studying low-frequency events. It has been difficult to reliably observe co-regulation in the lab, at least if it is defined as bidirectional mutual damping of negative arousal, with a number of studies finding little or no evidence for co-regulation (Ferrer & Steele, 2012, 2014; Madhyastha et al., 2011). But then, why should we see co-regulation in the lab if it only arises when mutual regulation is needed in response to a strong perturbation? Perhaps co-regulation is something that occurs once every three or four months in high functioning relationships. Further, perhaps different forms of co-regulation exist within different types of couples, making it important to distinguish different patterns of IED. Alternately, the opposite may be true and co-regulation may be so ubiquitous as to be invisible. As suggested by Social Baseline Theory (see Chapter 9 for a review), a state of co-regulation may the norm for functioning relationships and so we see little or no variability in the lab. If this were the case, we would be better off experimentally focusing on disrupting co-regulation to observe its consequences and the factors that reinstate it, rather than trying to find moderators of naturally occurring co-regulation.

## Summary

The next steps toward understanding IED can be summarized with a developmental analogy. In its infancy, the field of IED babbled chaotically, using one term to mean many things and multiple terms to mean the same thing. Now, in adolescence, the basic language has been acquired and is largely shared across the field, as can be seen in the contributions to this volume. Similarly, a basic tool kit of strong methodologies and rudimentary, but appropriate, statistical modeling approaches has been acquired. Perhaps we are prepared to transition to adulthood by achieving the developmental tasks of becoming increasingly systematic, refining and extending our conceptualization of IED, mastering the nuances of the tools we use, and acquiring more mature but powerful techniques for both data collection and mathematical modeling.

## References

Babiloni, F., & Astolfi, L. (2014). Social neuroscience and hyperscanning techniques: past, present and future. *Neuroscience & Biobehavioral Reviews*, 44, 76–93. https://doi.org/10.1016/j.neubiorev.2012.07.006

Beauchaine, T. (2001). Vagal tone, development, and Gray's motivational theory: toward an integrated model of autonomic nervous system functioning in psychopathology. *Development and Psychopathology*, 13, 183–214.

Boiger, M., & Mesquita, B. (2012). The construction of emotion in interactions, relationships, and cultures. *Emotion Review*, 4(3), 221–9. https://doi.org/10.1177/1754073912439765

Butler, E. A., Gross, J. J., & Barnard, K. (2014). Testing the effects of suppression and reappraisal on emotional concordance using a multivariate multilevel model. *Biological Psychology*, 98, 6–18.

Butler, E. A., & Randall, A. K. (2013). Emotional coregulation in close relationships. *Emotion Review*, 5, 202–10.

Butner, J. E., Berg, C. A., Baucom, B. R., & Wiebe, D. J. (2014). Modeling Coordination in multiple simultaneous latent change scores. *Multivariate Behavioral Research*, 49(6), 554–70. https://doi.org/10.1080/00273171.2014.934321

Chow, S., Ferrer, E., & Nesselroade, J. R. (2007). An unscented Kalman filter approach to the estimation of nonlinear dynamical systems models. *Multivariate Behavioral Research*, 42(2), 283–321.

Chow, S., Hamaker, E. L., Fujita, F., & Boker, S. M. (2009). Representing time-varying cyclic dynamics using multiple-subject state-space models. *British Journal of Mathematical and Statistical Psychology*, 62, 683–716.

Coviello, L., Sohn, Y., Kramer, A. D. I., et al. (2014). Detecting emotional contagion in massive social networks. *PLoS ONE*, 9(3). https://doi.org/10.1371/journal.pone.0090315

Ferrer, E., & Steele, J. S. (2012). Dynamic systems analysis of affective processes in dyadic interactions using differential equations. In G. R. Hancock & J. R. Harring (Eds.), *Advances in Longitudinal Methods in the Social and Behavioral Sciences* (pp. 111–34). Charlotte, NC: Information Age Publishing.

(2014). Differential equations for evaluating theoretical models of dyadic interactions. In P. C. M. Molenaar, K. M. Newell, & R. M. Lerner (Eds.), *Handbook of Developmental Systems Theory and Methodology* (pp. 345–68). New York, NY: Guilford Press.

Hamaker, E. L., & Grasman, R. P. (2012). Regime switching state-space models applied to psychological processes: handling missing data and making inferences. *Psychometrika*, 77(2), 400–22. https://doi.org/10.1007/S11336-012-9254-8

Hubbard, J. A., Parker, E. H., Ramsden, S. R., et al. (2004). The relations among observational, physiological, and self-report measures of children's anger. *Social Development*, 13(1), 14–39.

Ijzerman, H., Heine, E. C., Nagel, S. K., & Pronk, T. M. (2017). Modernizing relationship therapy through social thermoregulation theory: evidence, hypotheses, and explorations. *Frontiers in Psychology*. https://doi.org/10.3389/fpsyg.2017.00635

Lodewyckx, T., Tuerlinckx, F., Kuppens, P., Allen, N. B., & Sheeber, L. (2010). A hierarchical state space approach to affective dynamics. *Journal of Mathematical Psychology*, 55, 68–83.

Madhyastha, T. M., Hamaker, E. L., & Gottman, J. M. (2011). Investigating spousal influence using moment-to-moment affect data from marital conflict. *Journal of Family Psychology*, 25(2), 292–300.

Mesquita, B., & Boiger, M. (2014). Emotions in context: a sociodynamic model of emotions. *Emotion Review*, 6(4), 298–302. https://doi.org/10.1177/1754073914534480

Moscovitch, D. A., Suvak, M. K., & Hofmann, S. G. (2010). Emotional response patterns during social threat in individuals with generalized anxiety disorder and non-anxious controls. *Journal of Anxiety Disorders*, 24, 785–91. https://doi.org/10.1016/j.janxdis.2010.05.013

Reeck, C., Ames, D. R., & Ochsner, K. N. (2016). The social regulation of emotion: an integrative, cross-disciplinary model. *Trends in Cognitive Sciences*, 20(1), 47–63. https://doi.org/10.1016/j.tics.2015.09.003

Sbarra, D. A., & Hazan, C. (2008). Co-regulation, dysregulation, self-regulation: an integrative analysis and empirical agenda for understanding adult attachment, separation, loss, and recovery. *Personality and Social Psychology Review*, 12(2), 141–67.

Timmons, A. C., Margolin, G., & Saxbe, D. (2015). Physiological linkage in couples and its implications for individual and interpersonal functioning: a literature review. *Journal of Family Psychology*. https://doi.org/10.1037/fam0000115

Yang, M., & Chow, S. (2010). Using state-space model with regime switching to represent the dynamics of facial electromyography (EMG) data. *Psychometrika*, 75(4), 744–71. https://doi.org/10.1007/S11336-010-9176-2

# Author Index

# Subject Index

200  *Subject Index*

# STUDIES IN EMOTION AND SOCIAL INTERACTION

*The Interpersonal Dynamics of Emotion: Towards an Integrative Theory of Emotions as Social Information*, by
Gerban A. van Kleef

*From Self to Social Relationships: An Essentially Relational Perspective on Social Motivation*, by
Martijn van Zomeren

*The Aesthetics of Emotion: Up the Down Staircase of the Mind-Body*, by
Gerald C. Cupchik

*The Expression of Emotion: Philosophical, Psychological and Legal Perspectives*, edited by
Catharine Abell and Joel Smith

*Emotional Lives: Dramas of Identity in an Age of Mass Media*, by
E. Doyle McCarthy

*Interpersonal Emotion Dynamics in Close Relationships*, edited by
Ashley K. Randall and Dominik Schoebi